ROAD TO RIVERDALE®

VOLUME THREE

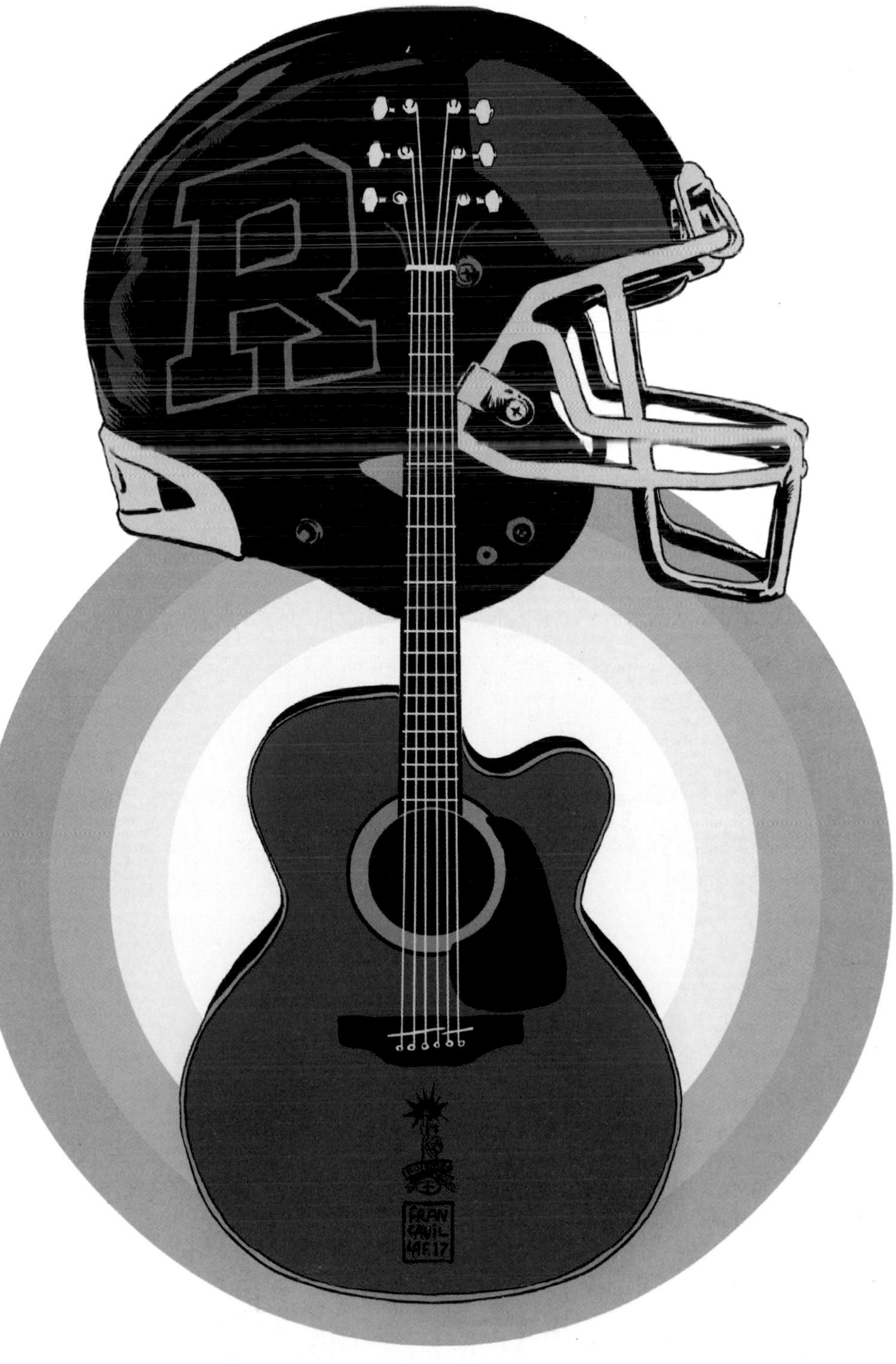

COVER ART BY
FRANCESCO FRANCAVILLA

FEATURING STORIES BY
MARK WAID, CHIP ZDARSKY,
ADAM HUGHES, MARGUERITE BENNETT,
CAMERON DeORDIO & TOM DeFALCO

WITH ART BY
FIONA STAPLES, ERICA HENDERSON,
ADAM HUGHES, AUDREY MOK, SANDY JARRELL,
ANDRE SZYMANOWICZ, JOSÉ VILLARRUBIA,
JEN VAUGHN, KELLY FITZPATRICK & JACK MORELLI

EDITOR
MIKE PELLERITO

CO-EDITOR (JOSIE)
ALEX SEGURA
ASSOCIATE EDITOR
STEPHEN OSWALD
ASSISTANT EDITOR
JAMIE LEE ROTANTE

EDITOR-IN-CHIEF
VICTOR GORELICK

GRAPHIC DESIGN BY
KARI McLACHLAN

PUBLISHER
JON GOLDWATER

ROAD TO RIVERDALE® INTRODUCTION

The CW *Riverdale* TV series, written by Archie Comics Chief Creative Officer Roberto Aguirre-Sacasa and produced by Warner Brothers Studios and Berlanti Productions, has not only rekindled the fire within lifelong Archie fans, but has also introduced new viewers and readers to the Archie Universe.

While *Riverdale* offers a subversive take on the Archie mythos and its characters, it is still an extension of the world cultivated in over 75 years' worth of comics. Within the past two years alone, under the leadership of Archie Comics Publisher/Co-CEO Jon Goldwater, the comics have been given new life, starting with relaunches of the company's most well-known and recognized properties and characters, including Archie, Jughead, Betty and Veronica, Josie and the Pussycats and Reggie. And that's only the beginning. Archie Comics is entering into a renaissance that will only continue and expand from here.

Speaking of which, you can tune into Season 2 of *Riverdale* on The CW network starting this Fall on Wednesdays, 8 PM EST/7 PM Central. You can also check out the ongoing *Riverdale* comic series by Roberto Aguirre-Sacasa and The CW writers room, which features ALL-NEW stories set between the episodes of the TV series, on sale now at your local comic shop.

If this is your first foray into the wider world of Archie Comics—thank you for picking up this graphic novel. We hope you've also enjoyed Volumes 1 and 2 and will continue to explore and enjoy what's ahead for Archie Comics in the future.

Welcome to Riverdale.

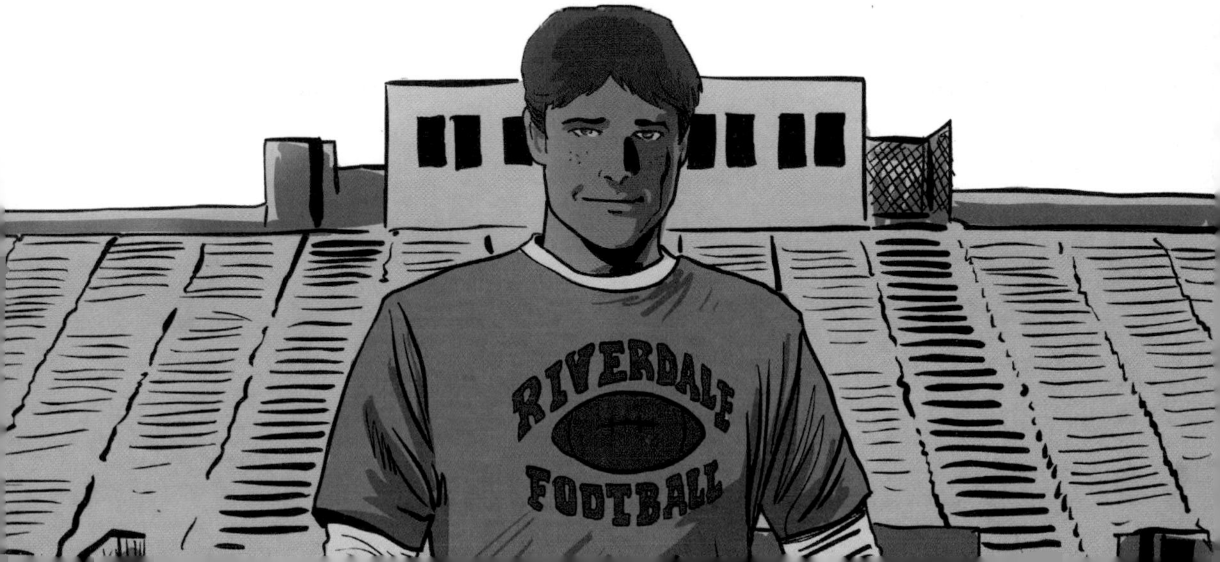
RIVERDALE
FOOTBALL

ROAD TO
RIVERDALE
CONTENTS

SECTION ONE
ARCHIE..6

PAGE

SECTION TWO
JUGHEAD...32

SECTION THREE
BETTY & VERONICA.......................................56

SECTION FOUR
JOSIE AND THE PUSSYCATS..........................80

SECTION FIVE
REGGIE AND ME...104

SPECIAL FEATURES
RIVERDALE PHOTO GALLERY..........................127

ARCHIE

PREVIOUSLY IN THE TOWN OF RIVERDALE...

When Archie joined the construction team working on the new Lodge Manor, he made a MAJOR mess of things! And Mr. Lodge's beautiful daughter, Veronica, caught Archie in the act of accidentally destroying their mansion-in-progress.

Now Archie's got to right his wrongs if he wants to get in good with Veronica, who's starting her first day at Riverdale High, and finally get over his breakup with Betty Cooper.

STORY BY
MARK WAID

ART BY
FIONA STAPLES

COLORING BY
ANDRE SZYMANOWICZ
WITH JEN VAUGHN

LETTERING BY
JACK MORELLI

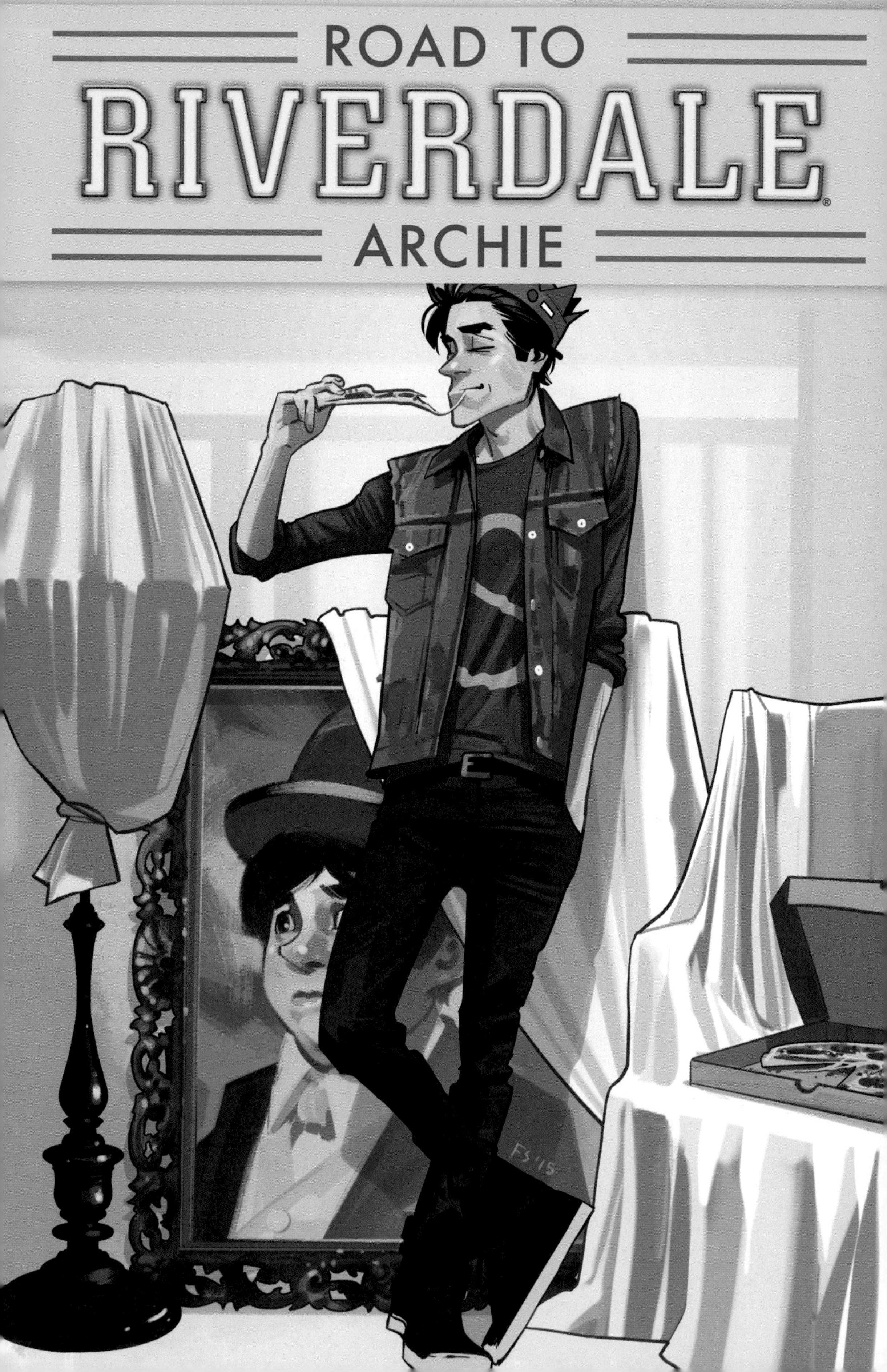
ROAD TO
RIVERDALE®
ARCHIE
FS '15

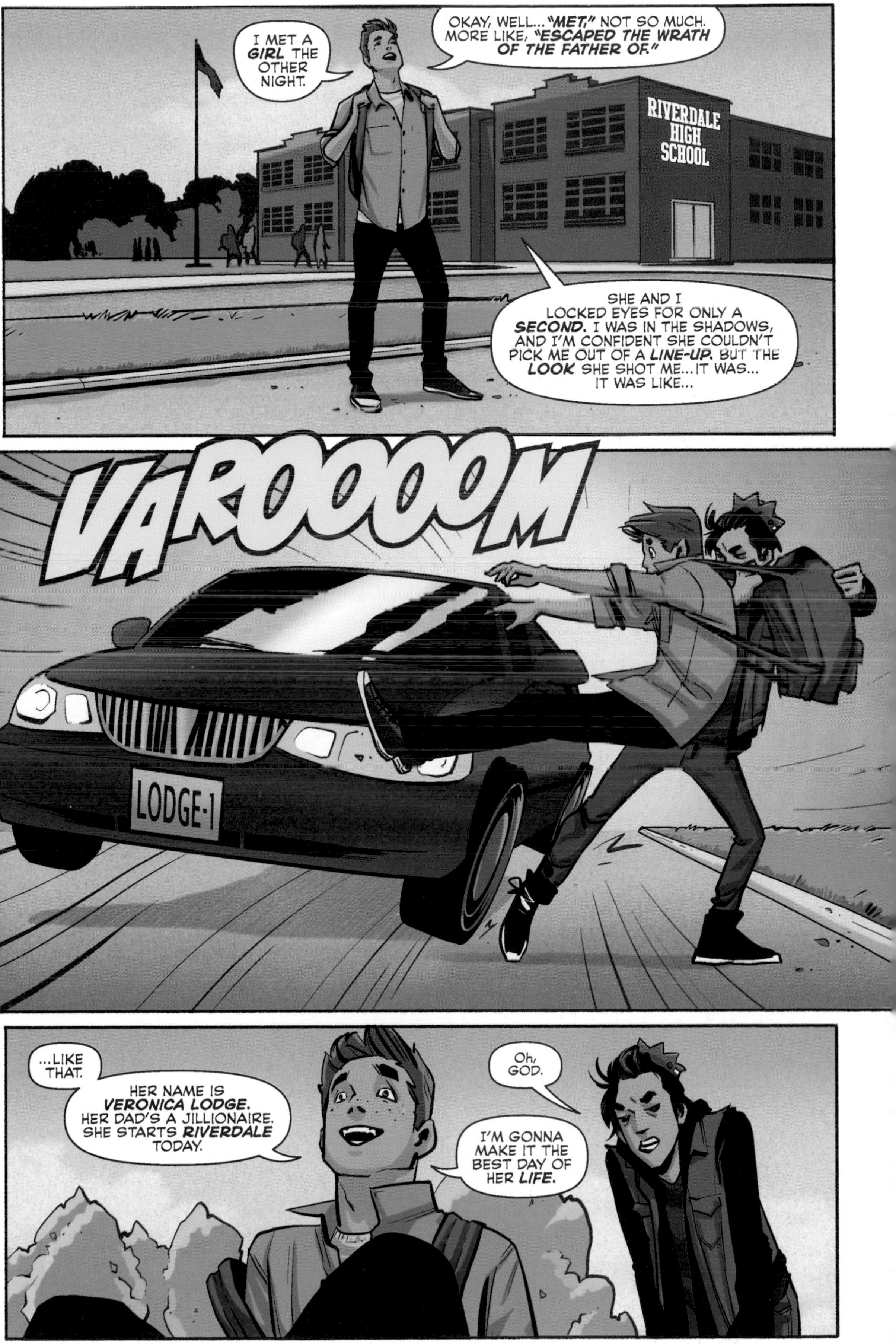
I MET A GIRL THE OTHER NIGHT.
OKAY, WELL... "MET," NOT SO MUCH. MORE LIKE, "ESCAPED THE WRATH OF THE FATHER OF."
RIVERDALE HIGH SCHOOL
SHE AND I LOCKED EYES FOR ONLY A SECOND. I WAS IN THE SHADOWS, AND I'M CONFIDENT SHE COULDN'T PICK ME OUT OF A LINE-UP. BUT THE LOOK SHE SHOT ME...IT WAS... IT WAS LIKE...
VAROOOOM
LODGE-1
...LIKE THAT.
HER NAME IS VERONICA LODGE. HER DAD'S A JILLIONAIRE. SHE STARTS RIVERDALE TODAY.
Oh, GOD.
I'M GONNA MAKE IT THE BEST DAY OF HER LIFE.

CHAPTER ONE: NICE Purse, ANDREWS

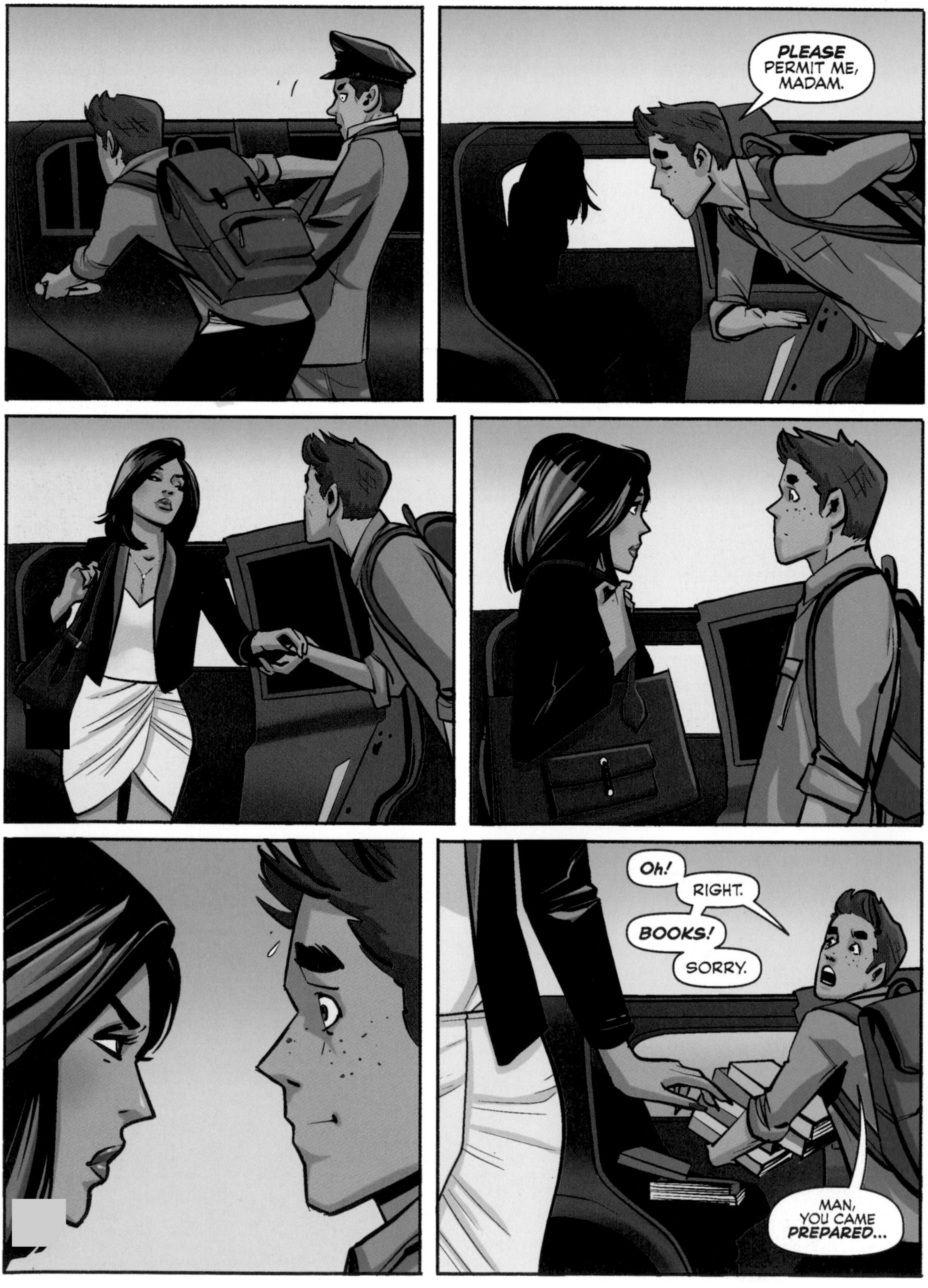
PLEASE PERMIT ME, MADAM.
Oh!
RIGHT.
BOOKS!
SORRY.
MAN, YOU CAME PREPARED...

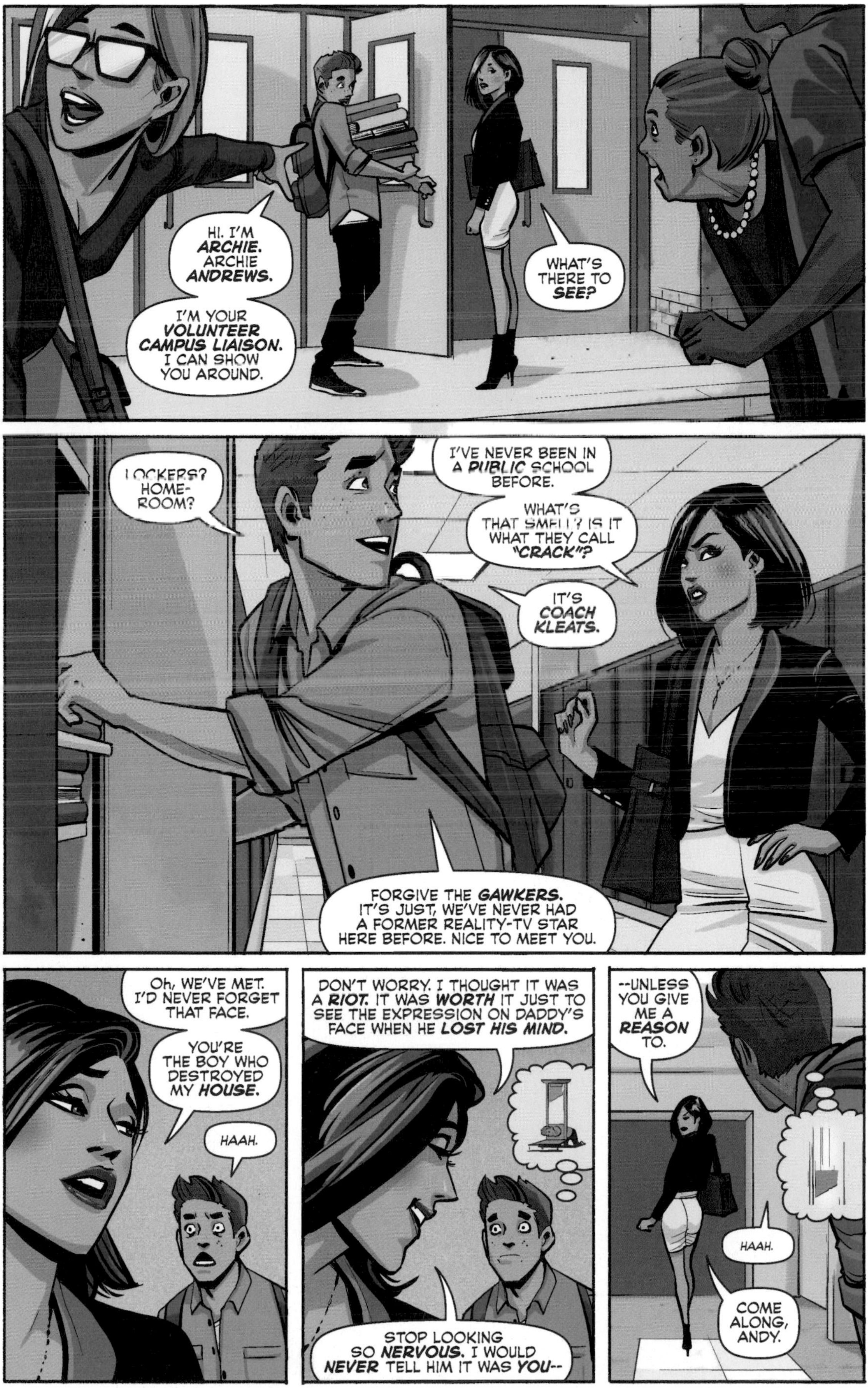
HI. I'M ARCHIE. ARCHIE ANDREWS.
I'M YOUR VOLUNTEER CAMPUS LIAISON. I CAN SHOW YOU AROUND.
WHAT'S THERE TO SEE?
LOCKERS? HOME-ROOM?
I'VE NEVER BEEN IN A PUBLIC SCHOOL BEFORE.
WHAT'S THAT SMELL? IS IT WHAT THEY CALL "CRACK"?
IT'S COACH KLEATS.
FORGIVE THE GAWKERS. IT'S JUST, WE'VE NEVER HAD A FORMER REALITY-TV STAR HERE BEFORE. NICE TO MEET YOU.
Oh, WE'VE MET. I'D NEVER FORGET THAT FACE.
YOU'RE THE BOY WHO DESTROYED MY HOUSE.
HAAH.
DON'T WORRY. I THOUGHT IT WAS A RIOT. IT WAS WORTH IT JUST TO SEE THE EXPRESSION ON DADDY'S FACE WHEN HE LOST HIS MIND.
STOP LOOKING SO NERVOUS. I WOULD NEVER TELL HIM IT WAS YOU--
--UNLESS YOU GIVE ME A REASON TO.
HAAH.
COME ALONG, ANDY.

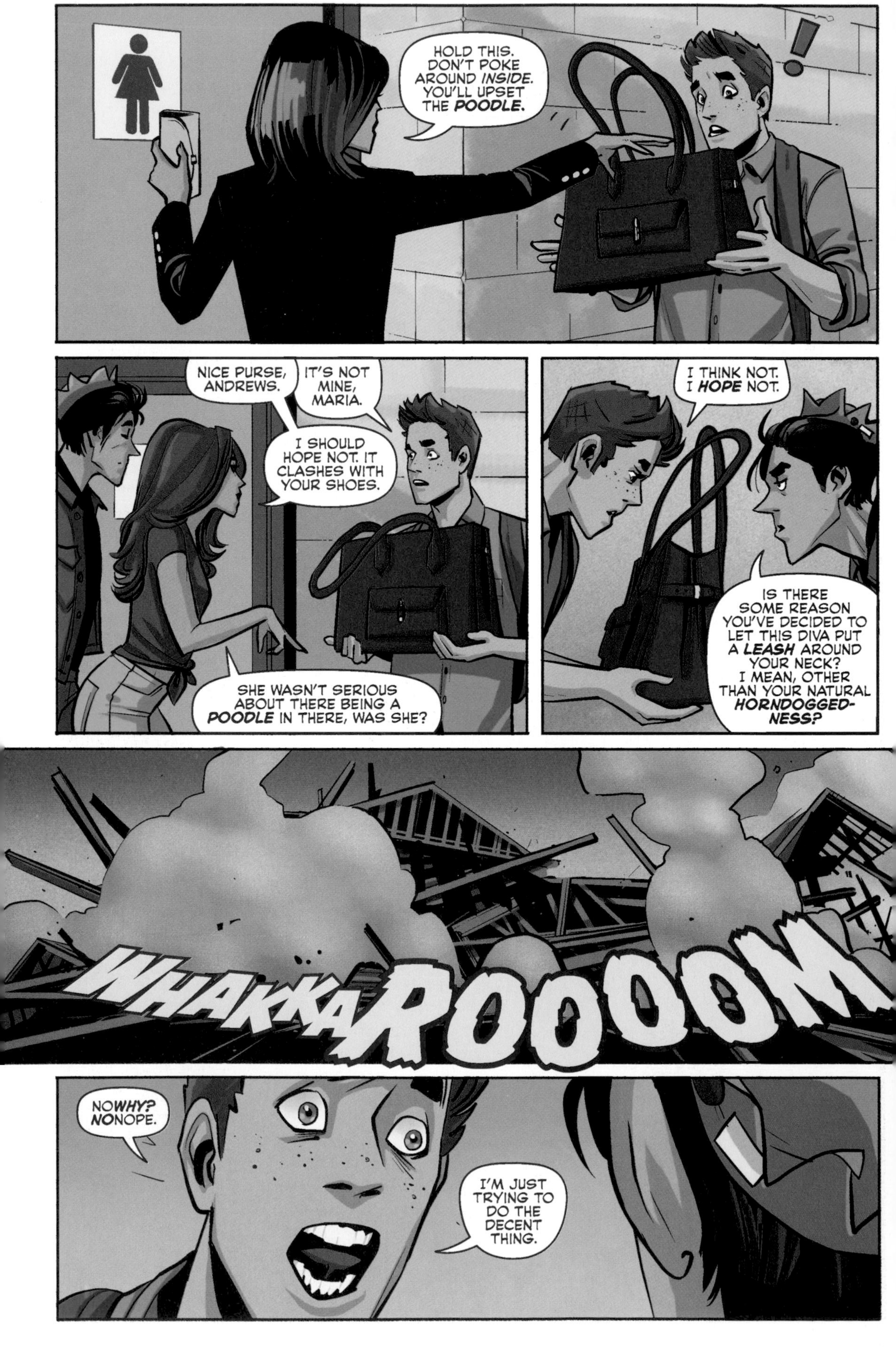
HOLD THIS. DON'T POKE AROUND *INSIDE.* YOU'LL UPSET THE ***POODLE.***
!
NICE PURSE, ANDREWS.
IT'S NOT MINE, MARIA.
I SHOULD HOPE NOT. IT CLASHES WITH YOUR SHOES.
SHE WASN'T SERIOUS ABOUT THERE BEING A ***POODLE*** IN THERE, WAS SHE?
I THINK NOT. I ***HOPE*** NOT.
IS THERE SOME REASON YOU'VE DECIDED TO LET THIS DIVA PUT A ***LEASH*** AROUND YOUR NECK? I MEAN, OTHER THAN YOUR NATURAL ***HORNDOGGED-NESS?***
WHAKKAROOOOM
NO***WHY?*** ***NO***NOPE.
I'M JUST TRYING TO DO THE DECENT THING.

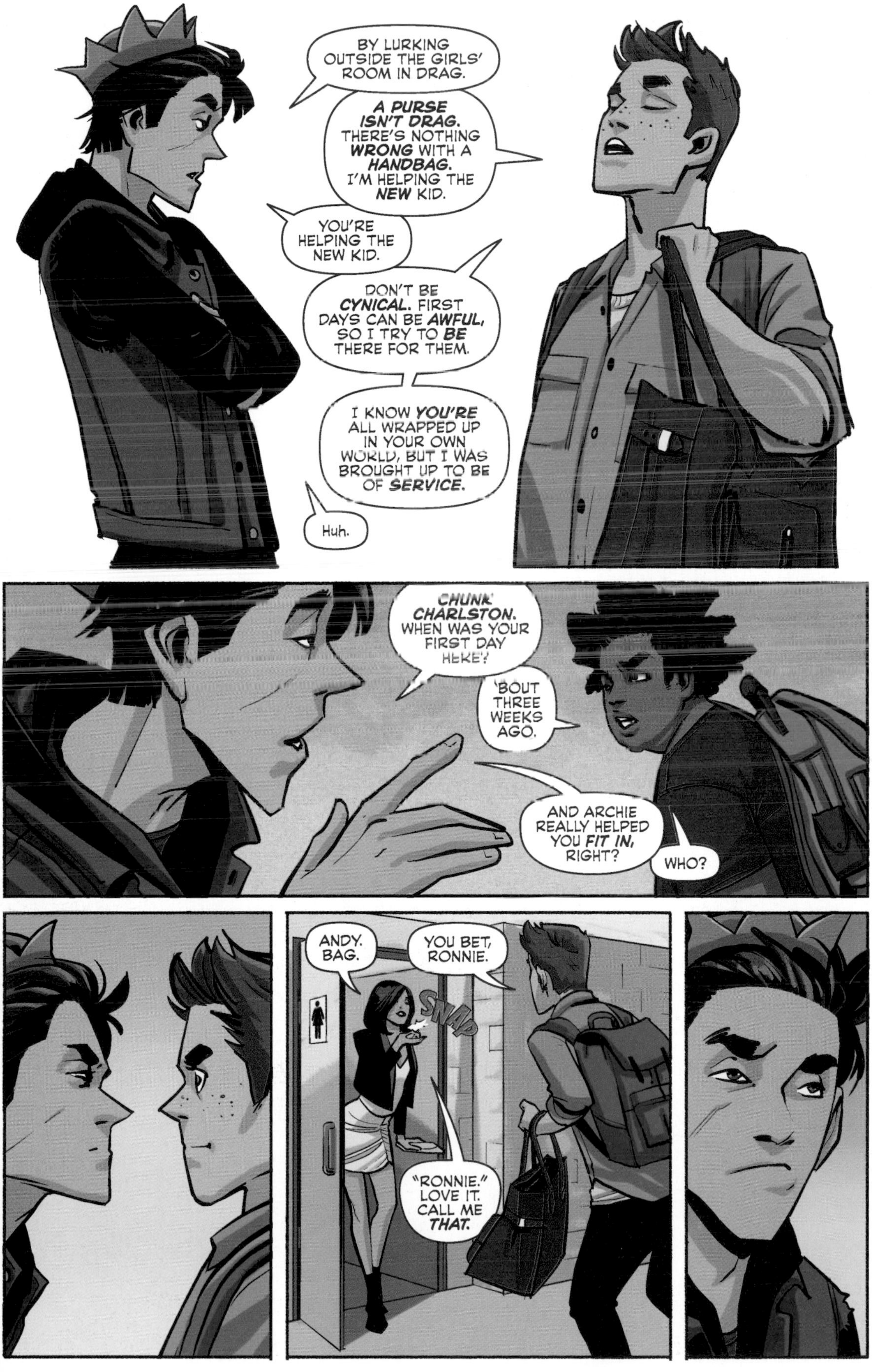
BY LURKING OUTSIDE THE GIRLS' ROOM IN DRAG.
A PURSE ISN'T DRAG. THERE'S NOTHING WRONG WITH A HANDBAG. I'M HELPING THE NEW KID.
YOU'RE HELPING THE NEW KID.
DON'T BE CYNICAL. FIRST DAYS CAN BE AWFUL, SO I TRY TO BE THERE FOR THEM.
I KNOW YOU'RE ALL WRAPPED UP IN YOUR OWN WORLD, BUT I WAS BROUGHT UP TO BE OF SERVICE.
Huh.
CHUNK CHARLSTON. WHEN WAS YOUR FIRST DAY HERE?
'BOUT THREE WEEKS AGO.
AND ARCHIE REALLY HELPED YOU FIT IN, RIGHT?
WHO?
ANDY. BAG.
YOU BET, RONNIE.
SNAP
"RONNIE." LOVE IT. CALL ME THAT.

CHAPTER TWO: THEN Taylor SANG TO Katie

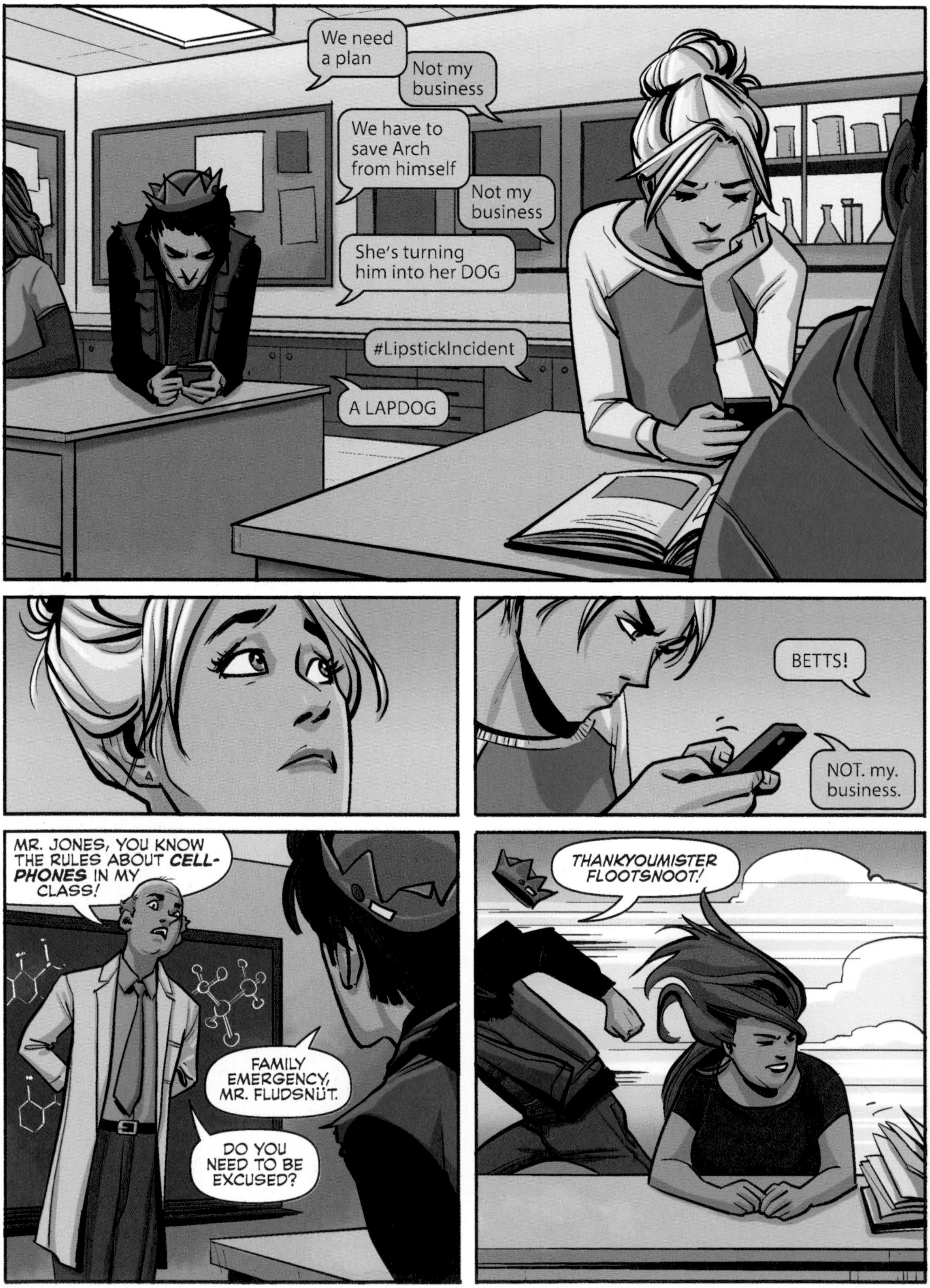
We need a plan
Not my business
We have to save Arch from himself
Not my business
She's turning him into her DOG
#LipstickIncident
A LAPDOG
BETTS!
NOT. my. business.
MR. JONES, YOU KNOW THE RULES ABOUT CELL-PHONES IN MY CLASS!
FAMILY EMERGENCY, MR. FLUDSNÜT.
DO YOU NEED TO BE EXCUSED?
THANKYOUMISTER FLOOTSNOOT!

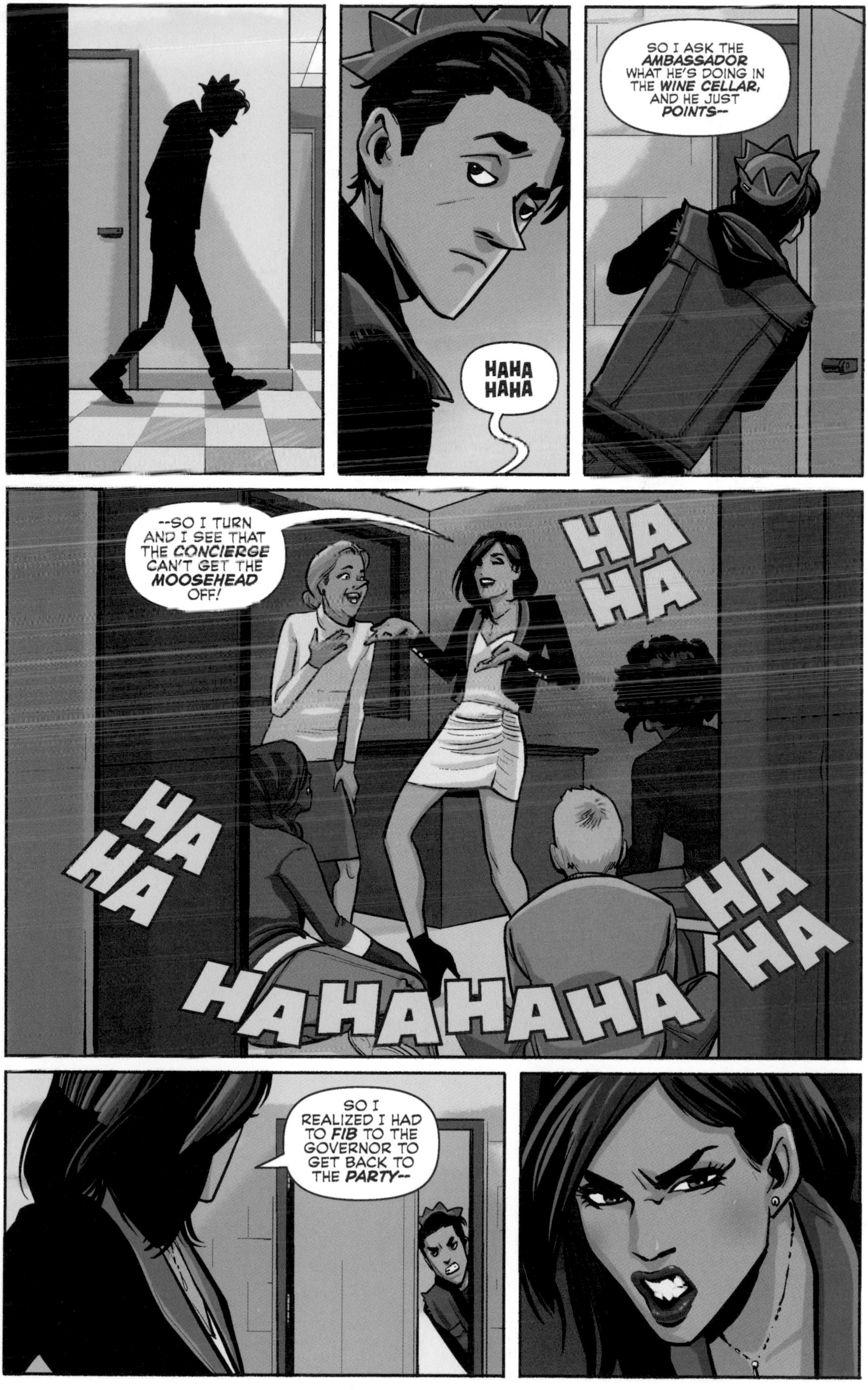
HAHA HAHA
SO I ASK THE AMBASSADOR WHAT HE'S DOING IN THE WINE CELLAR, AND HE JUST POINTS--
--SO I TURN AND I SEE THAT THE CONCIERGE CAN'T GET THE MOOSEHEAD OFF!
HA HA HA
HA HA
HA HA
HAHAHAHAHAHA
SO I REALIZED I HAD TO FIB TO THE GOVERNOR TO GET BACK TO THE PARTY--

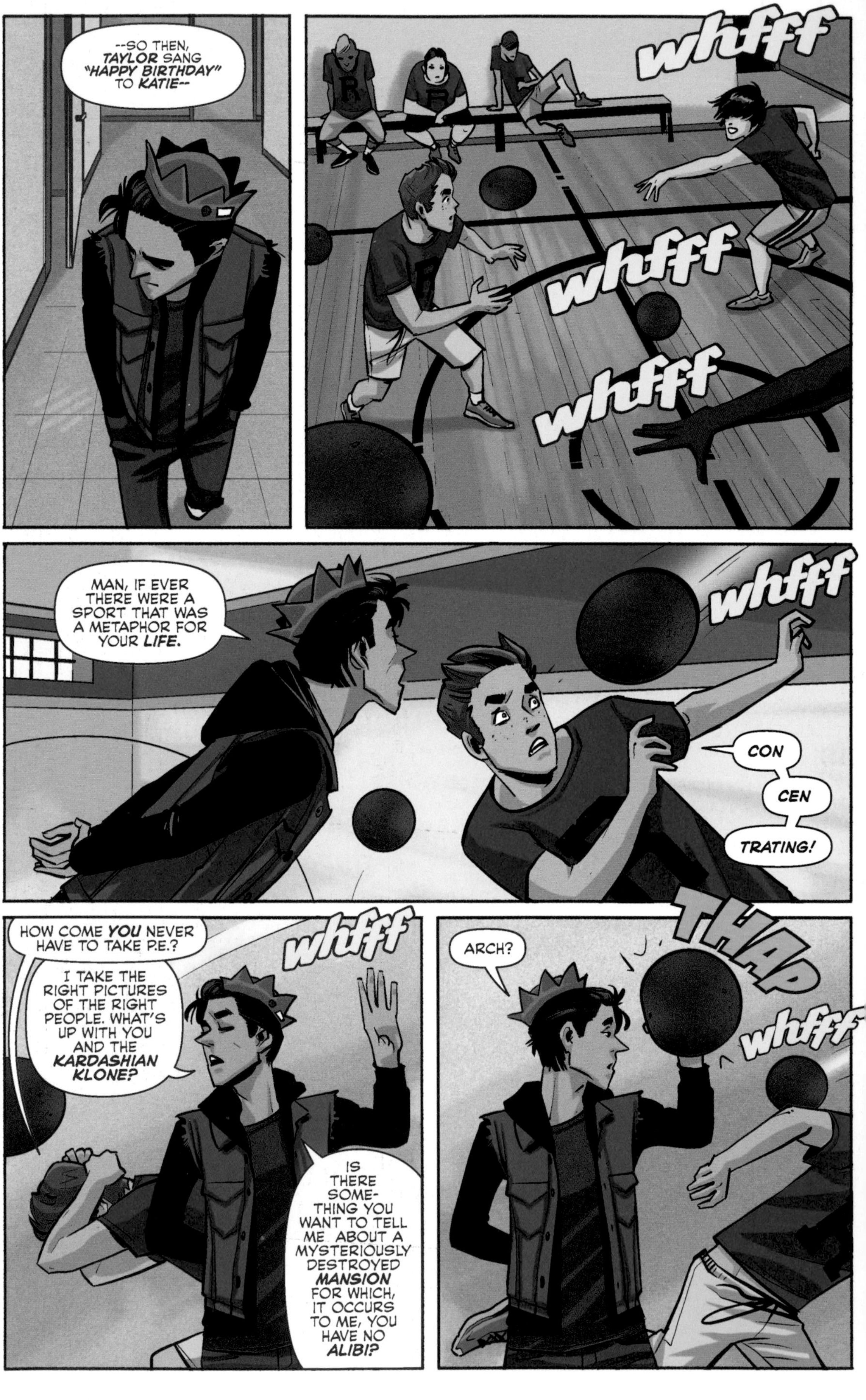
--SO THEN, TAYLOR SANG "HAPPY BIRTHDAY" TO KATIE--
whfff
whfff
whfff
MAN, IF EVER THERE WERE A SPORT THAT WAS A METAPHOR FOR YOUR LIFE.
whfff
CON
CEN
TRATING!
HOW COME YOU NEVER HAVE TO TAKE P.E.?
I TAKE THE RIGHT PICTURES OF THE RIGHT PEOPLE. WHAT'S UP WITH YOU AND THE KARDASHIAN KLONE?
whfff
IS THERE SOME-THING YOU WANT TO TELL ME ABOUT A MYSTERIOUSLY DESTROYED MANSION FOR WHICH, IT OCCURS TO ME, YOU HAVE NO ALIBI?
ARCH?
THAP
whfff

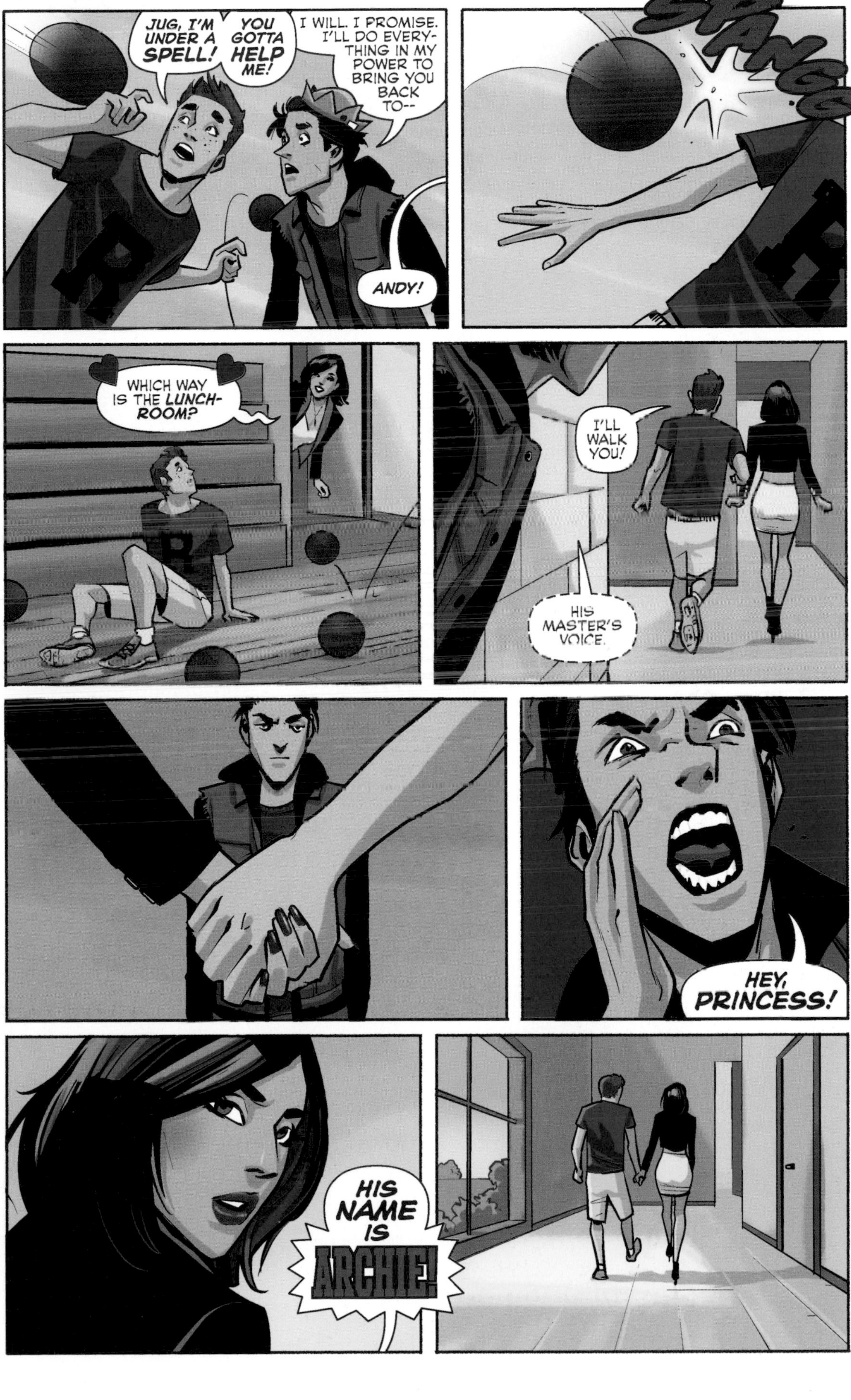
JUG, I'M UNDER A SPELL!
YOU GOTTA HELP ME!
I WILL. I PROMISE. I'LL DO EVERY-THING IN MY POWER TO BRING YOU BACK TO--
ANDY!
SPANGG
WHICH WAY IS THE LUNCH-ROOM?
I'LL WALK YOU!
HIS MASTER'S VOICE.
HEY, PRINCESS!
HIS NAME IS ARCHIE!

CHAPTER THREE: WHO'S YOUR Chef?

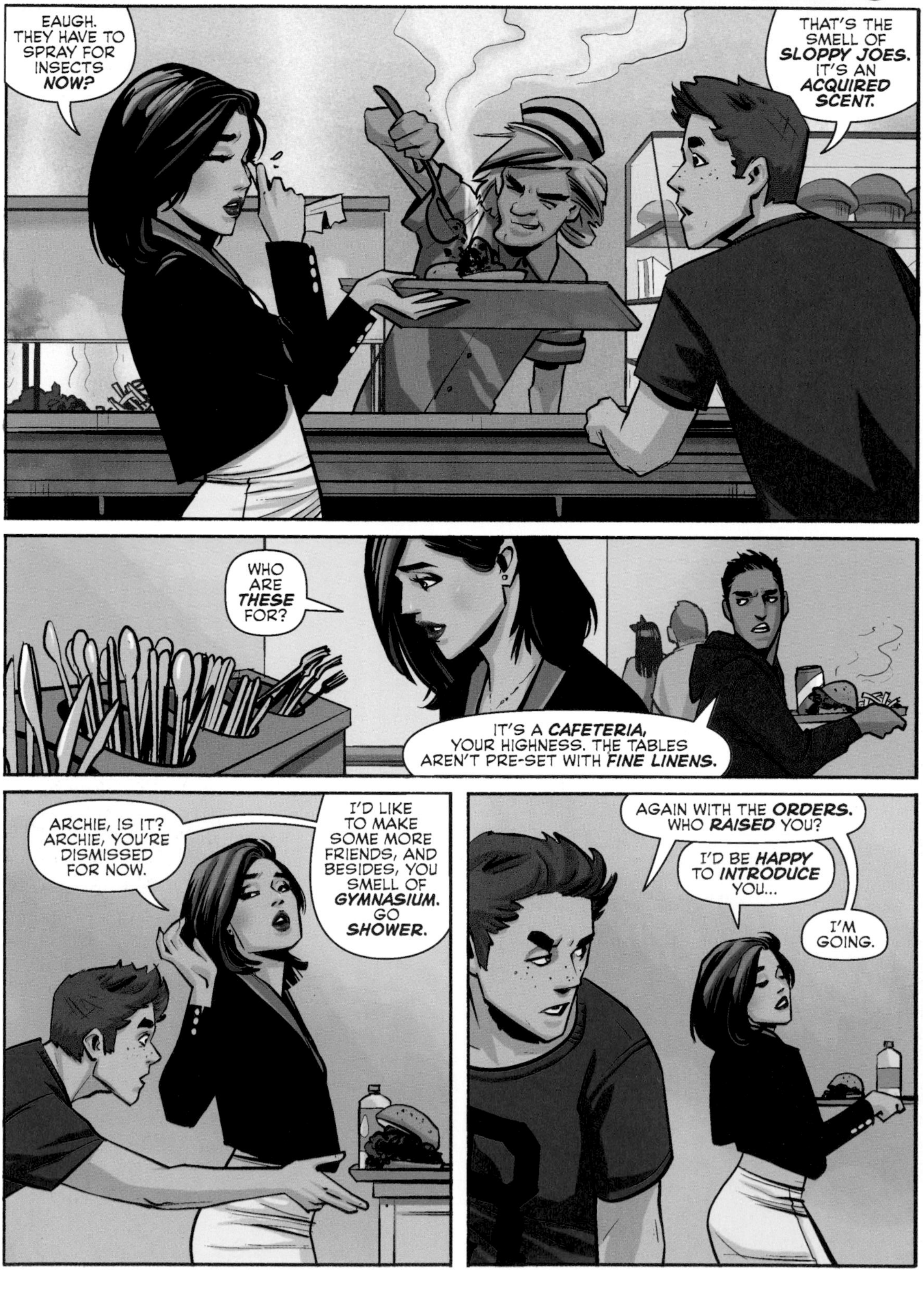
EAUGH. THEY HAVE TO SPRAY FOR INSECTS NOW?
THAT'S THE SMELL OF SLOPPY JOES. IT'S AN ACQUIRED SCENT.
WHO ARE THESE FOR?
IT'S A CAFETERIA, YOUR HIGHNESS. THE TABLES AREN'T PRE-SET WITH FINE LINENS.
ARCHIE, IS IT? ARCHIE, YOU'RE DISMISSED FOR NOW.
I'D LIKE TO MAKE SOME MORE FRIENDS, AND BESIDES, YOU SMELL OF GYMNASIUM. GO SHOWER.
AGAIN WITH THE ORDERS. WHO RAISED YOU?
I'D BE HAPPY TO INTRODUCE YOU...
I'M GOING.

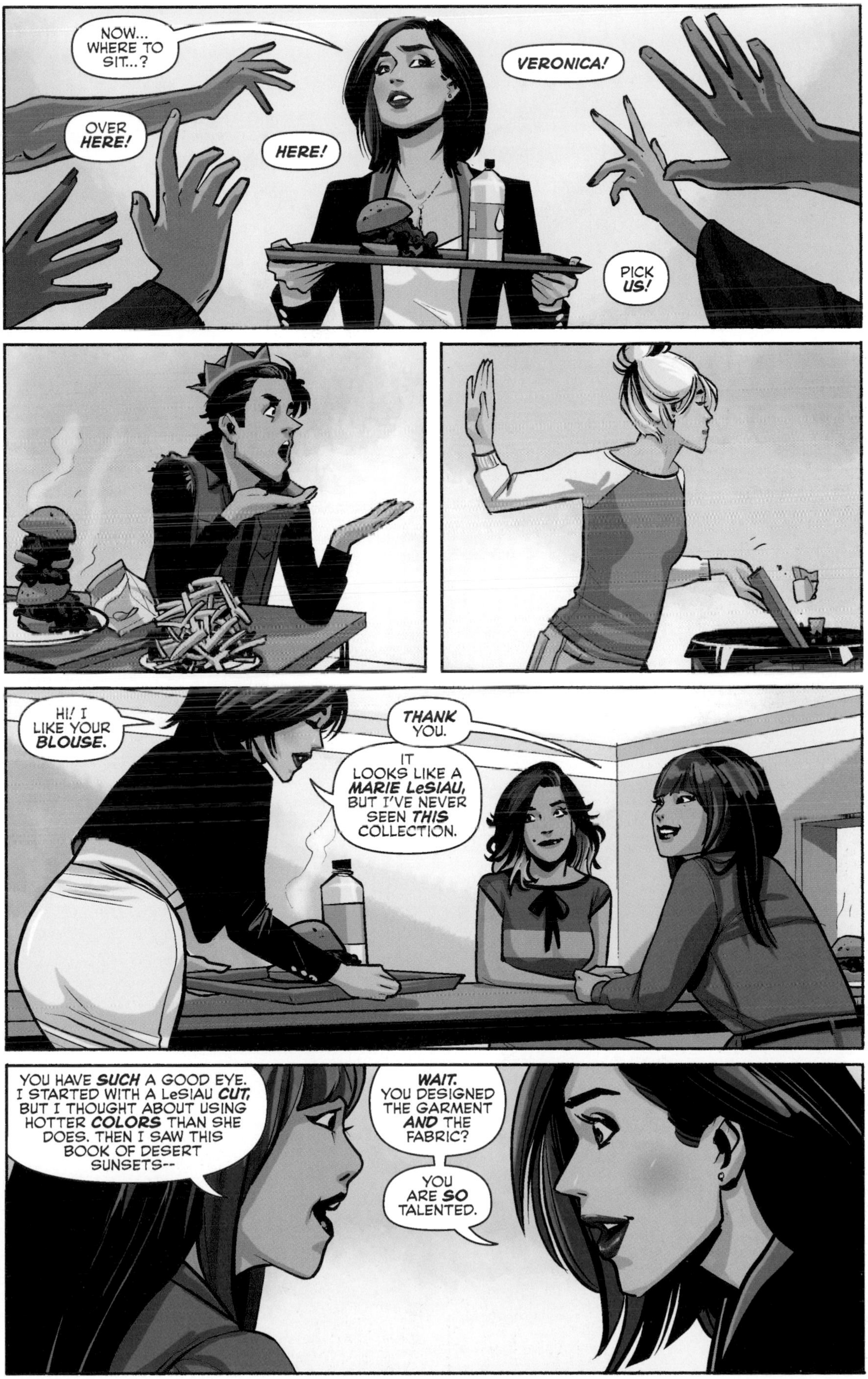
NOW... WHERE TO SIT...?
VERONICA!
OVER HERE!
HERE!
PICK US!
HI! I LIKE YOUR BLOUSE.
THANK YOU.
IT LOOKS LIKE A MARIE LeSIAU, BUT I'VE NEVER SEEN THIS COLLECTION.
YOU HAVE SUCH A GOOD EYE. I STARTED WITH A LeSIAU CUT, BUT I THOUGHT ABOUT USING HOTTER COLORS THAN SHE DOES. THEN I SAW THIS BOOK OF DESERT SUNSETS--
WAIT. YOU DESIGNED THE GARMENT AND THE FABRIC?
YOU ARE SO TALENTED.

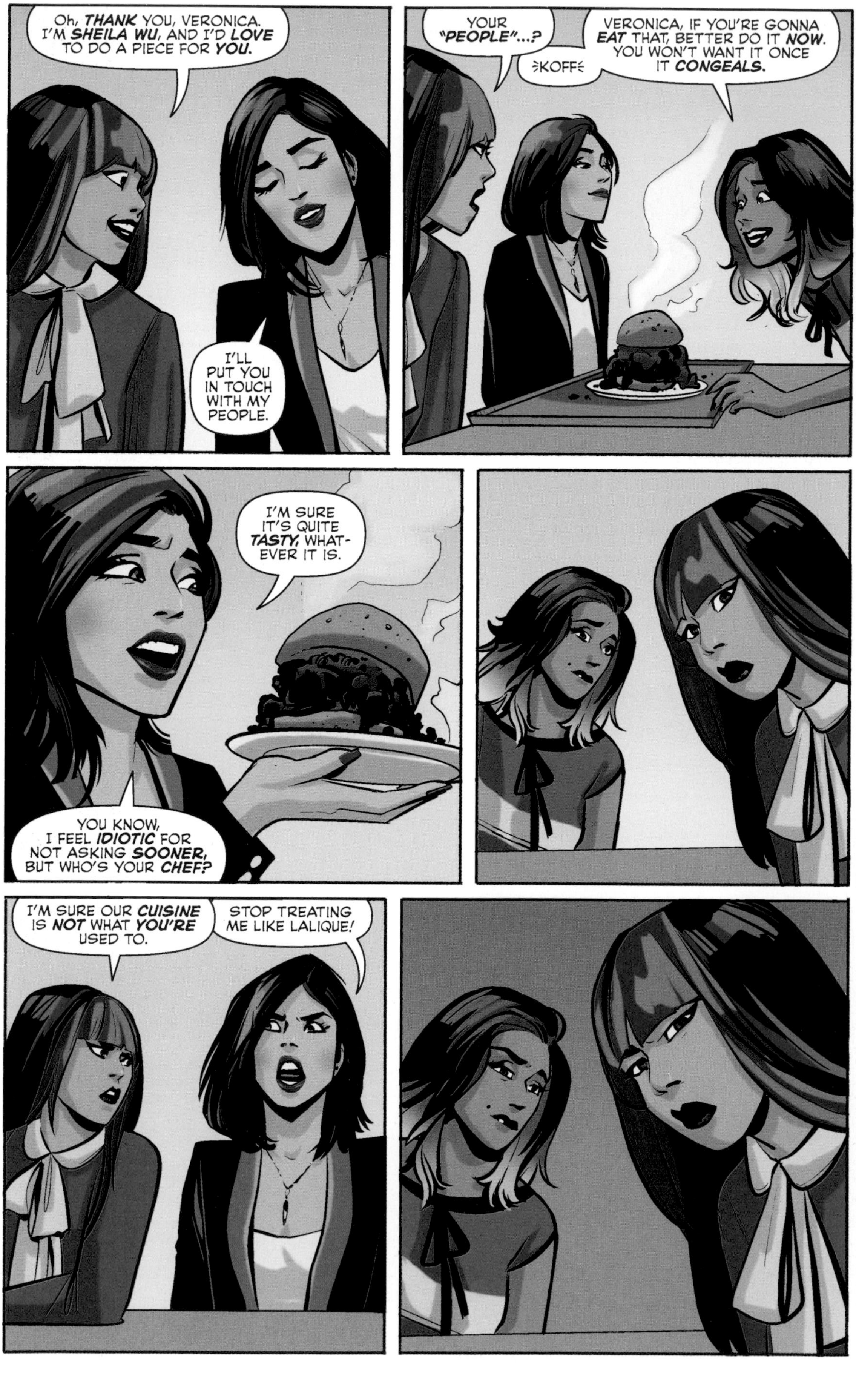
Oh, THANK YOU, VERONICA. I'M SHEILA WU, AND I'D LOVE TO DO A PIECE FOR YOU.
I'LL PUT YOU IN TOUCH WITH MY PEOPLE.
YOUR "PEOPLE"...?
KOFF
VERONICA, IF YOU'RE GONNA EAT THAT, BETTER DO IT NOW. YOU WON'T WANT IT ONCE IT CONGEALS.
I'M SURE IT'S QUITE TASTY, WHATEVER IT IS.
YOU KNOW, I FEEL IDIOTIC FOR NOT ASKING SOONER, BUT WHO'S YOUR CHEF?
I'M SURE OUR CUISINE IS NOT WHAT YOU'RE USED TO.
STOP TREATING ME LIKE LALIQUE!

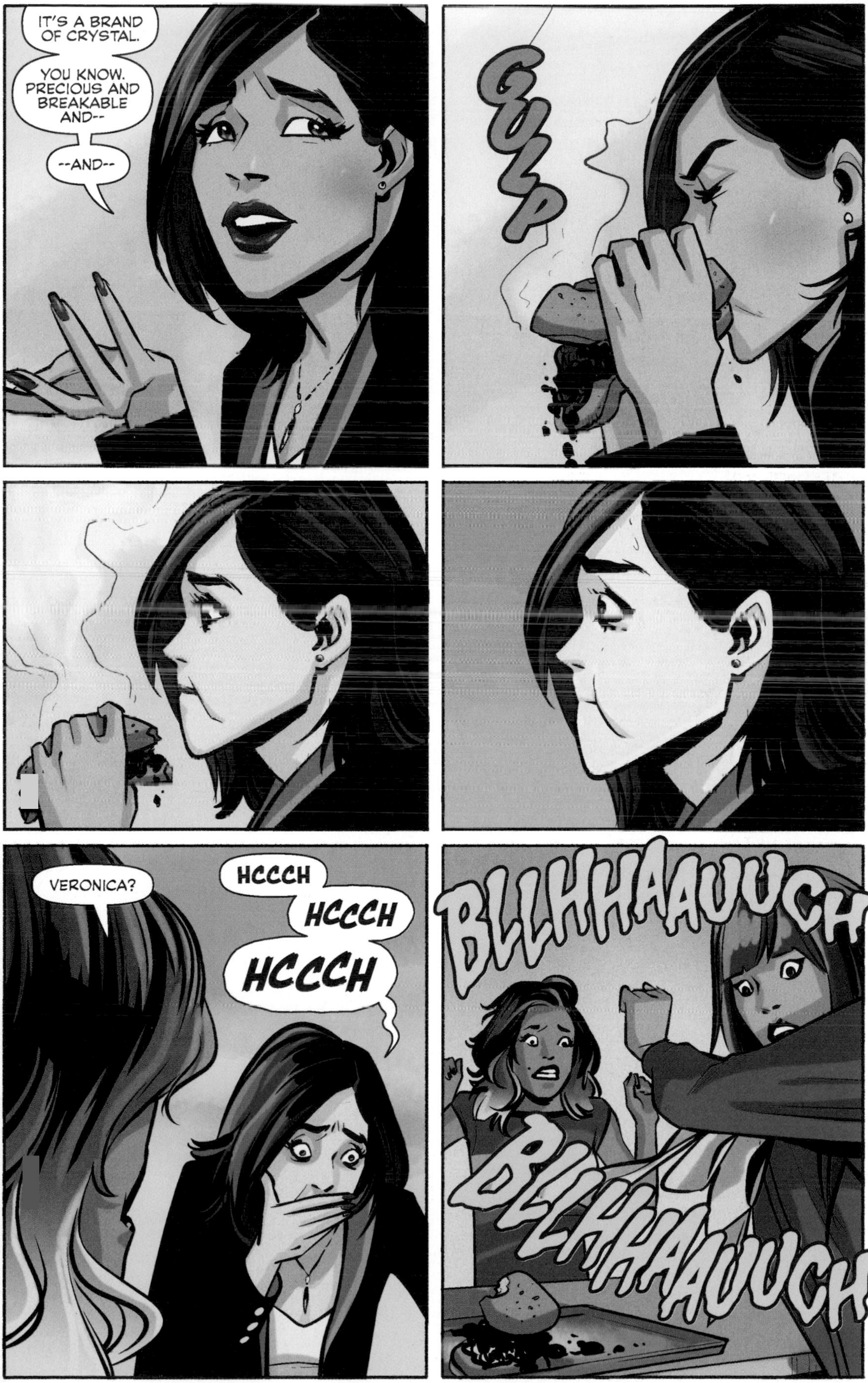
IT'S A BRAND OF CRYSTAL.
YOU KNOW. PRECIOUS AND BREAKABLE AND--
--AND--
GULP
VERONICA?
HCCCH
HCCCH
HCCCH
BLLHHAAUUCH
BLLHHAAUUCH

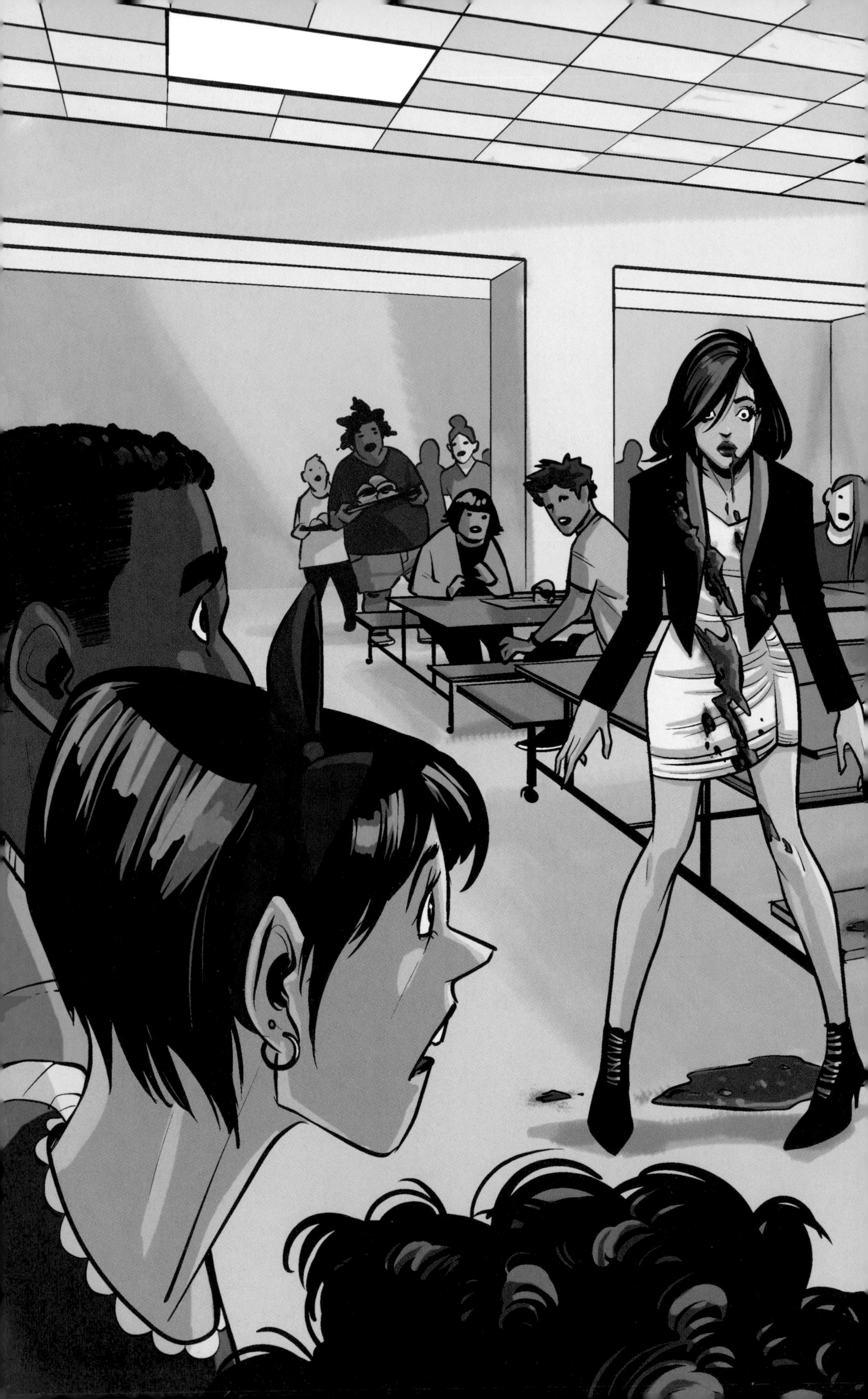

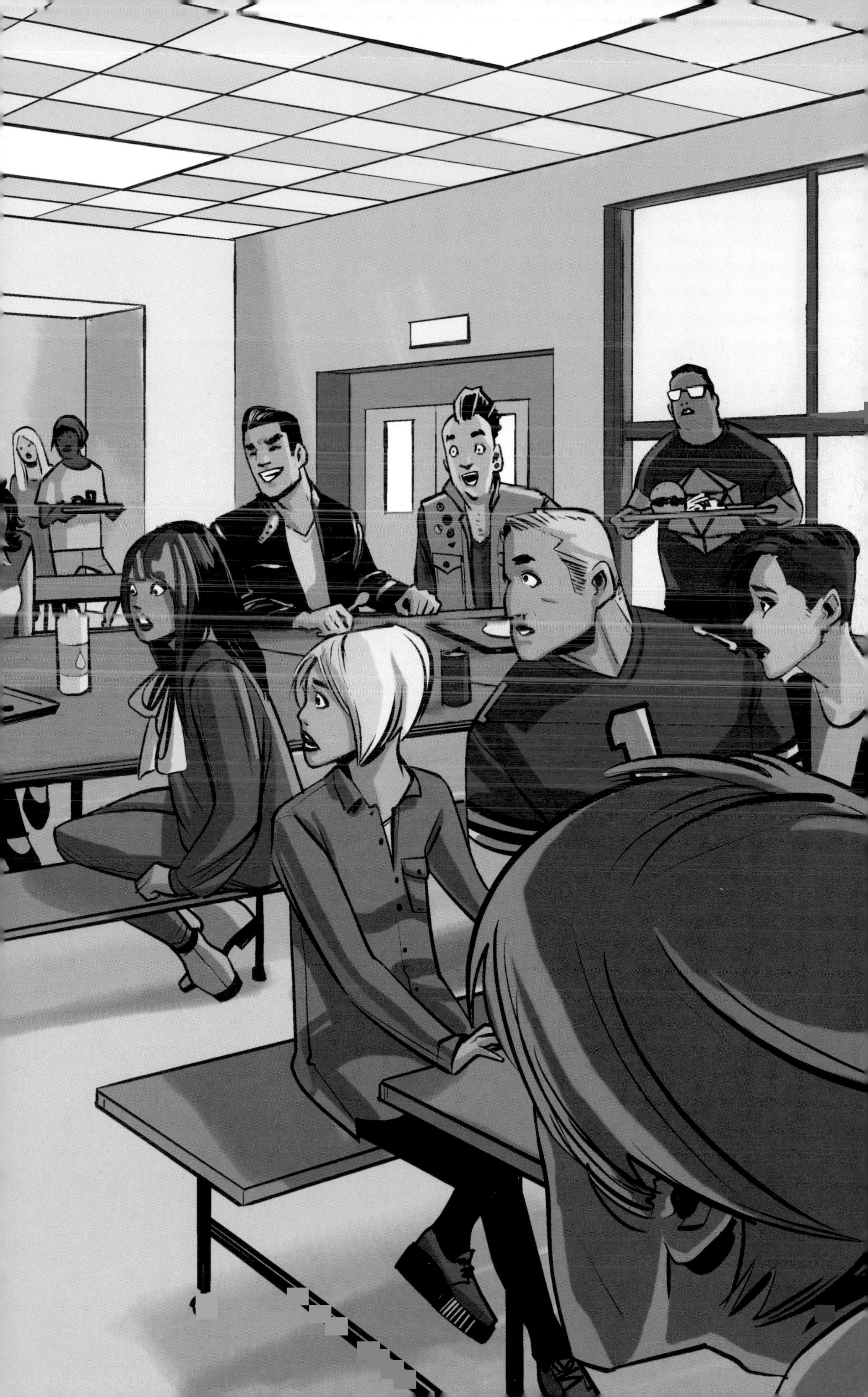

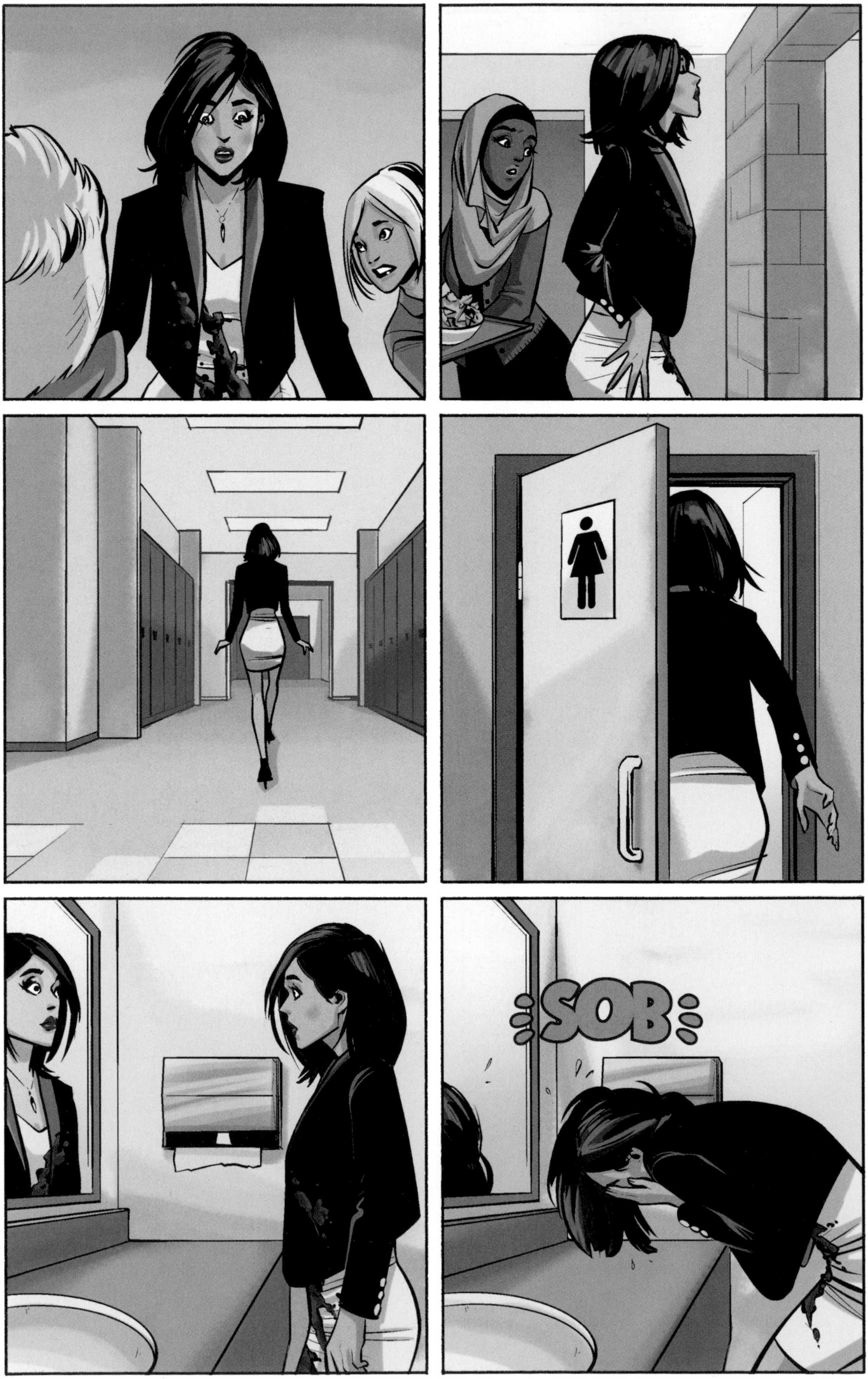
SOB

CHAPTER FOUR: PARADE FLOAT

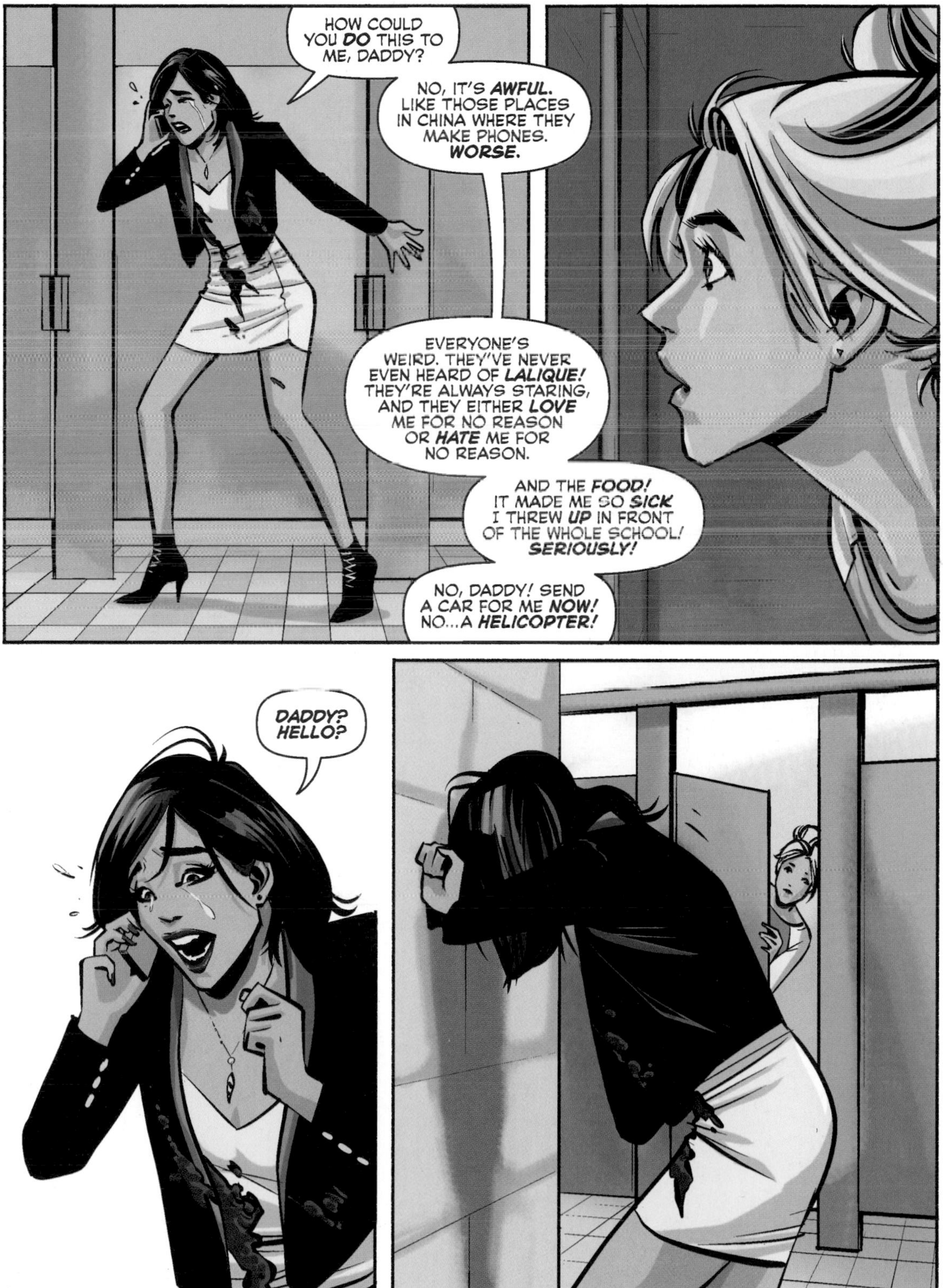
HOW COULD YOU **DO** THIS TO ME, DADDY?
NO, IT'S **AWFUL.** LIKE THOSE PLACES IN CHINA WHERE THEY MAKE PHONES. **WORSE.**
EVERYONE'S WEIRD. THEY'VE NEVER EVEN HEARD OF **LALIQUE!** THEY'RE ALWAYS STARING, AND THEY EITHER **LOVE** ME FOR NO REASON OR **HATE** ME FOR NO REASON.
AND THE **FOOD!** IT MADE ME SO **SICK** I THREW **UP** IN FRONT OF THE WHOLE SCHOOL! **SERIOUSLY!**
NO, DADDY! SEND A CAR FOR ME **NOW!** NO...A **HELICOPTER!**
DADDY? HELLO?

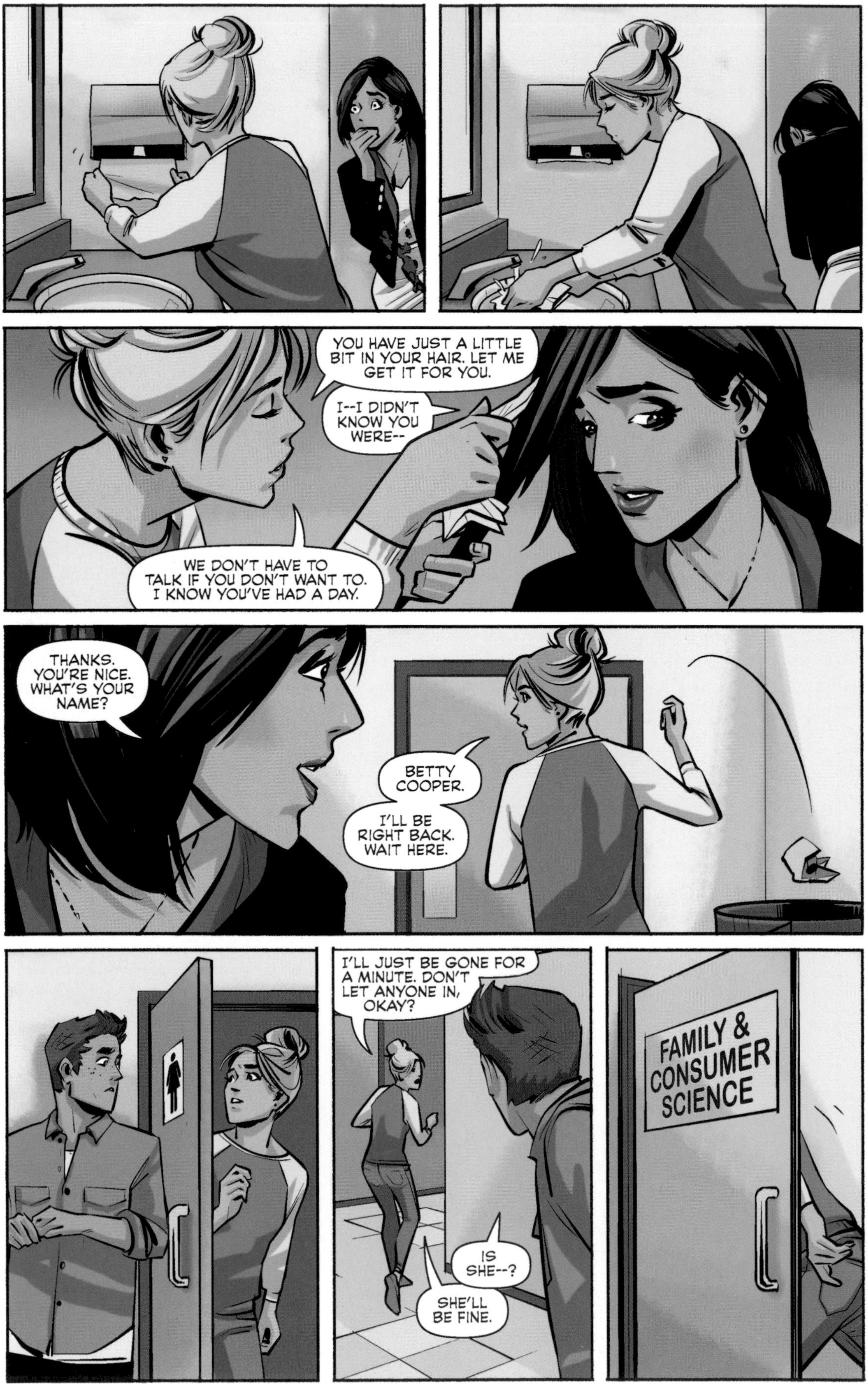
YOU HAVE JUST A LITTLE BIT IN YOUR HAIR. LET ME GET IT FOR YOU.
I--I DIDN'T KNOW YOU WERE--
WE DON'T HAVE TO TALK IF YOU DON'T WANT TO. I KNOW YOU'VE HAD A DAY.
THANKS. YOU'RE NICE. WHAT'S YOUR NAME?
BETTY COOPER.
I'LL BE RIGHT BACK. WAIT HERE.
I'LL JUST BE GONE FOR A MINUTE. DON'T LET ANYONE IN, OKAY?
IS SHE--?
SHE'LL BE FINE.
FAMILY & CONSUMER SCIENCE

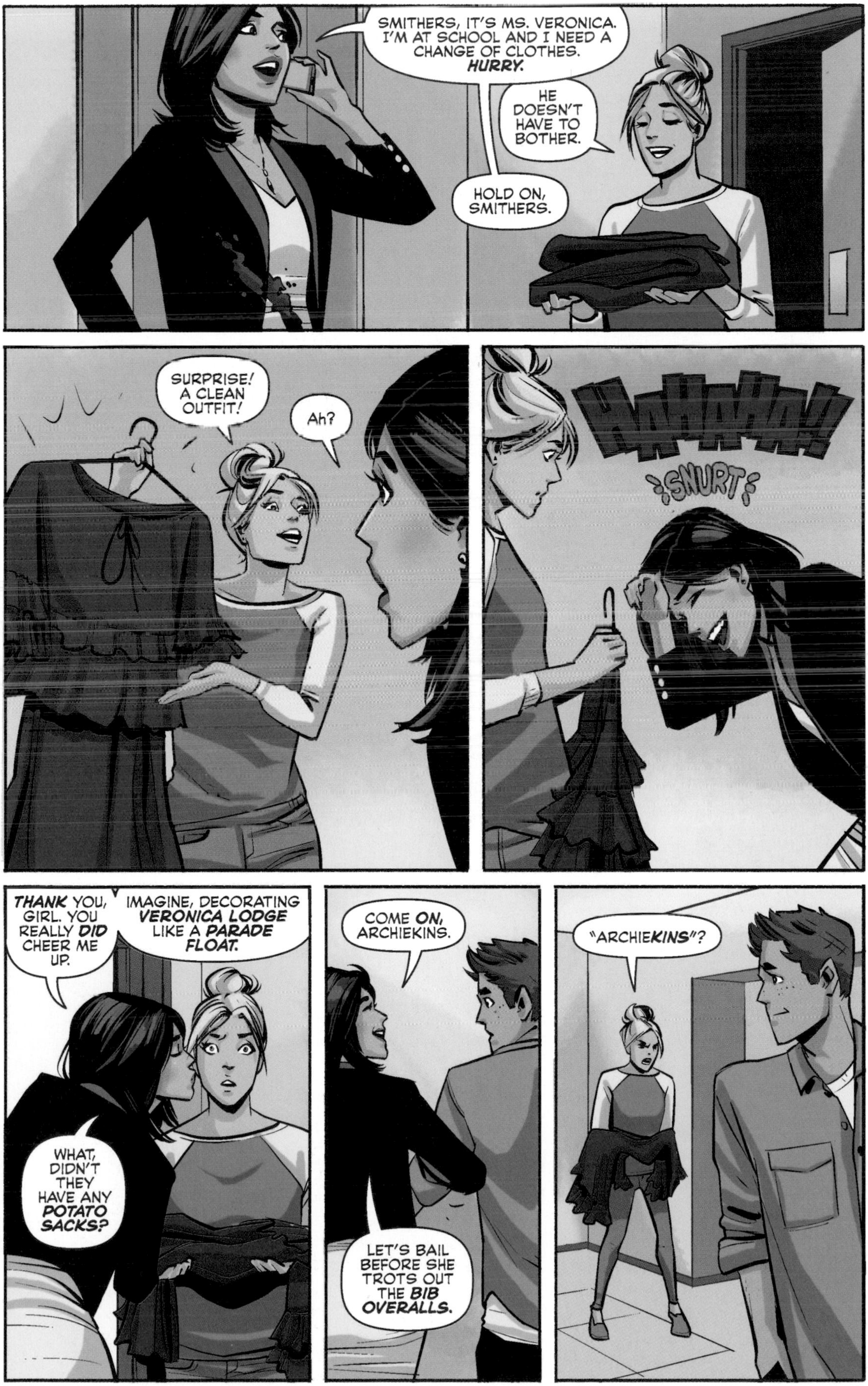
SMITHERS, IT'S MS. VERONICA. I'M AT SCHOOL AND I NEED A CHANGE OF CLOTHES. **HURRY.**
HE DOESN'T HAVE TO BOTHER.
HOLD ON, SMITHERS.
SURPRISE! A CLEAN OUTFIT!
Ah?
HAHAHAH!
SNURT
THANK YOU, GIRL. YOU REALLY **DID** CHEER ME UP.
IMAGINE, DECORATING **VERONICA LODGE** LIKE A **PARADE FLOAT.**
WHAT, DIDN'T THEY HAVE ANY **POTATO SACKS?**
COME **ON,** ARCHIEKINS.
LET'S BAIL BEFORE SHE TROTS OUT THE **BIB OVERALLS.**
"ARCHIE**KINS**"?

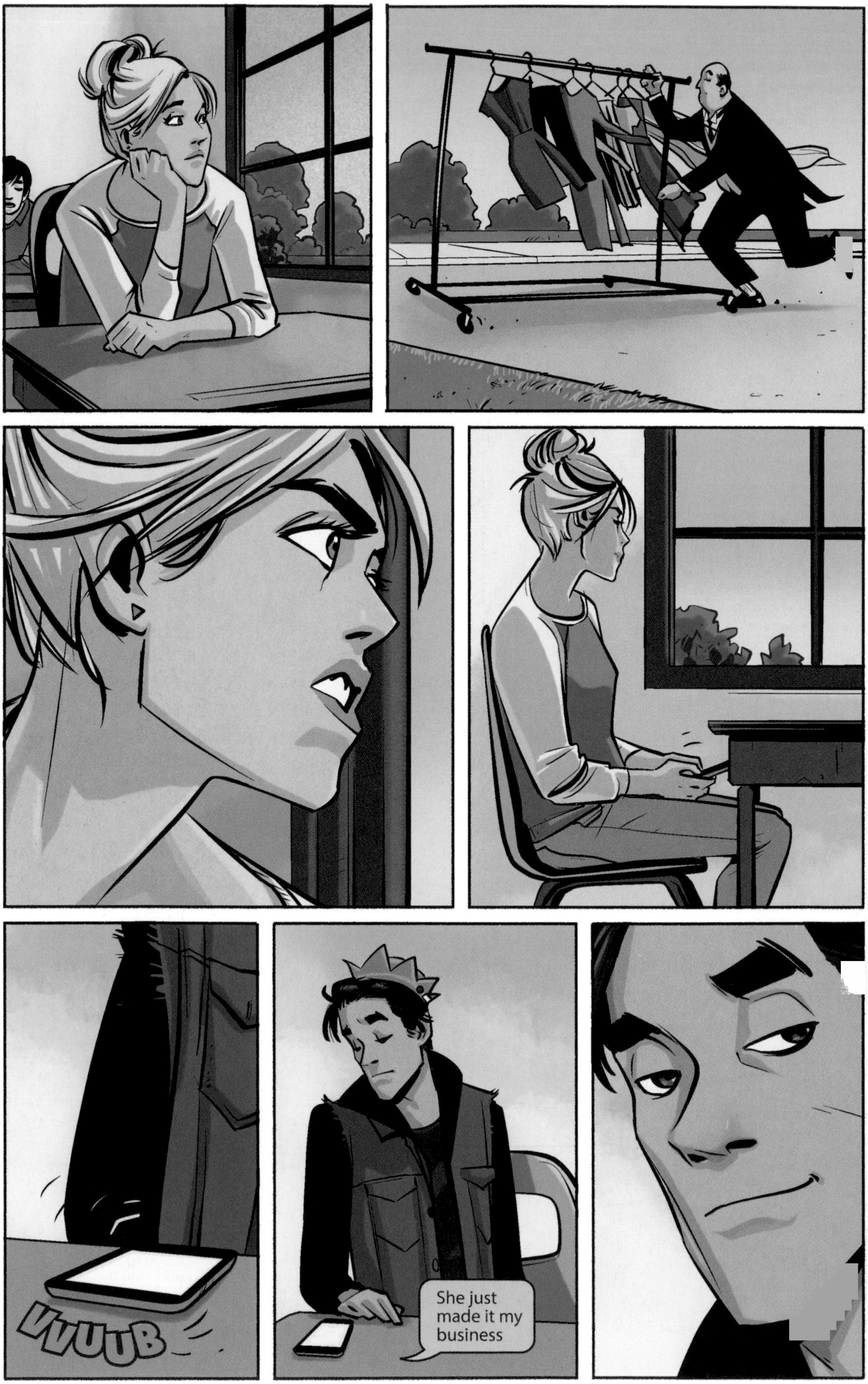
VVUUB
She just made it my business

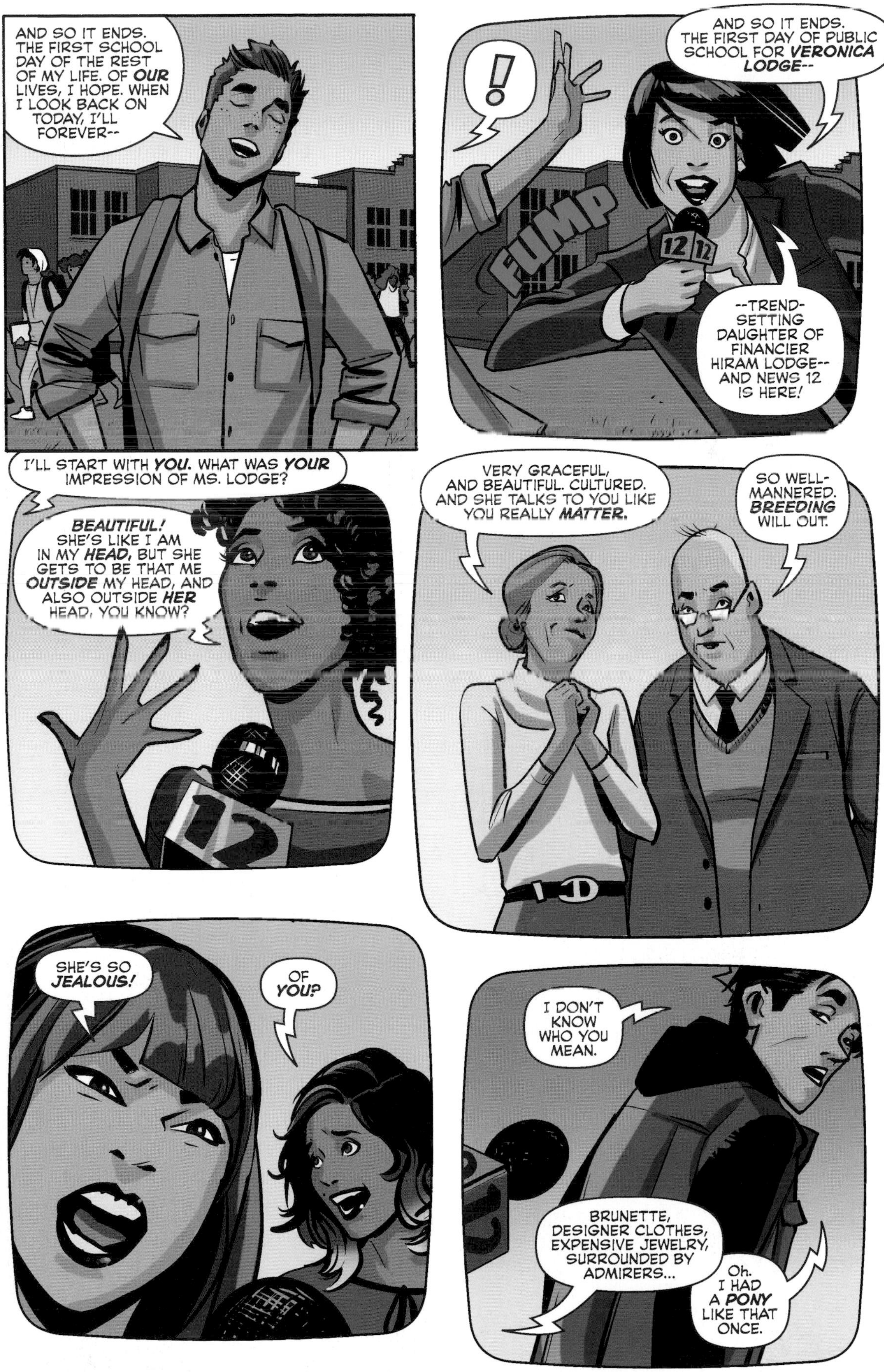
AND SO IT ENDS. THE FIRST SCHOOL DAY OF THE REST OF MY LIFE. OF OUR LIVES, I HOPE. WHEN I LOOK BACK ON TODAY, I'LL FOREVER--
!
AND SO IT ENDS. THE FIRST DAY OF PUBLIC SCHOOL FOR VERONICA LODGE--
FUMP
--TREND-SETTING DAUGHTER OF FINANCIER HIRAM LODGE--AND NEWS 12 IS HERE!
I'LL START WITH YOU. WHAT WAS YOUR IMPRESSION OF MS. LODGE?
BEAUTIFUL! SHE'S LIKE I AM IN MY HEAD, BUT SHE GETS TO BE THAT ME OUTSIDE MY HEAD, AND ALSO OUTSIDE HER HEAD, YOU KNOW?
VERY GRACEFUL, AND BEAUTIFUL. CULTURED. AND SHE TALKS TO YOU LIKE YOU REALLY MATTER.
SO WELL-MANNERED. BREEDING WILL OUT.
SHE'S SO JEALOUS!
OF YOU?
I DON'T KNOW WHO YOU MEAN.
BRUNETTE, DESIGNER CLOTHES, EXPENSIVE JEWELRY, SURROUNDED BY ADMIRERS...
Oh. I HAD A PONY LIKE THAT ONCE.

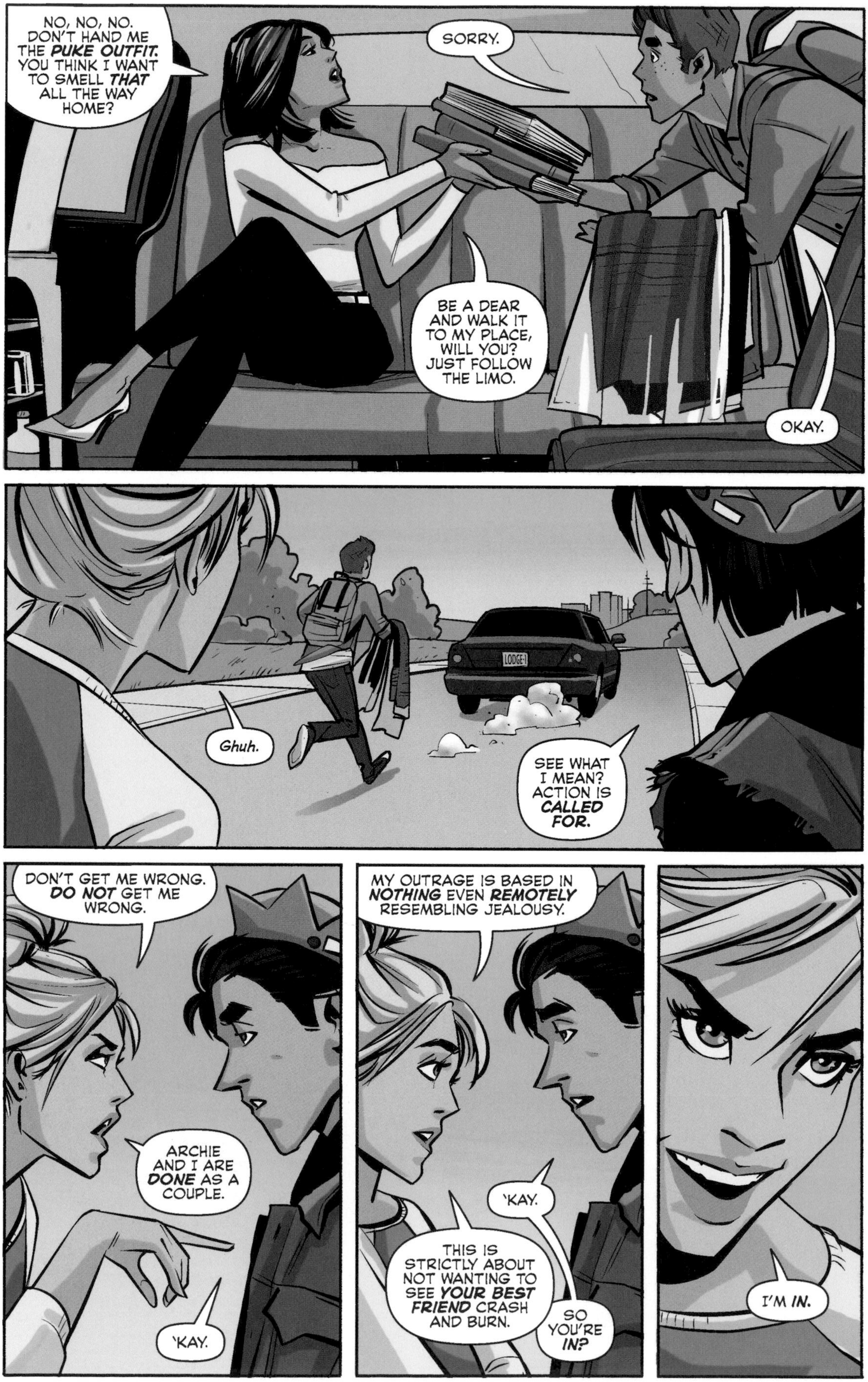
NO, NO, NO. DON'T HAND ME THE PUKE OUTFIT. YOU THINK I WANT TO SMELL THAT ALL THE WAY HOME?
SORRY.
BE A DEAR AND WALK IT TO MY PLACE, WILL YOU? JUST FOLLOW THE LIMO.
OKAY.
LODGE-1
Ghuh.
SEE WHAT I MEAN? ACTION IS CALLED FOR.
DON'T GET ME WRONG. DO NOT GET ME WRONG.
ARCHIE AND I ARE DONE AS A COUPLE.
'KAY.
MY OUTRAGE IS BASED IN NOTHING EVEN REMOTELY RESEMBLING JEALOUSY.
'KAY.
THIS IS STRICTLY ABOUT NOT WANTING TO SEE YOUR BEST FRIEND CRASH AND BURN.
SO YOU'RE IN?
I'M IN.

CATCH UP WITH THE ONGOING
ARCHIE SERIES
ON SALE NOW!

PREVIOUSLY IN THE TOWN OF RIVERDALE...

Riverdale High's new Principal, Mr. Stanger, isn't the only faculty member with an all-business, no-fun attitude. He's assembled a team of new teachers that are just as hard on the students, and find their entertainment in doling out punishments!

Jughead managed to find every loophole he could to avoid the dreaded detention room, but a mysterious knife has landed him in hot water, and now he's been expelled! But why would Jughead have a knife on him, anyway?

Everyone knows he swallows his food whole...

STORY BY
CHIP ZDARSKY

ART BY
ERICA HENDERSON

LETTERING BY
JACK MORELLI

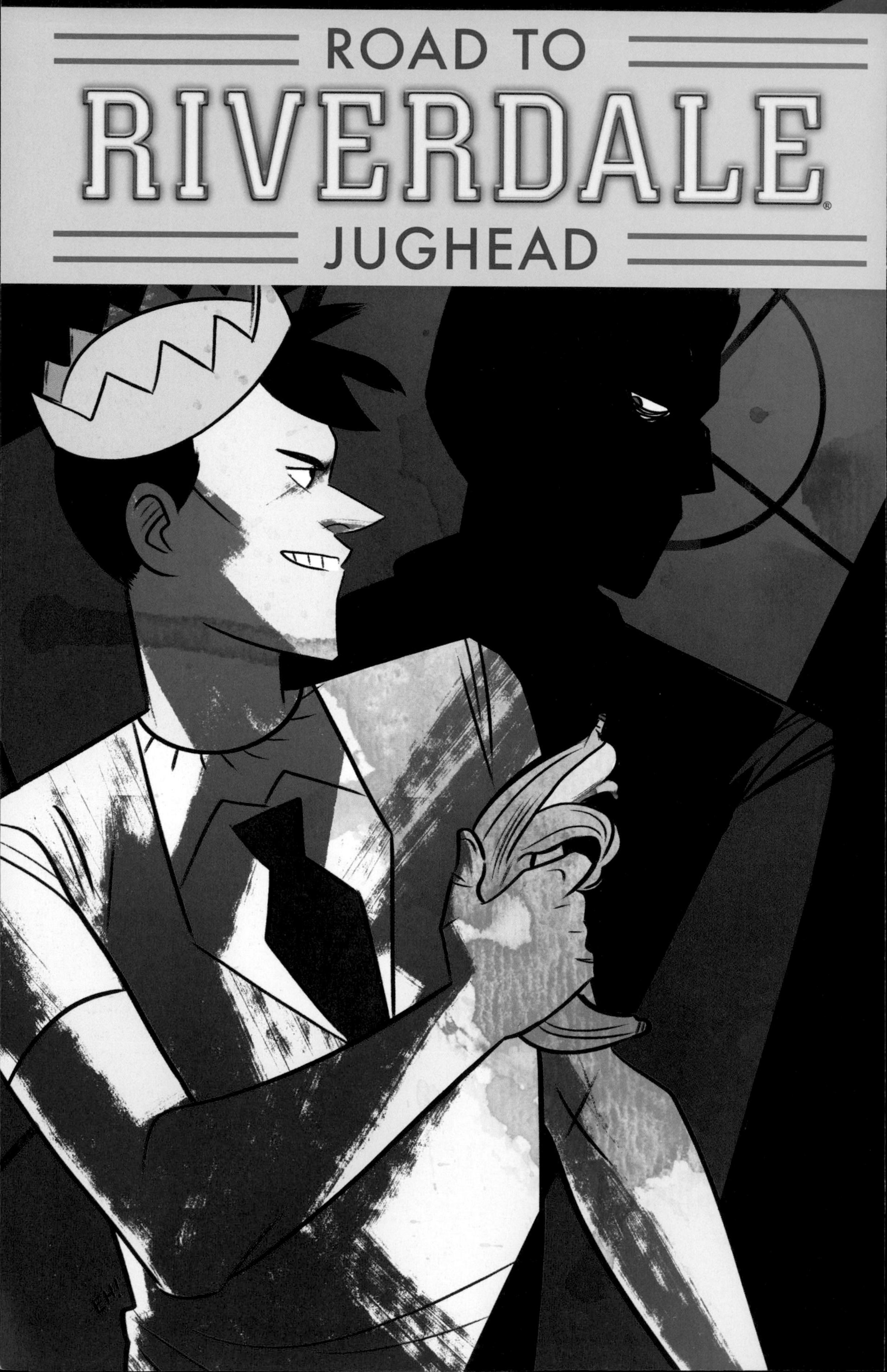
ROAD TO
RIVERDALE®
JUGHEAD

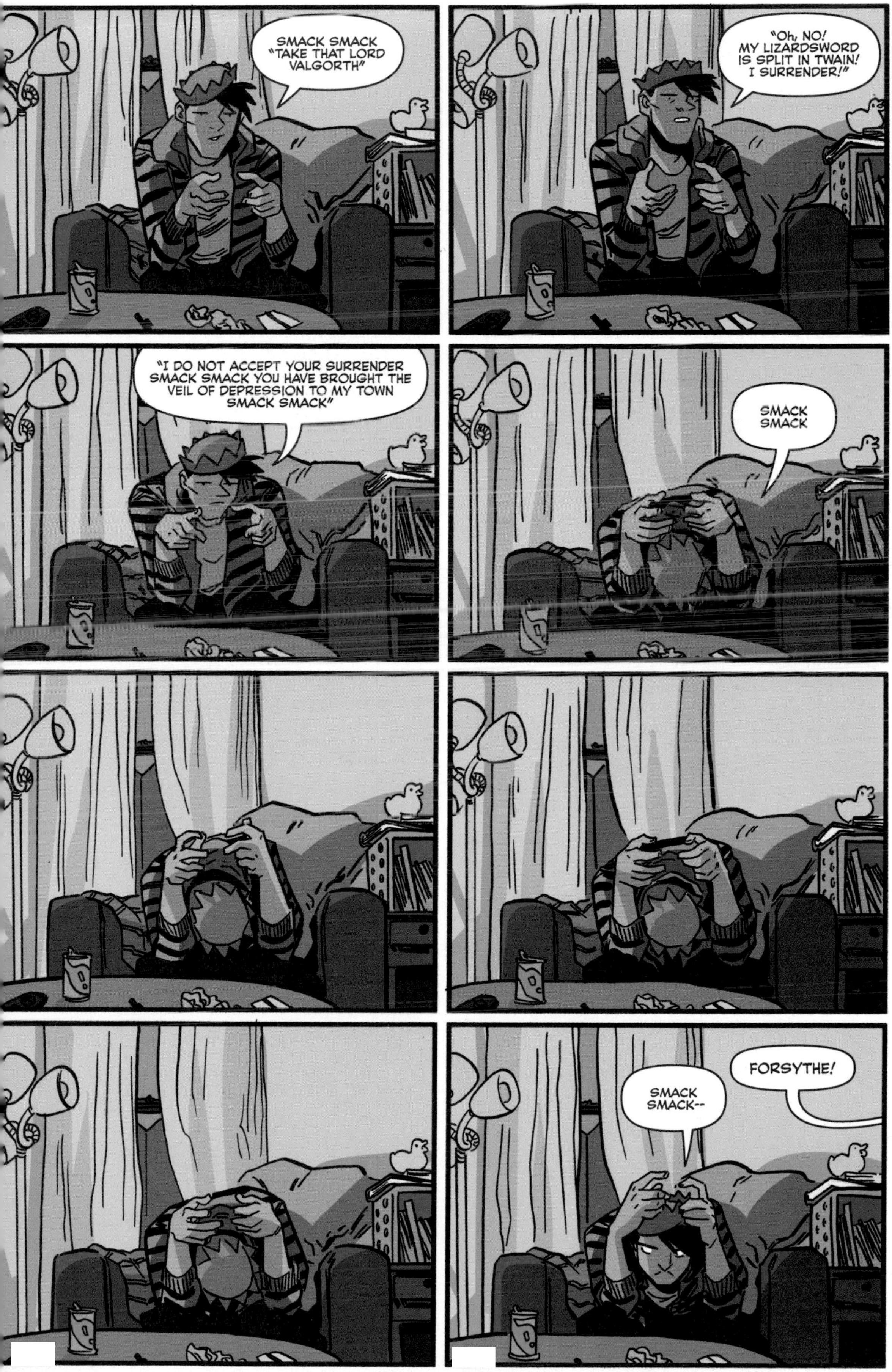
SMACK SMACK "TAKE THAT LORD VALGORTH"
"Oh, NO! MY LIZARDSWORD IS SPLIT IN TWAIN! I SURRENDER!"
"I DO NOT ACCEPT YOUR SURRENDER SMACK SMACK YOU HAVE BROUGHT THE VEIL OF DEPRESSION TO MY TOWN SMACK SMACK"
SMACK SMACK
SMACK SMACK--
FORSYTHE!

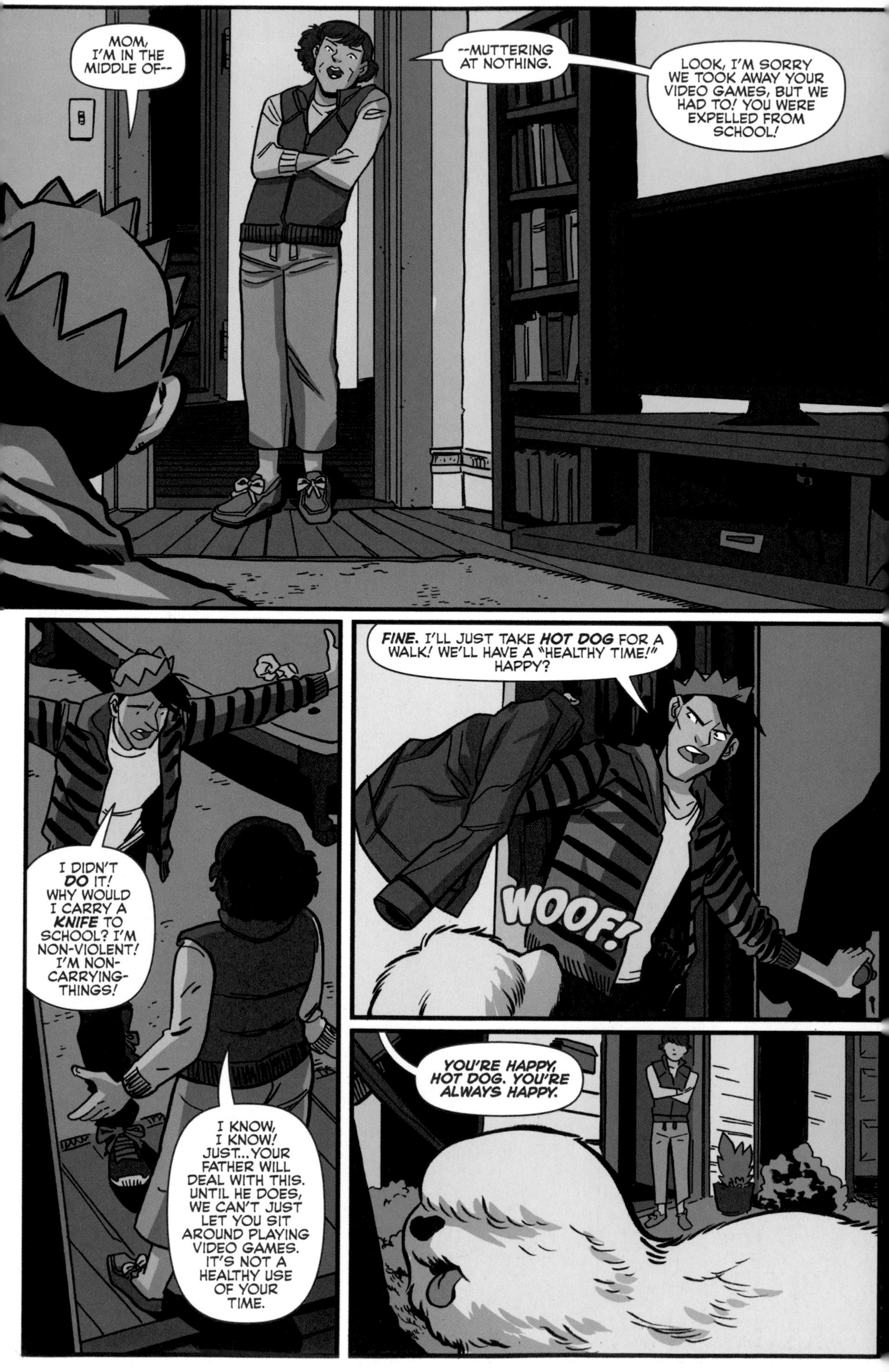
MOM, I'M IN THE MIDDLE OF--
--MUTTERING AT NOTHING.
LOOK, I'M SORRY WE TOOK AWAY YOUR VIDEO GAMES, BUT WE HAD TO! YOU WERE EXPELLED FROM SCHOOL!
I DIDN'T DO IT! WHY WOULD I CARRY A KNIFE TO SCHOOL? I'M NON-VIOLENT! I'M NON-CARRYING-THINGS!
I KNOW, I KNOW! JUST...YOUR FATHER WILL DEAL WITH THIS. UNTIL HE DOES, WE CAN'T JUST LET YOU SIT AROUND PLAYING VIDEO GAMES. IT'S NOT A HEALTHY USE OF YOUR TIME.
FINE. I'LL JUST TAKE HOT DOG FOR A WALK! WE'LL HAVE A "HEALTHY TIME!" HAPPY?
WOOF!
YOU'RE HAPPY, HOT DOG. YOU'RE ALWAYS HAPPY.

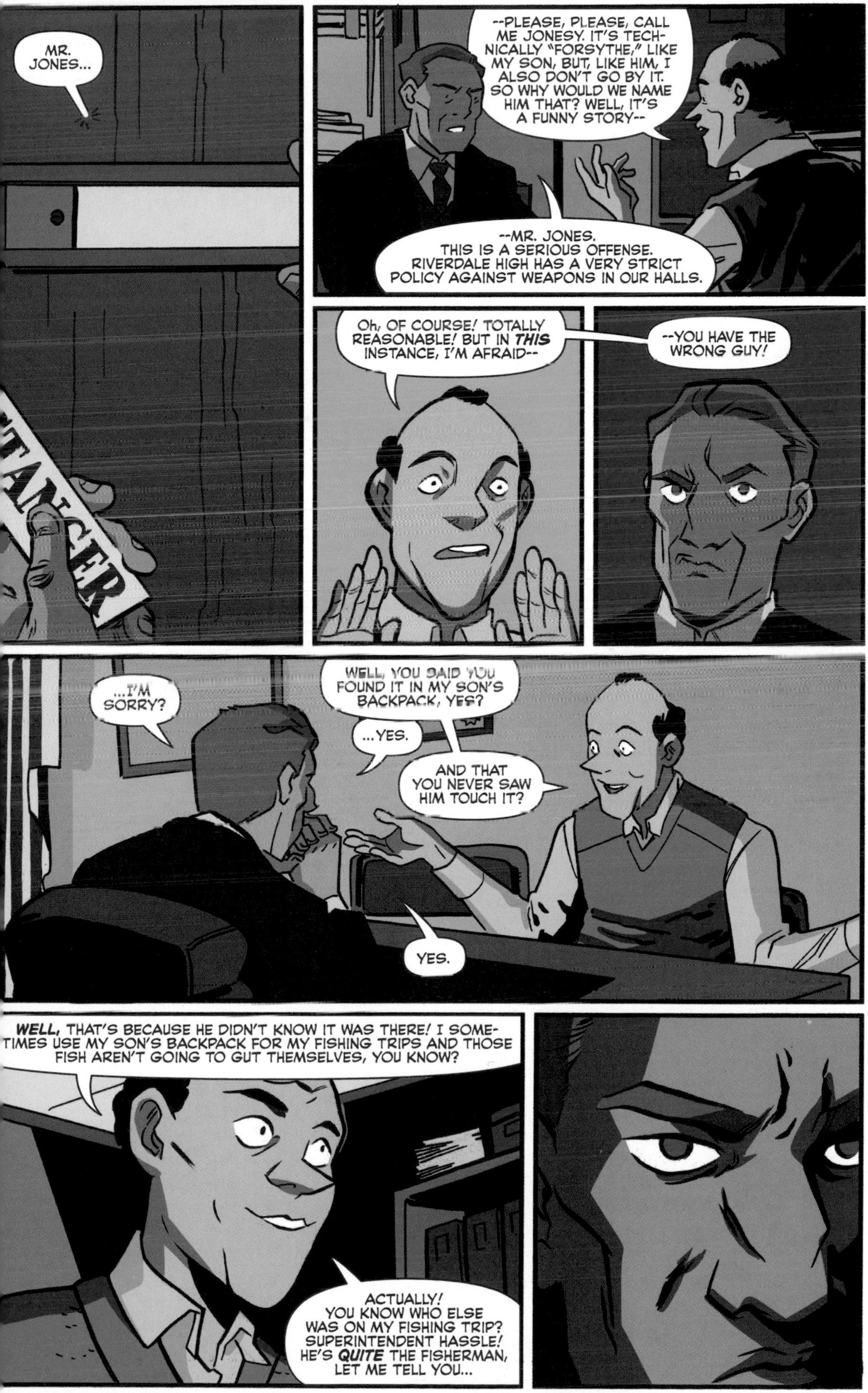
MR. JONES...
--PLEASE, PLEASE, CALL ME JONESY. IT'S TECHNICALLY "FORSYTHE," LIKE MY SON, BUT, LIKE HIM, I ALSO DON'T GO BY IT. SO WHY WOULD WE NAME HIM THAT? WELL, IT'S A FUNNY STORY--
--MR. JONES. THIS IS A SERIOUS OFFENSE. RIVERDALE HIGH HAS A VERY STRICT POLICY AGAINST WEAPONS IN OUR HALLS.
Oh, OF COURSE! TOTALLY REASONABLE! BUT IN *THIS* INSTANCE, I'M AFRAID--
--YOU HAVE THE WRONG GUY!
...I'M SORRY?
WELL, YOU SAID YOU FOUND IT IN MY SON'S BACKPACK, YES?
...YES.
AND THAT YOU NEVER SAW HIM TOUCH IT?
YES.
WELL, THAT'S BECAUSE HE DIDN'T KNOW IT WAS THERE! I SOMETIMES USE MY SON'S BACKPACK FOR MY FISHING TRIPS AND THOSE FISH AREN'T GOING TO GUT THEMSELVES, YOU KNOW?
ACTUALLY! YOU KNOW WHO ELSE WAS ON MY FISHING TRIP? SUPERINTENDENT HASSLE! HE'S ***QUITE*** THE FISHERMAN, LET ME TELL YOU...

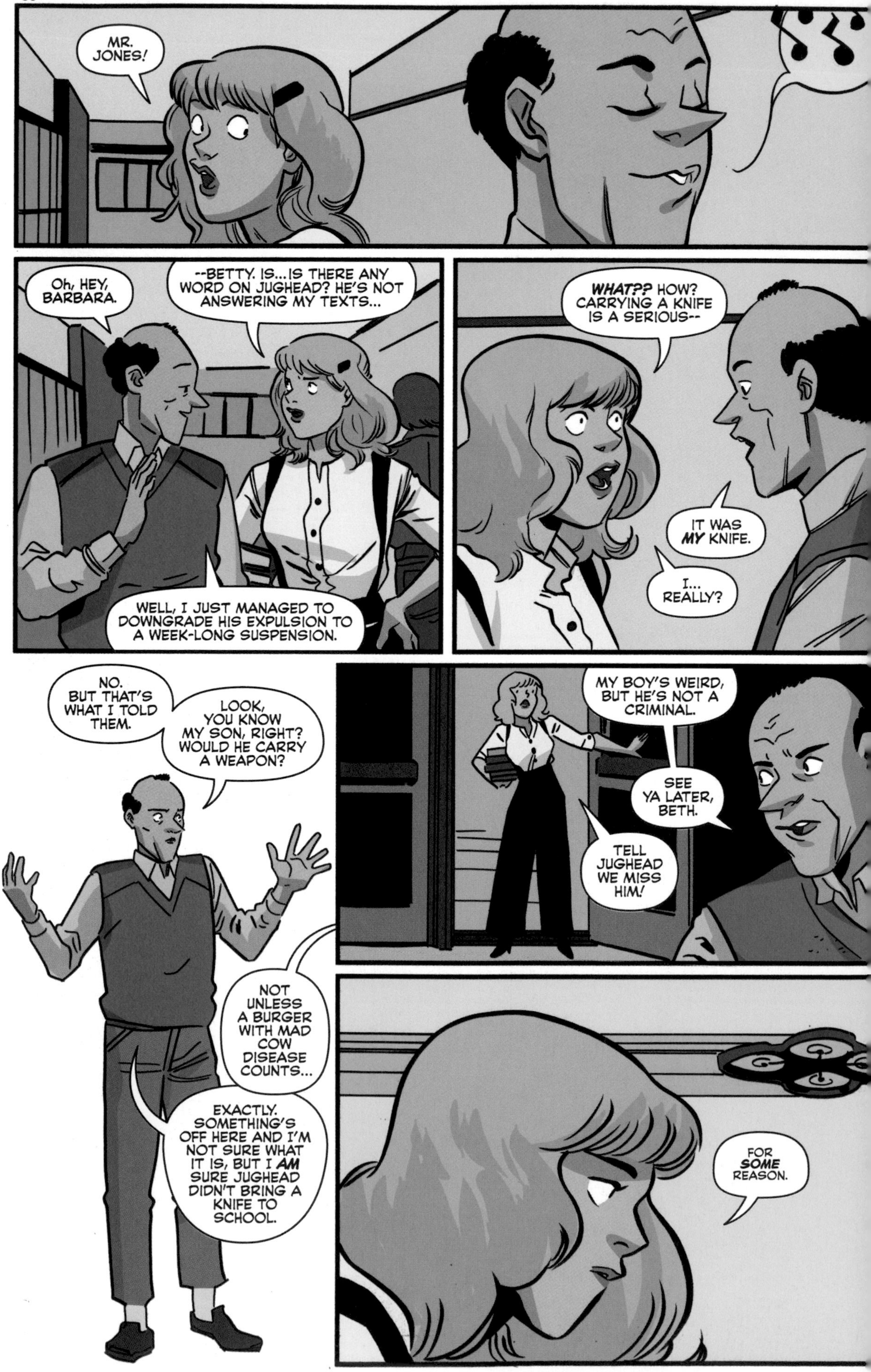
MR. JONES!
Oh, HEY, BARBARA.
--BETTY. IS...IS THERE ANY WORD ON JUGHEAD? HE'S NOT ANSWERING MY TEXTS...
WELL, I JUST MANAGED TO DOWNGRADE HIS EXPULSION TO A WEEK-LONG SUSPENSION.
WHAT?? HOW? CARRYING A KNIFE IS A SERIOUS--
IT WAS MY KNIFE.
I... REALLY?
NO. BUT THAT'S WHAT I TOLD THEM.
LOOK, YOU KNOW MY SON, RIGHT? WOULD HE CARRY A WEAPON?
NOT UNLESS A BURGER WITH MAD COW DISEASE COUNTS...
EXACTLY. SOMETHING'S OFF HERE AND I'M NOT SURE WHAT IT IS, BUT I AM SURE JUGHEAD DIDN'T BRING A KNIFE TO SCHOOL.
MY BOY'S WEIRD, BUT HE'S NOT A CRIMINAL.
SEE YA LATER, BETH.
TELL JUGHEAD WE MISS HIM!
FOR SOME REASON.

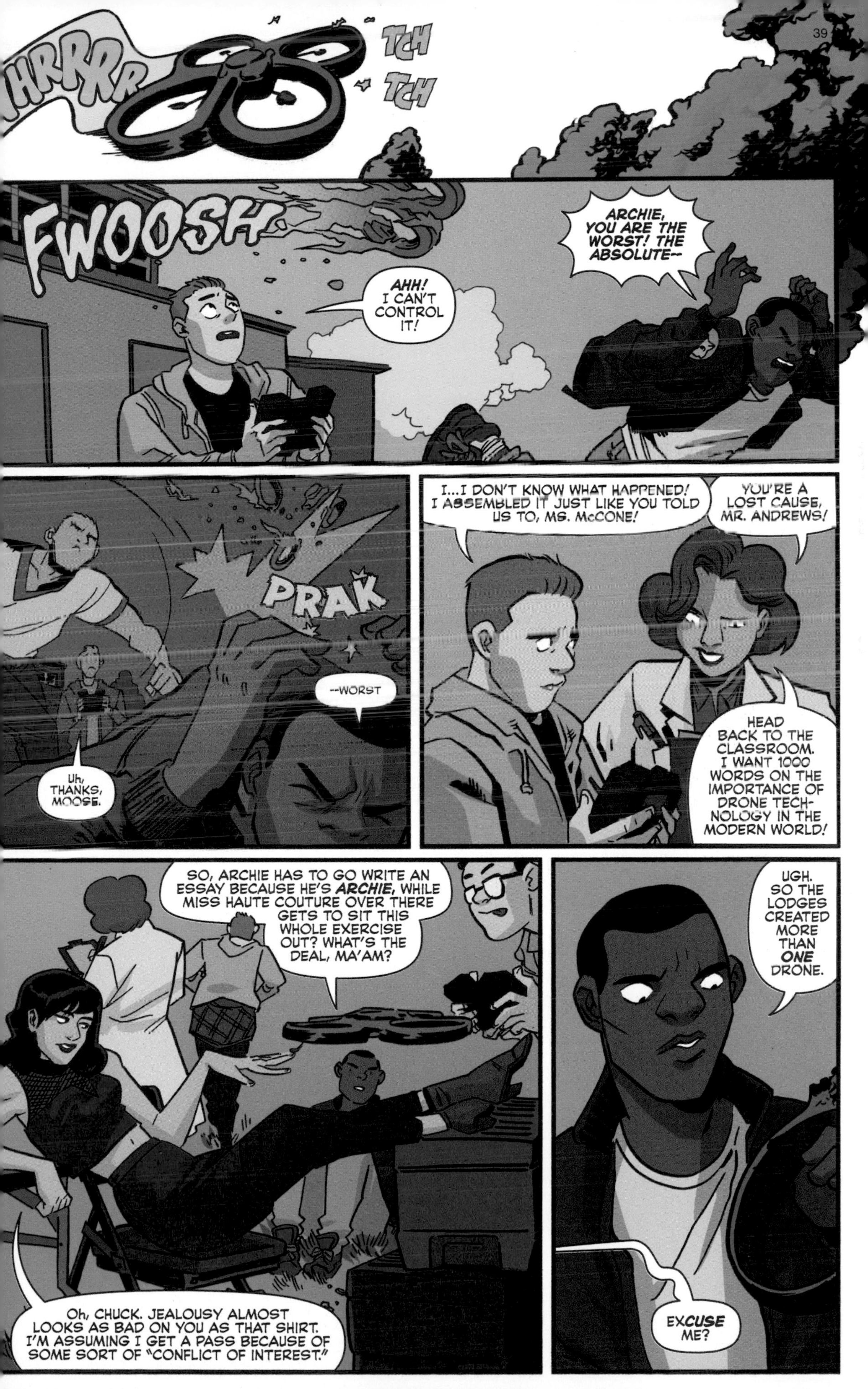
HRRRRR
TCH
TCH
FWOOSH
AHH! I CAN'T CONTROL IT!
ARCHIE, YOU ARE THE WORST! THE ABSOLUTE--
PRAK
--WORST
Uh, THANKS, MOOSE.
I...I DON'T KNOW WHAT HAPPENED! I ASSEMBLED IT JUST LIKE YOU TOLD US TO, MS. McCONE!
YOU'RE A LOST CAUSE, MR. ANDREWS!
HEAD BACK TO THE CLASSROOM. I WANT 1000 WORDS ON THE IMPORTANCE OF DRONE TECHNOLOGY IN THE MODERN WORLD!
SO, ARCHIE HAS TO GO WRITE AN ESSAY BECAUSE HE'S ARCHIE, WHILE MISS HAUTE COUTURE OVER THERE GETS TO SIT THIS WHOLE EXERCISE OUT? WHAT'S THE DEAL, MA'AM?
Oh, CHUCK. JEALOUSY ALMOST LOOKS AS BAD ON YOU AS THAT SHIRT. I'M ASSUMING I GET A PASS BECAUSE OF SOME SORT OF "CONFLICT OF INTEREST."
UGH. SO THE LODGES CREATED MORE THAN ONE DRONE.
EXCUSE ME?

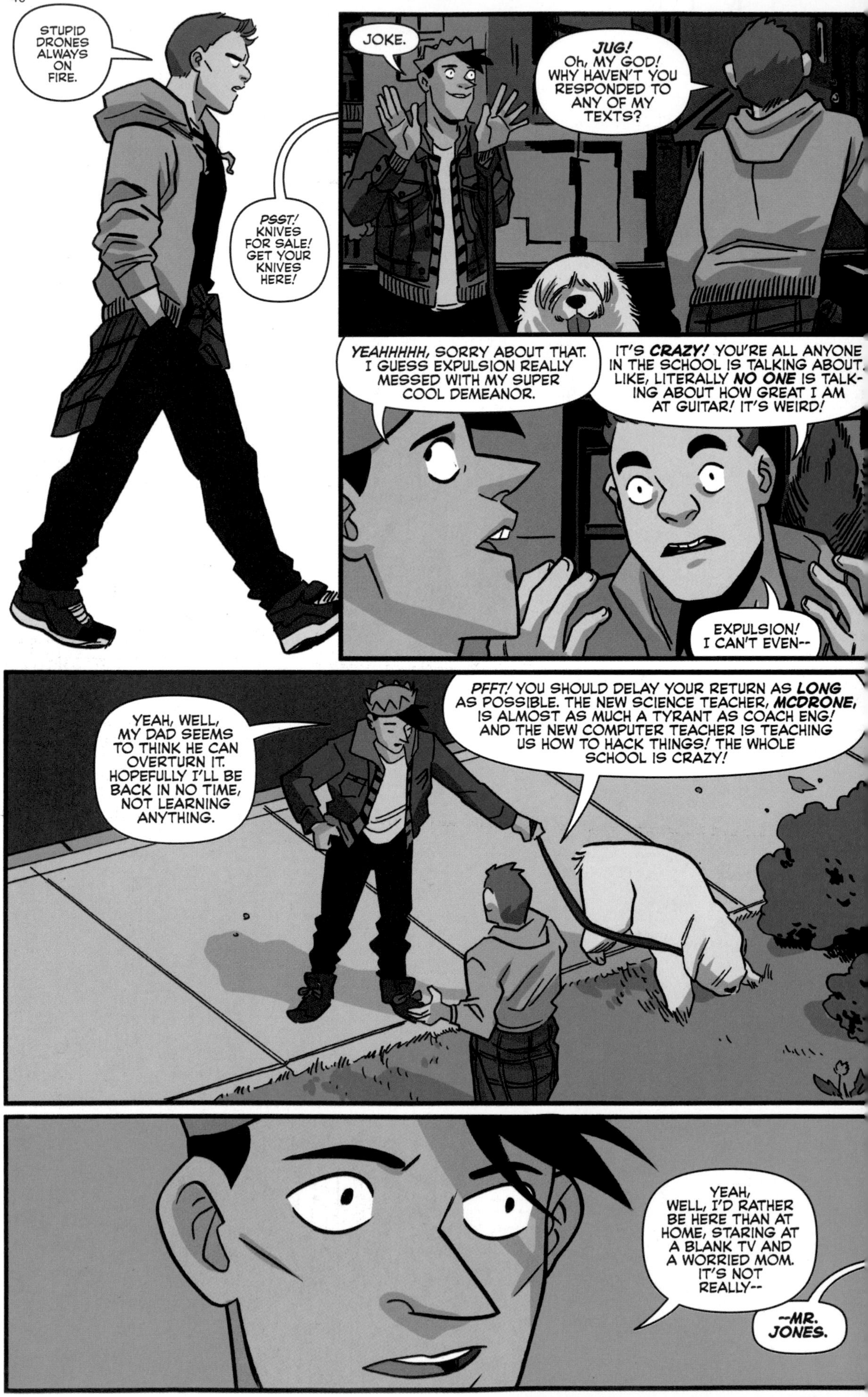
STUPID DRONES ALWAYS ON FIRE.
JOKE.
JUG! Oh, MY GOD! WHY HAVEN'T YOU RESPONDED TO ANY OF MY TEXTS?
PSST! KNIVES FOR SALE! GET YOUR KNIVES HERE!
YEAHHHHH, SORRY ABOUT THAT. I GUESS EXPULSION REALLY MESSED WITH MY SUPER COOL DEMEANOR.
IT'S CRAZY! YOU'RE ALL ANYONE IN THE SCHOOL IS TALKING ABOUT. LIKE, LITERALLY NO ONE IS TALKING ABOUT HOW GREAT I AM AT GUITAR! IT'S WEIRD!
EXPULSION! I CAN'T EVEN--
YEAH, WELL, MY DAD SEEMS TO THINK HE CAN OVERTURN IT. HOPEFULLY I'LL BE BACK IN NO TIME, NOT LEARNING ANYTHING.
PFFT! YOU SHOULD DELAY YOUR RETURN AS LONG AS POSSIBLE. THE NEW SCIENCE TEACHER, MCDRONE, IS ALMOST AS MUCH A TYRANT AS COACH ENG! AND THE NEW COMPUTER TEACHER IS TEACHING US HOW TO HACK THINGS! THE WHOLE SCHOOL IS CRAZY!
YEAH, WELL, I'D RATHER BE HERE THAN AT HOME, STARING AT A BLANK TV AND A WORRIED MOM. IT'S NOT REALLY--
--MR. JONES.

Oh, HEY, *MR.* STANGER. WHAT'S UP? WHAT ARE YOU DOING OUTSIDE? PLANTING? I HEARD YOU'RE REALLY GOOD AT *PLANTING THINGS.*

I JUST MET WITH YOUR *FATHER,* WHO, LIKE YOU, IS A *NUISANCE.*

'OU'LL BE PLEASED TO KNOW WE REACHED AN... AGREEMENT... THAT YOU MAY COME BACK TO RIVERDALE HIGH IN A WEEK'S TIME.

OR AT LEAST, YOU *WOULD HAVE--*

--UNTIL YOU *BROKE* THE EXPULSION RULES BY VISITING THE SCHOOL! I'M AFRAID YOU JUST ADDED ANOTHER WEEK TO YOUR SUSPENSION, MR. JONES.

AHEM.

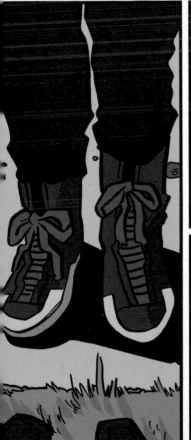

I WOULD *NEVER* BREAK YOUR RULES, SIR! I WISH I COULD, SO I COULD WALK ONTO YOUR GRASS AND PICK UP THE VILE LEAVINGS OF MY PRECIOUS DOG! BUT, ALAS!

IT'S A SHAME THERE'S A WITNESS THIS TIME, ISN'T IT, MR. STANGER? I MEAN, BESIDES YOUR *REPUTABLE* COACH ENG!

I'LL BE AT POP'S, ARCH. THINKING ABOUT HOW I NEVER BREAK THE RULES.

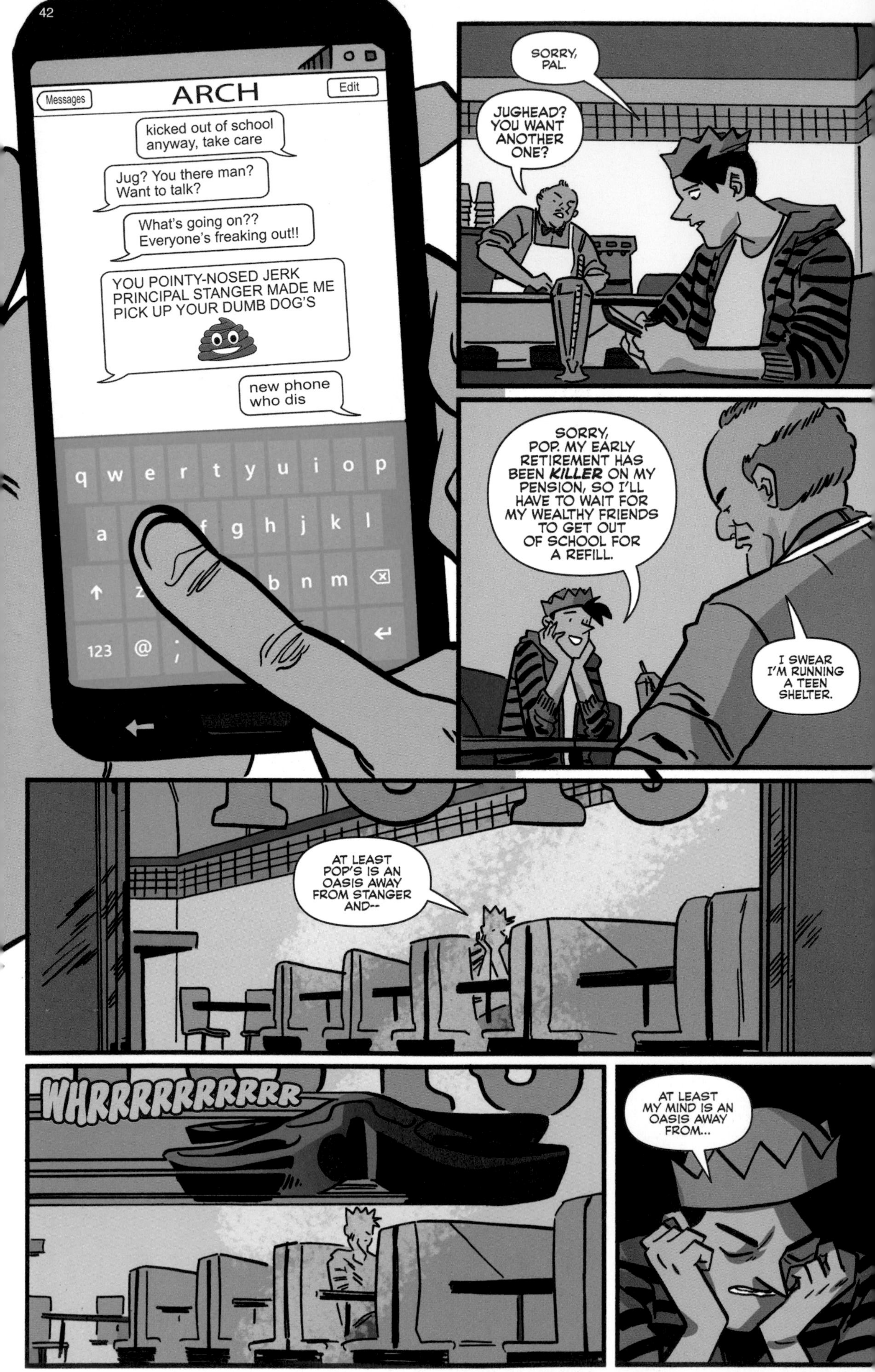
Messages
ARCH
Edit
kicked out of school anyway, take care
Jug? You there man? Want to talk?
What's going on?? Everyone's freaking out!!
YOU POINTY-NOSED JERK PRINCIPAL STANGER MADE ME PICK UP YOUR DUMB DOG'S
new phone who dis
SORRY, PAL.
JUGHEAD? YOU WANT ANOTHER ONE?
SORRY, POP. MY EARLY RETIREMENT HAS BEEN KILLER ON MY PENSION, SO I'LL HAVE TO WAIT FOR MY WEALTHY FRIENDS TO GET OUT OF SCHOOL FOR A REFILL.
I SWEAR I'M RUNNING A TEEN SHELTER.
AT LEAST POP'S IS AN OASIS AWAY FROM STANGER AND--
WHRRRRRRRRRR
AT LEAST MY MIND IS AN OASIS AWAY FROM...

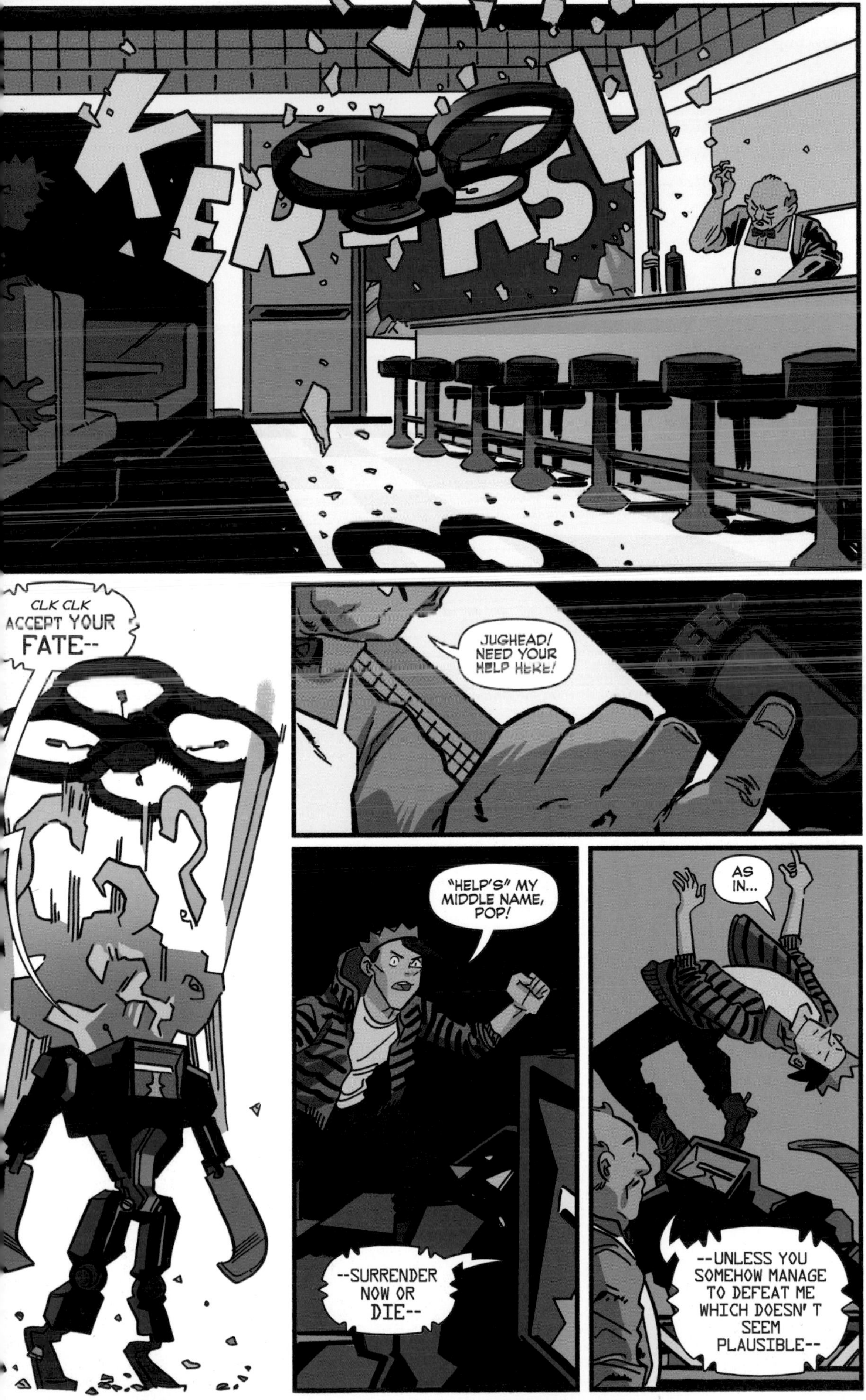
KER-RASH
CLK CLK ACCEPT YOUR FATE--
JUGHEAD! NEED YOUR HELP HERE!
"HELP'S" MY MIDDLE NAME, POP!
--SURRENDER NOW OR DIE--
AS IN...
--UNLESS YOU SOMEHOW MANAGE TO DEFEAT ME WHICH DOESN'T SEEM PLAUSIBLE--

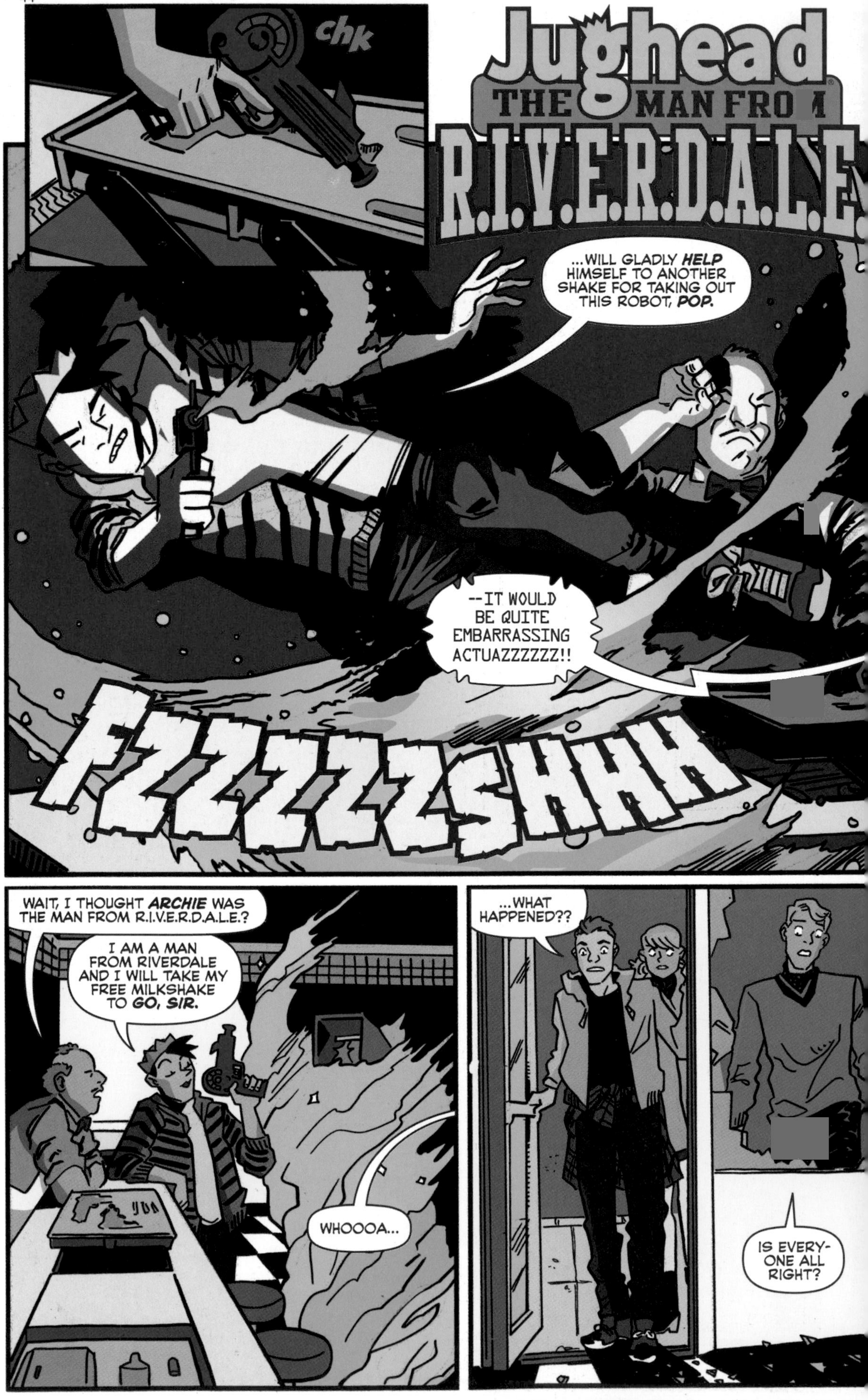
chk
Jughead
THE MAN FROM
R.I.V.E.R.D.A.L.E.
...WILL GLADLY HELP HIMSELF TO ANOTHER SHAKE FOR TAKING OUT THIS ROBOT, POP.
--IT WOULD BE QUITE EMBARRASSING ACTUAZZZZZZ!!
FZZZZZSHHH
WAIT, I THOUGHT ARCHIE WAS THE MAN FROM R.I.V.E.R.D.A.L.E.?
I AM A MAN FROM RIVERDALE AND I WILL TAKE MY FREE MILKSHAKE TO GO, SIR.
WHOOOA...
...WHAT HAPPENED??
IS EVERY-ONE ALL RIGHT?

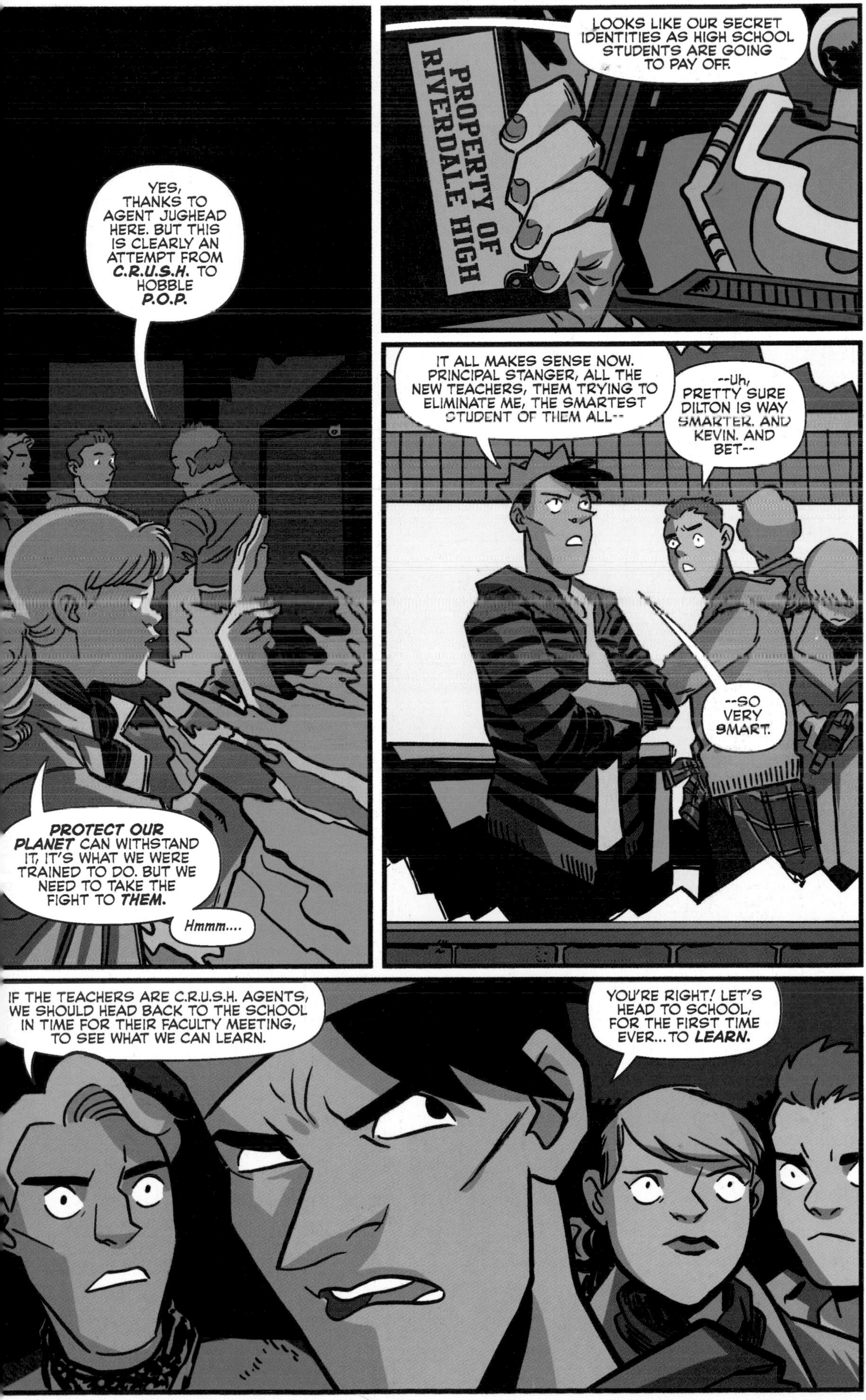
LOOKS LIKE OUR SECRET IDENTITIES AS HIGH SCHOOL STUDENTS ARE GOING TO PAY OFF.
PROPERTY OF RIVERDALE HIGH
YES, THANKS TO AGENT JUGHEAD HERE. BUT THIS IS CLEARLY AN ATTEMPT FROM C.R.U.S.H. TO HOBBLE P.O.P.
PROTECT OUR PLANET CAN WITHSTAND IT, IT'S WHAT WE WERE TRAINED TO DO. BUT WE NEED TO TAKE THE FIGHT TO THEM.
Hmmm....
IT ALL MAKES SENSE NOW. PRINCIPAL STANGER, ALL THE NEW TEACHERS, THEM TRYING TO ELIMINATE ME, THE SMARTEST STUDENT OF THEM ALL--
--Uh, PRETTY SURE DILTON IS WAY SMARTER. AND KEVIN. AND BET--
--SO VERY SMART.
IF THE TEACHERS ARE C.R.U.S.H. AGENTS, WE SHOULD HEAD BACK TO THE SCHOOL IN TIME FOR THEIR FACULTY MEETING, TO SEE WHAT WE CAN LEARN.
YOU'RE RIGHT! LET'S HEAD TO SCHOOL, FOR THE FIRST TIME EVER...TO LEARN.

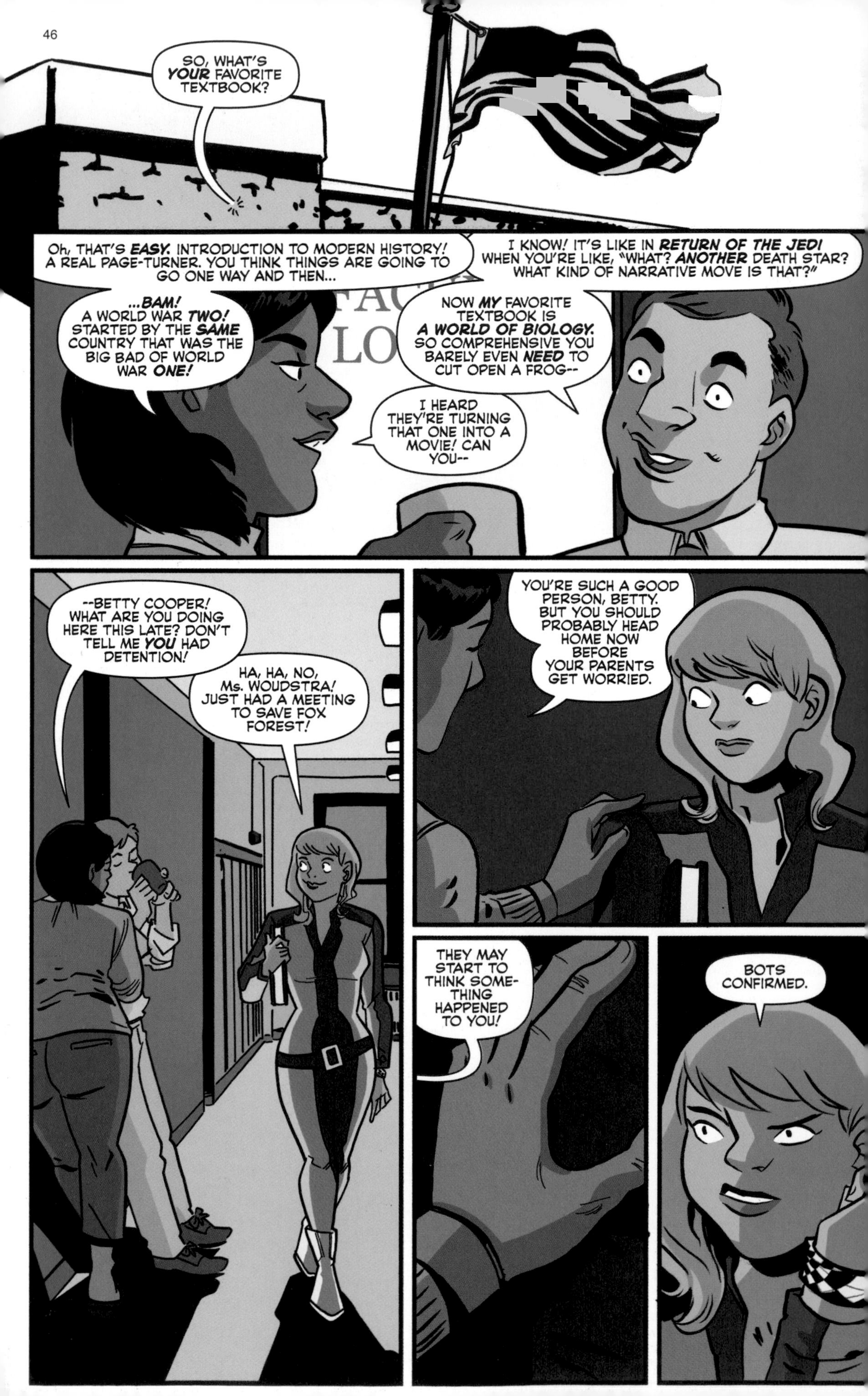
SO, WHAT'S YOUR FAVORITE TEXTBOOK?
Oh, THAT'S EASY. INTRODUCTION TO MODERN HISTORY! A REAL PAGE-TURNER. YOU THINK THINGS ARE GOING TO GO ONE WAY AND THEN...
...BAM! A WORLD WAR TWO! STARTED BY THE SAME COUNTRY THAT WAS THE BIG BAD OF WORLD WAR ONE!
I KNOW! IT'S LIKE IN RETURN OF THE JEDI WHEN YOU'RE LIKE, "WHAT? ANOTHER DEATH STAR? WHAT KIND OF NARRATIVE MOVE IS THAT?"
NOW MY FAVORITE TEXTBOOK IS A WORLD OF BIOLOGY. SO COMPREHENSIVE YOU BARELY EVEN NEED TO CUT OPEN A FROG--
I HEARD THEY'RE TURNING THAT ONE INTO A MOVIE! CAN YOU--
--BETTY COOPER! WHAT ARE YOU DOING HERE THIS LATE? DON'T TELL ME YOU HAD DETENTION!
HA, HA, NO, Ms. WOUDSTRA! JUST HAD A MEETING TO SAVE FOX FOREST!
YOU'RE SUCH A GOOD PERSON, BETTY. BUT YOU SHOULD PROBABLY HEAD HOME NOW BEFORE YOUR PARENTS GET WORRIED.
THEY MAY START TO THINK SOME-THING HAPPENED TO YOU!
BOTS CONFIRMED.

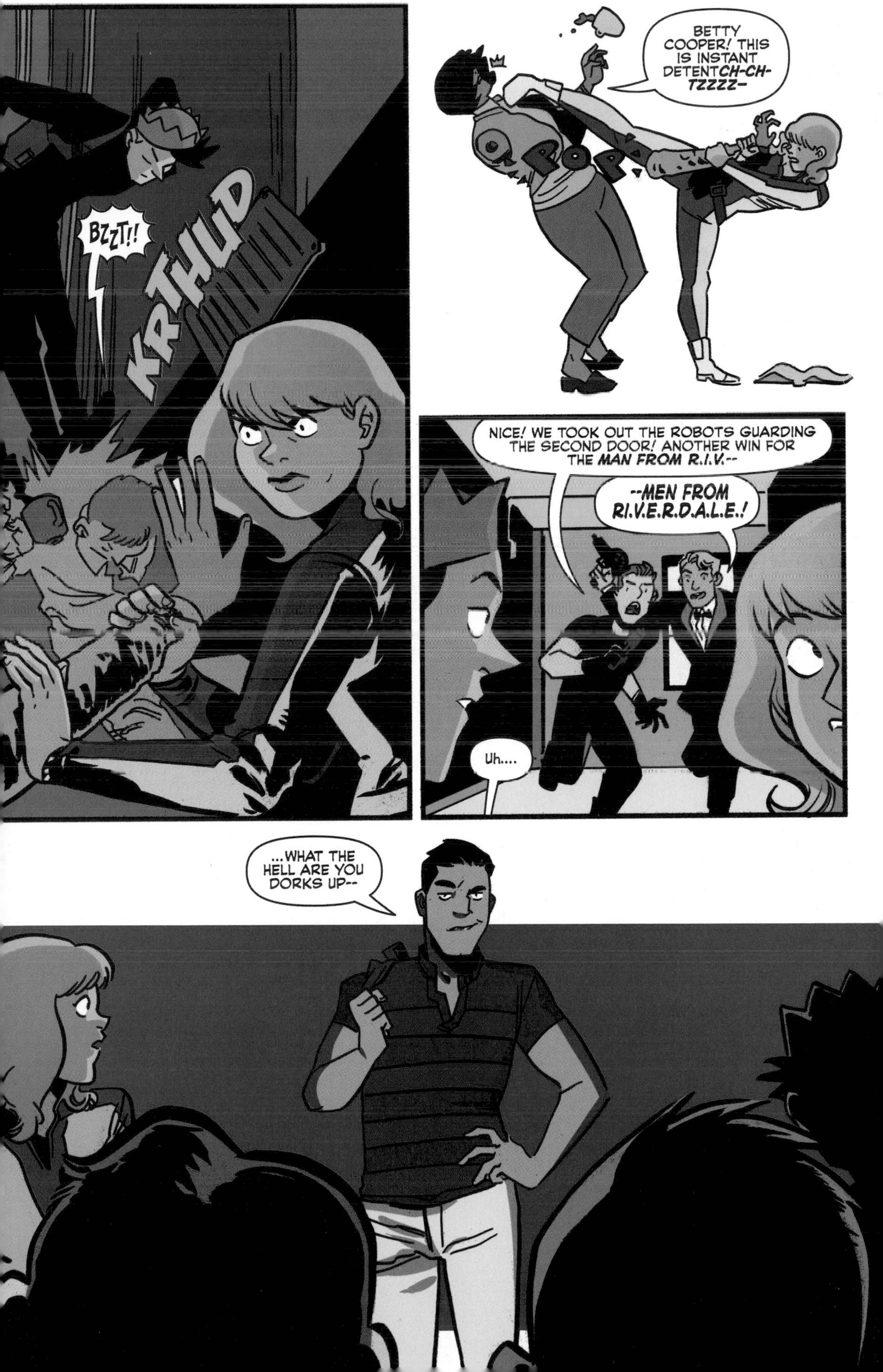
BZZT!!
KRTHUD
BETTY COOPER! THIS IS INSTANT DETENTCH-CH-TZZZZ–
POP
NICE! WE TOOK OUT THE ROBOTS GUARDING THE SECOND DOOR! ANOTHER WIN FOR THE MAN FROM R.I.V.--
--MEN FROM R.I.V.E.R.D.A.L.E.!
Uh....
...WHAT THE HELL ARE YOU DORKS UP--

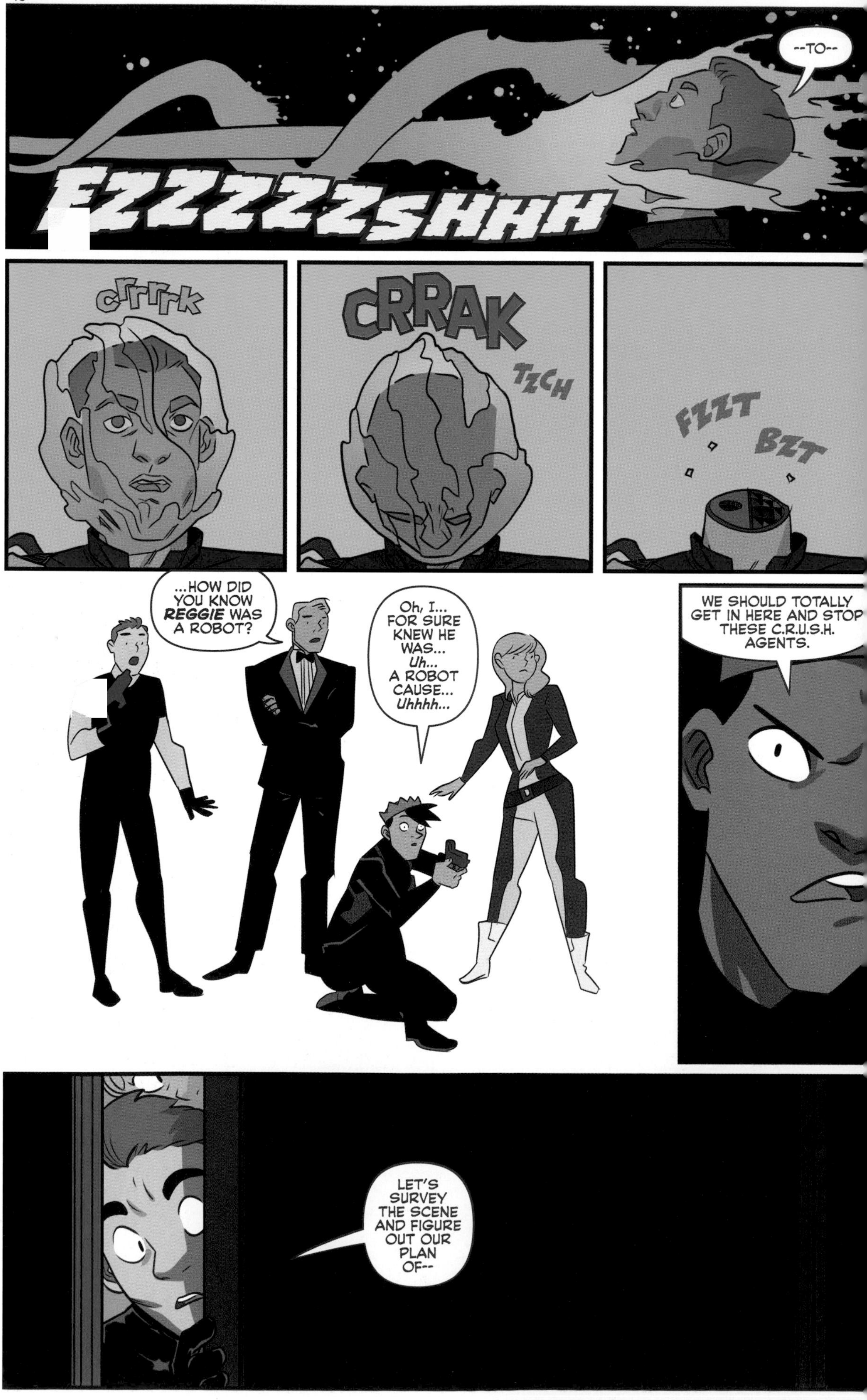
--TO--
FZZZZZZSHHH
crrrrk
CRRAK
TZCH
FZZT
BZT
...HOW DID YOU KNOW REGGIE WAS A ROBOT?
Oh, I... FOR SURE KNEW HE WAS... Uh... A ROBOT CAUSE... Uhhhh...
WE SHOULD TOTALLY GET IN HERE AND STOP THESE C.R.U.S.H. AGENTS.
LET'S SURVEY THE SCENE AND FIGURE OUT OUR PLAN OF--

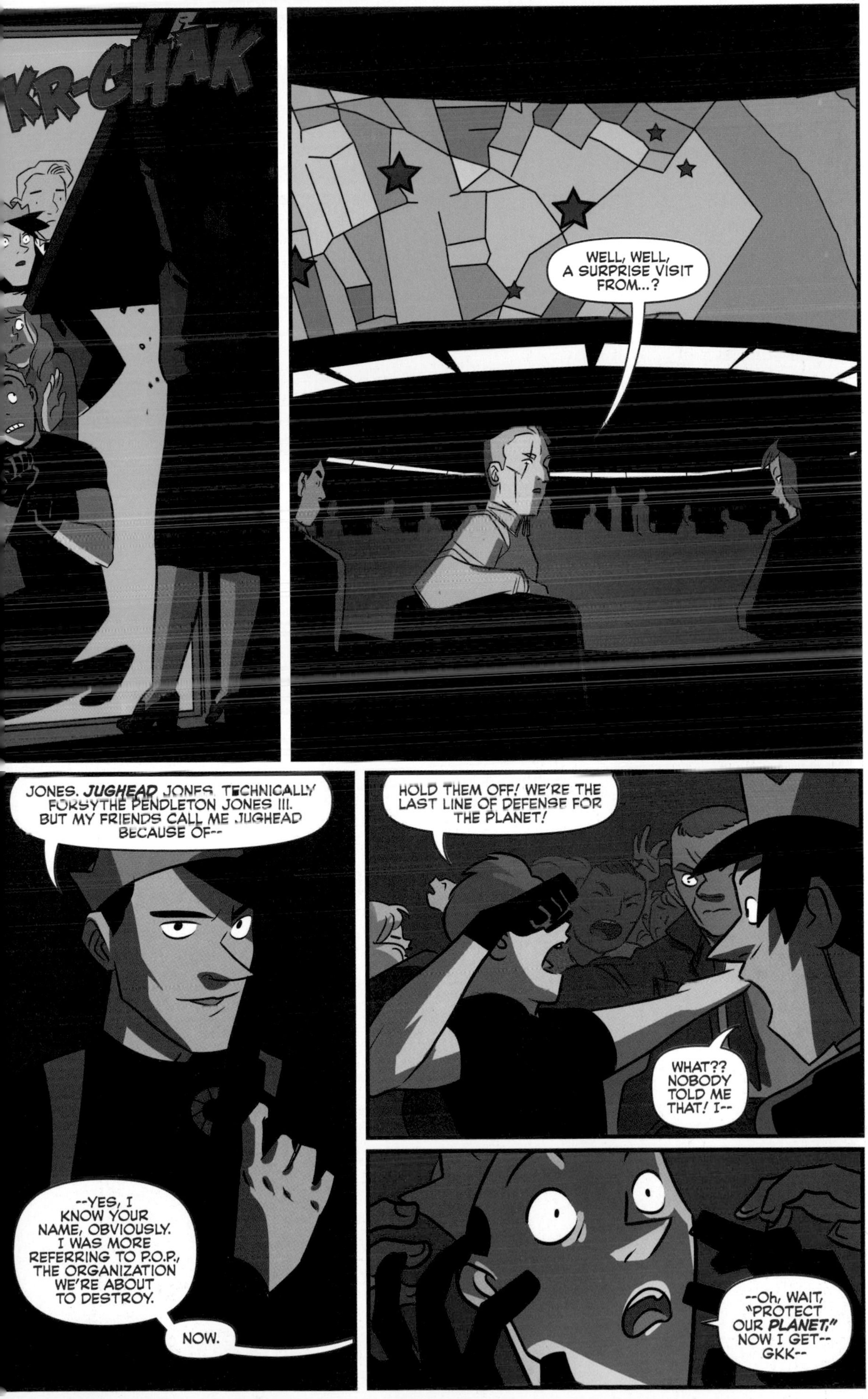
KR-CHAK
WELL, WELL, A SURPRISE VISIT FROM...?
JONES. JUGHEAD JONES. TECHNICALLY FORSYTHE PENDLETON JONES III. BUT MY FRIENDS CALL ME JUGHEAD BECAUSE OF--
--YES, I KNOW YOUR NAME, OBVIOUSLY. I WAS MORE REFERRING TO P.O.P., THE ORGANIZATION WE'RE ABOUT TO DESTROY.
NOW.
HOLD THEM OFF! WE'RE THE LAST LINE OF DEFENSE FOR THE PLANET!
WHAT?? NOBODY TOLD ME THAT! I--
--Oh, WAIT, "PROTECT OUR PLANET," NOW I GET-- GKK--

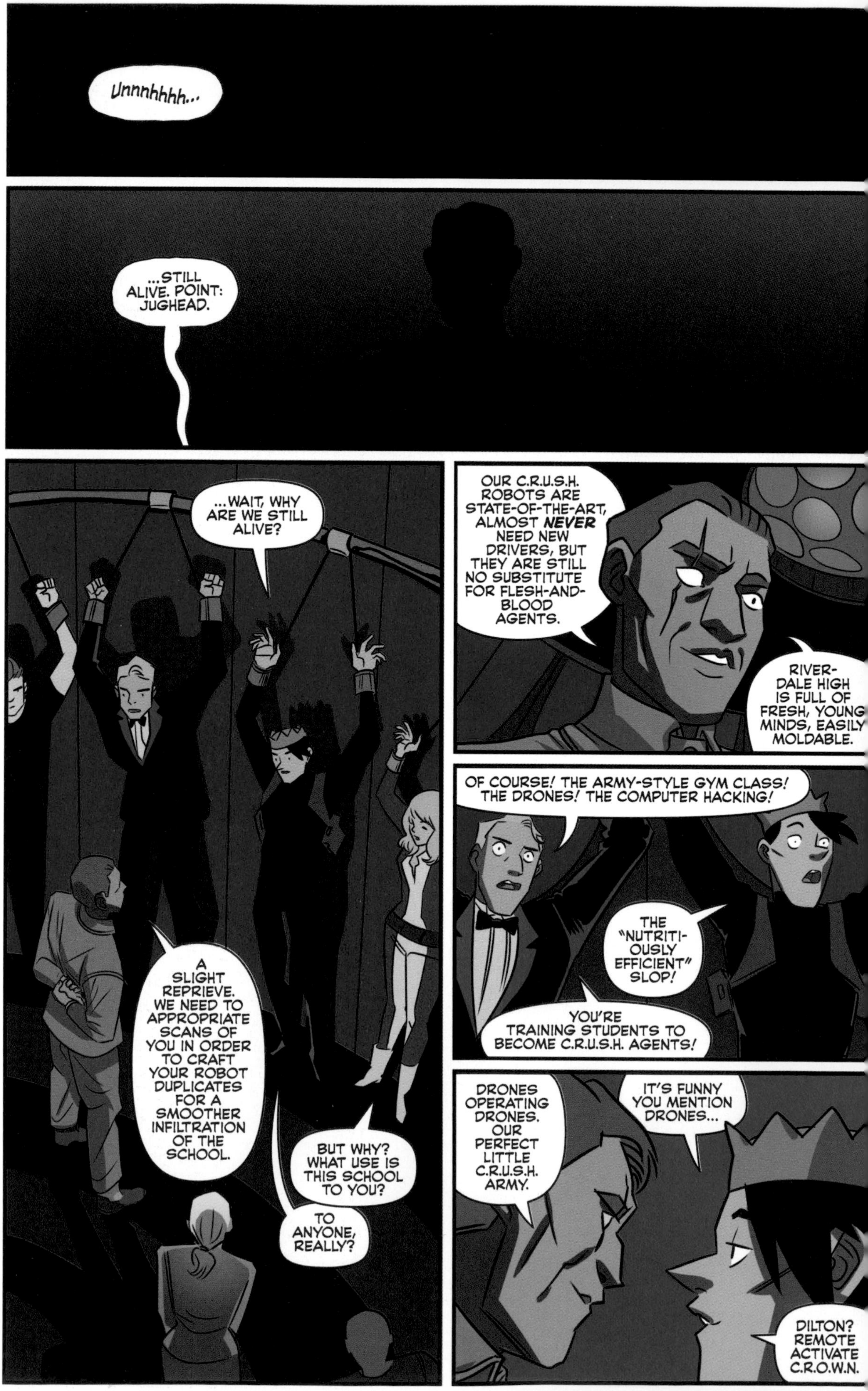
Unnnhhhh...
...STILL ALIVE. POINT: JUGHEAD.
...WAIT, WHY ARE WE STILL ALIVE?
A SLIGHT REPRIEVE. WE NEED TO APPROPRIATE SCANS OF YOU IN ORDER TO CRAFT YOUR ROBOT DUPLICATES FOR A SMOOTHER INFILTRATION OF THE SCHOOL.
BUT WHY? WHAT USE IS THIS SCHOOL TO YOU?
TO ANYONE, REALLY?
OUR C.R.U.S.H. ROBOTS ARE STATE-OF-THE-ART, ALMOST NEVER NEED NEW DRIVERS, BUT THEY ARE STILL NO SUBSTITUTE FOR FLESH-AND-BLOOD AGENTS.
RIVER-DALE HIGH IS FULL OF FRESH, YOUNG MINDS, EASILY MOLDABLE.
OF COURSE! THE ARMY-STYLE GYM CLASS! THE DRONES! THE COMPUTER HACKING!
THE "NUTRITI-OUSLY EFFICIENT" SLOP!
YOU'RE TRAINING STUDENTS TO BECOME C.R.U.S.H. AGENTS!
DRONES OPERATING DRONES. OUR PERFECT LITTLE C.R.U.S.H. ARMY.
IT'S FUNNY YOU MENTION DRONES...
DILTON? REMOTE ACTIVATE C.R.O.W.N.

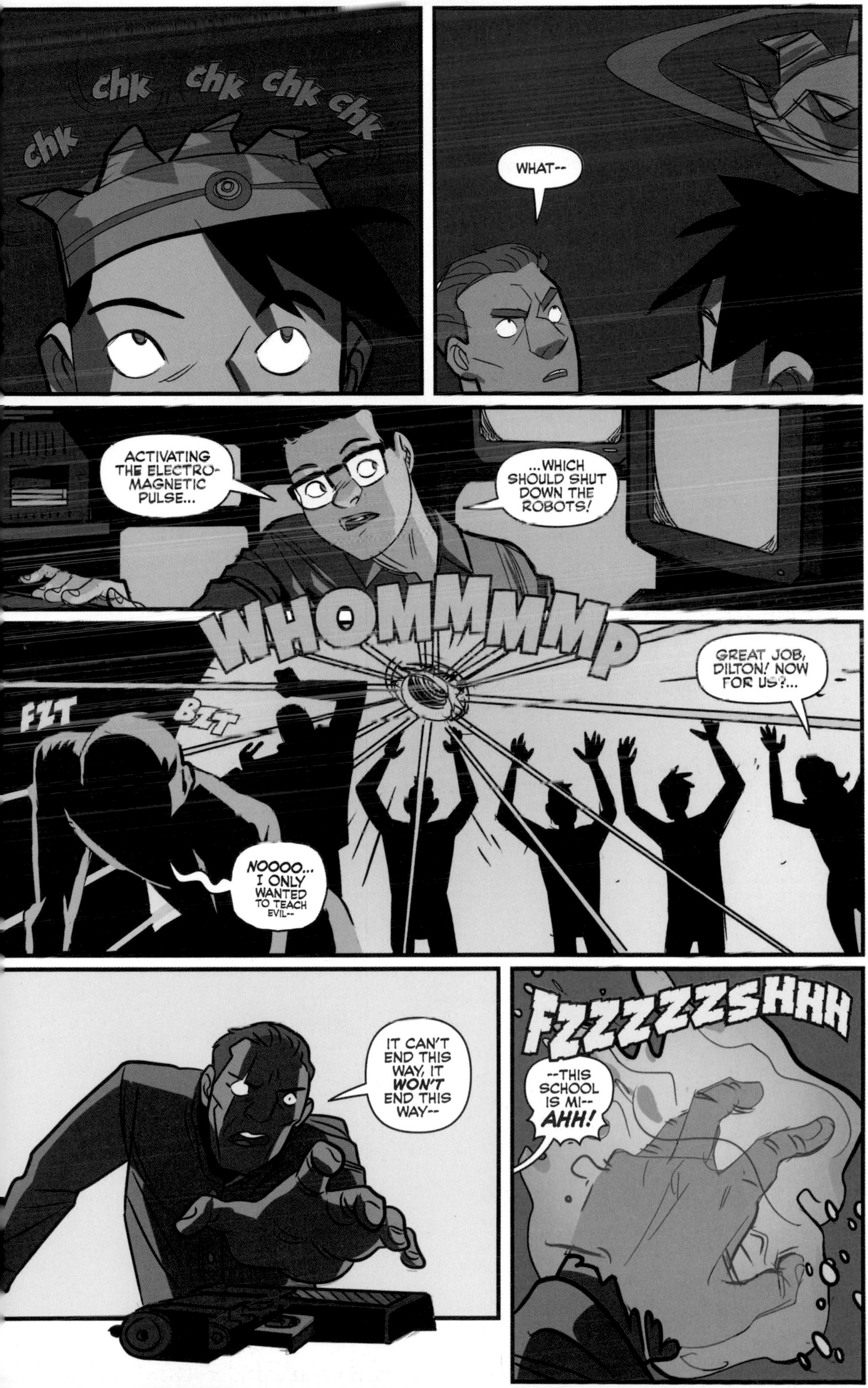
chk chk chk chk chk
WHAT--
ACTIVATING THE ELECTRO-MAGNETIC PULSE...
...WHICH SHOULD SHUT DOWN THE ROBOTS!
WHOMMMMMP
GREAT JOB, DILTON! NOW FOR US?...
FZT
BZT
NOOOO... I ONLY WANTED TO TEACH EVIL--
IT CAN'T END THIS WAY, IT *WON'T* END THIS WAY--
FZZZZZZSHHH
--THIS SCHOOL IS MI-- *AHH!*

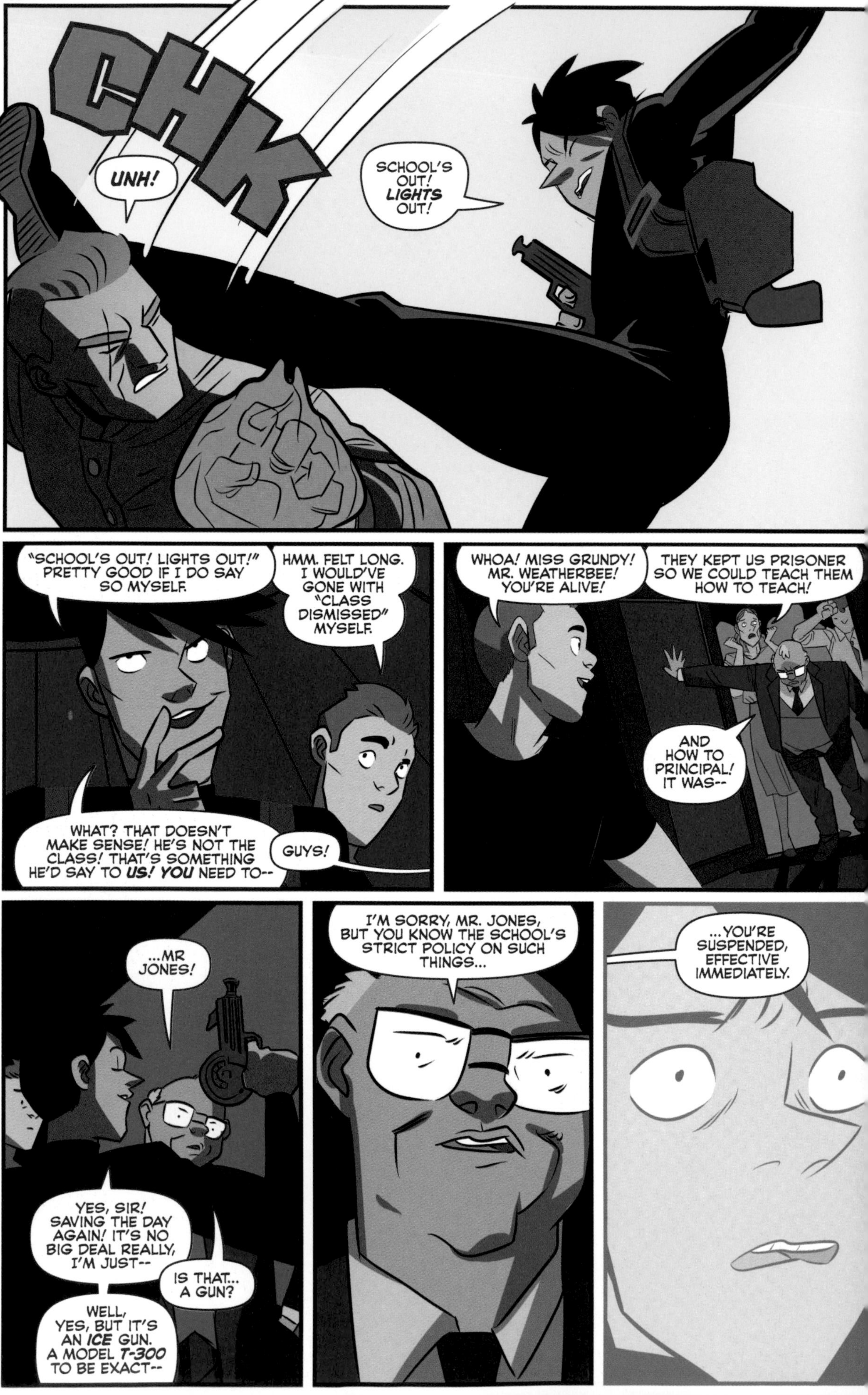
CHK
UNH!
SCHOOL'S OUT! LIGHTS OUT!
"SCHOOL'S OUT! LIGHTS OUT!" PRETTY GOOD IF I DO SAY SO MYSELF.
HMM. FELT LONG. I WOULD'VE GONE WITH "CLASS DISMISSED" MYSELF.
WHAT? THAT DOESN'T MAKE SENSE! HE'S NOT THE CLASS! THAT'S SOMETHING HE'D SAY TO US! YOU NEED TO--
GUYS!
WHOA! MISS GRUNDY! MR. WEATHERBEE! YOU'RE ALIVE!
THEY KEPT US PRISONER SO WE COULD TEACH THEM HOW TO TEACH!
AND HOW TO PRINCIPAL! IT WAS--
...MR JONES!
YES, SIR! SAVING THE DAY AGAIN! IT'S NO BIG DEAL REALLY, I'M JUST--
IS THAT... A GUN?
WELL, YES, BUT IT'S AN ICE GUN. A MODEL T-300 TO BE EXACT--
I'M SORRY, MR. JONES, BUT YOU KNOW THE SCHOOL'S STRICT POLICY ON SUCH THINGS...
...YOU'RE SUSPENDED, EFFECTIVE IMMEDIATELY.

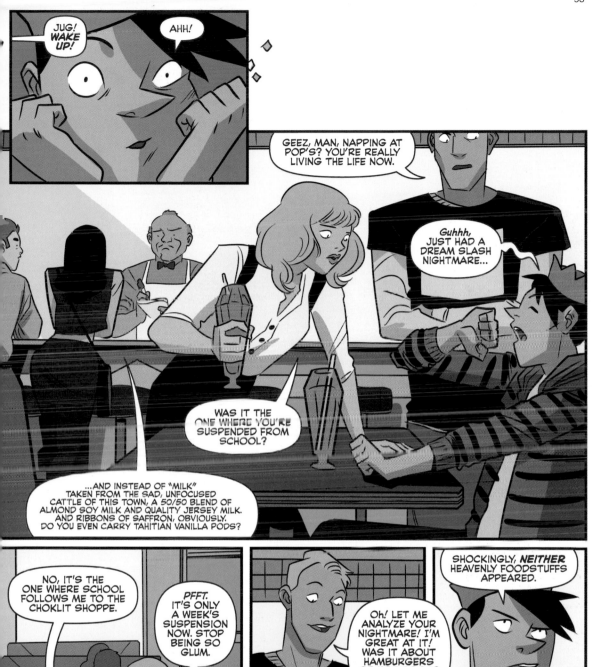

JUG! *WAKE UP!*

AHH!

GEEZ, MAN, NAPPING AT POP'S? YOU'RE REALLY LIVING THE LIFE NOW.

Guhhh, JUST HAD A DREAM SLASH NIGHTMARE...

WAS IT THE ONE WHERE YOU'RE SUSPENDED FROM SCHOOL?

...AND INSTEAD OF "MILK" TAKEN FROM THE SAD, UNFOCUSED CATTLE OF THIS TOWN, A 50/50 BLEND OF ALMOND SOY MILK AND QUALITY JERSEY MILK. AND RIBBONS OF SAFFRON, OBVIOUSLY. DO YOU EVEN CARRY TAHITIAN VANILLA PODS?

NO, IT'S THE ONE WHERE SCHOOL FOLLOWS ME TO THE CHOKLIT SHOPPE.

PFFT. IT'S ONLY A WEEK'S SUSPENSION NOW. STOP BEING SO GLUM.

OH! LET ME ANALYZE YOUR NIGHTMARE! I'M GREAT AT IT! WAS IT ABOUT HAMBURGERS OR HOT DOGS? CAUSE FREUD SAYS--

SHOCKINGLY, *NEITHER* HEAVENLY FOODSTUFFS APPEARED.

STANGER WAS INFILTRATING THE SCHOOL TO CREATE EVIL SECRET AGENTS! REPLACING TEACHERS, TWISTING THE CLASSES TO BE ALL ABOUT SPY AND ARMY STUFF...

...LIKE CREATING AND PILOTING DRONES...

...INTRO-DUCING RATIONS...

...HACKING MILITARY OBSTACLE COURSES...

...JUGHEAD?

Oh, MY GOD... GUYS...

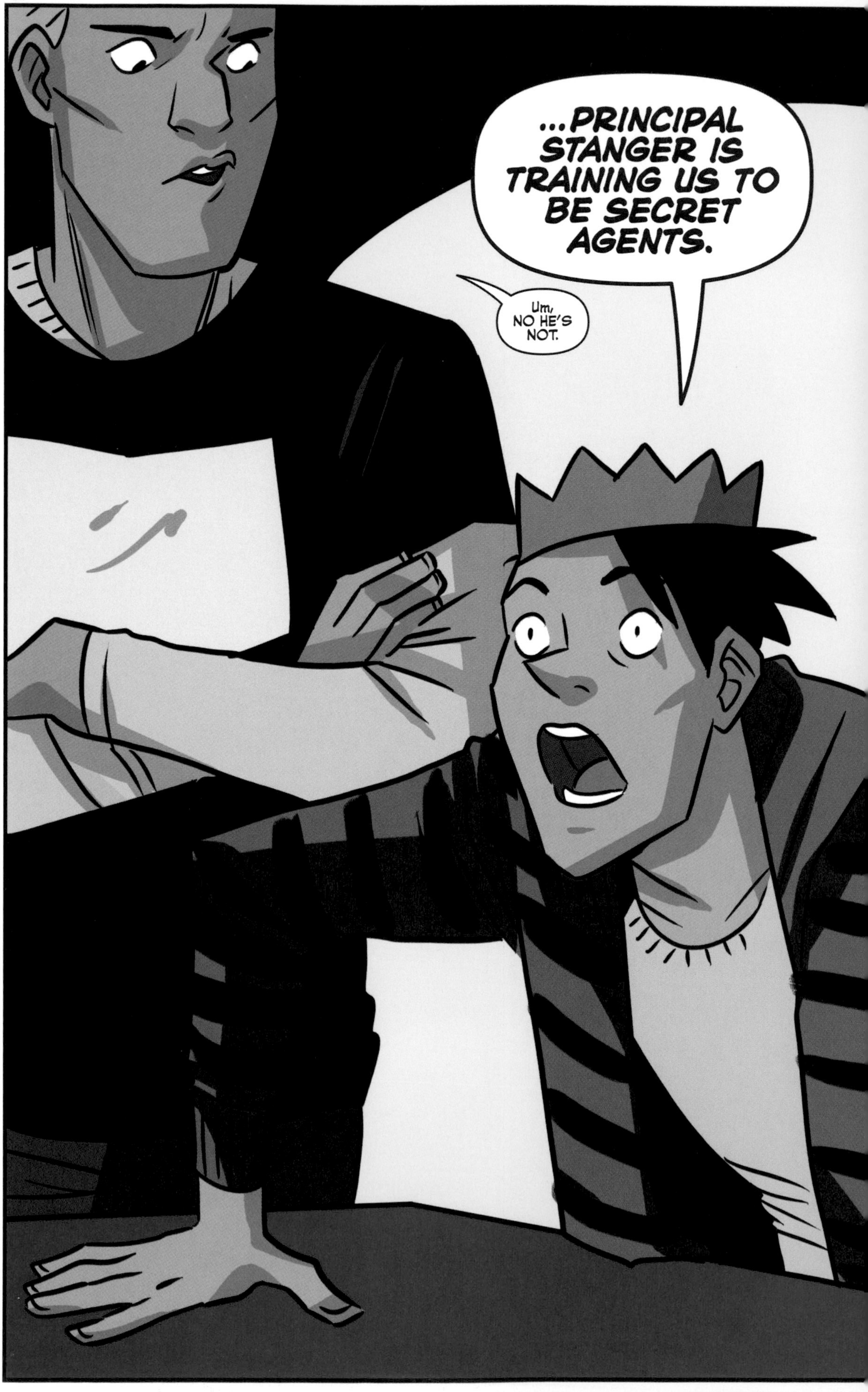
...PRINCIPAL STANGER IS TRAINING US TO BE SECRET AGENTS.
Um, NO HE'S NOT.

BETTY & VERONICA

PREVIOUSLY IN THE TOWN OF RIVERDALE...

Betty and Veronica have waged war on one another!

In one corner, it's Betty Cooper fighting for everything her hometown stands for: local artisans, community charities and hard, honest work. In the other corner is Veronica Lodge, rallying for high-end corporate chain takeovers and the hipster agenda. With the entire town split in two, which BFF will prevail?

It all comes down to a Halloween dance...

STORY & ART BY
ADAM HUGHES

COLORING BY
JOSÉ VILLARRUBIA

LETTERING BY
JACK MORELLI

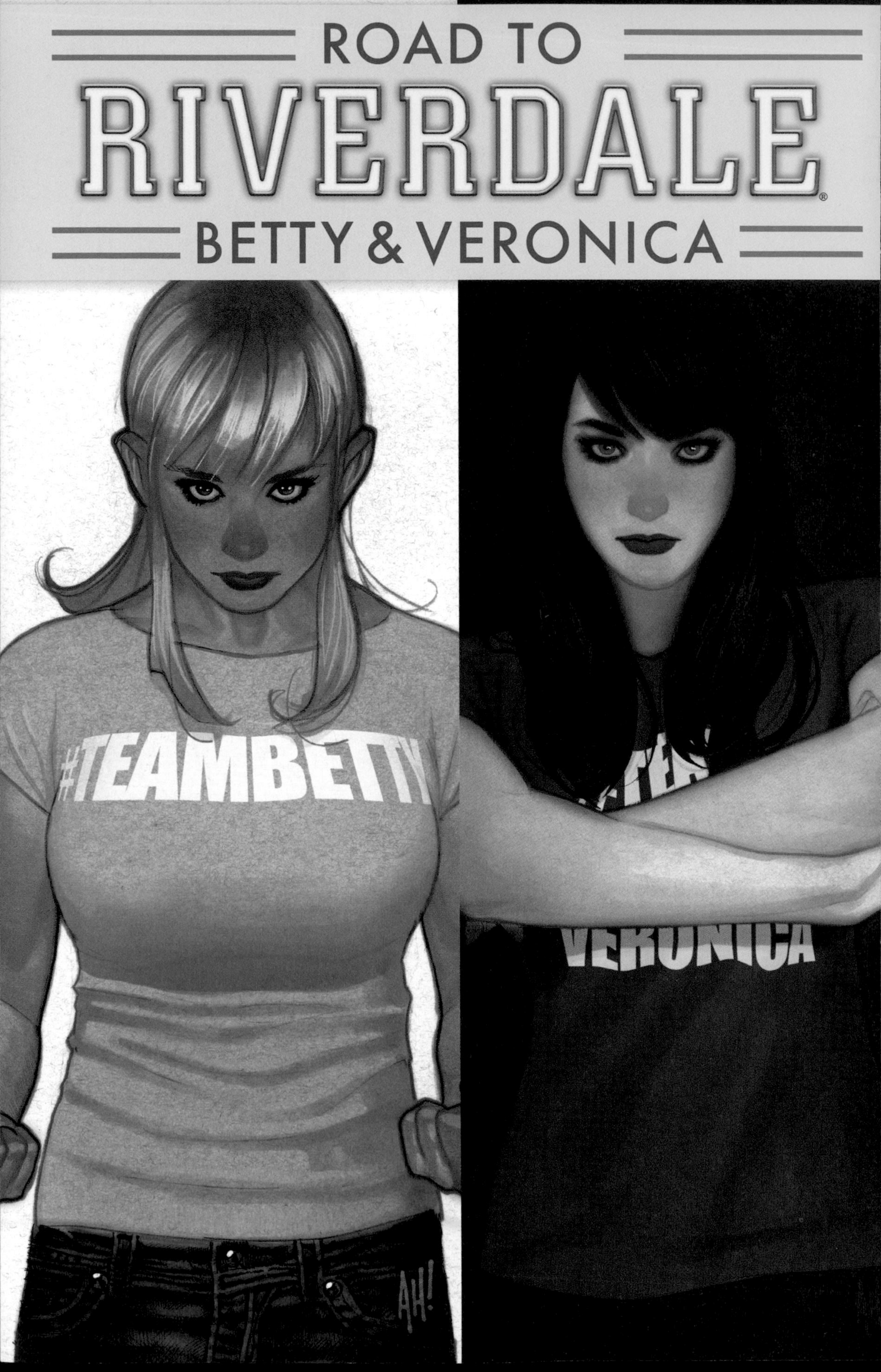
ROAD TO
RIVERDALE
BETTY & VERONICA
#TEAMBETTY
VERONICA

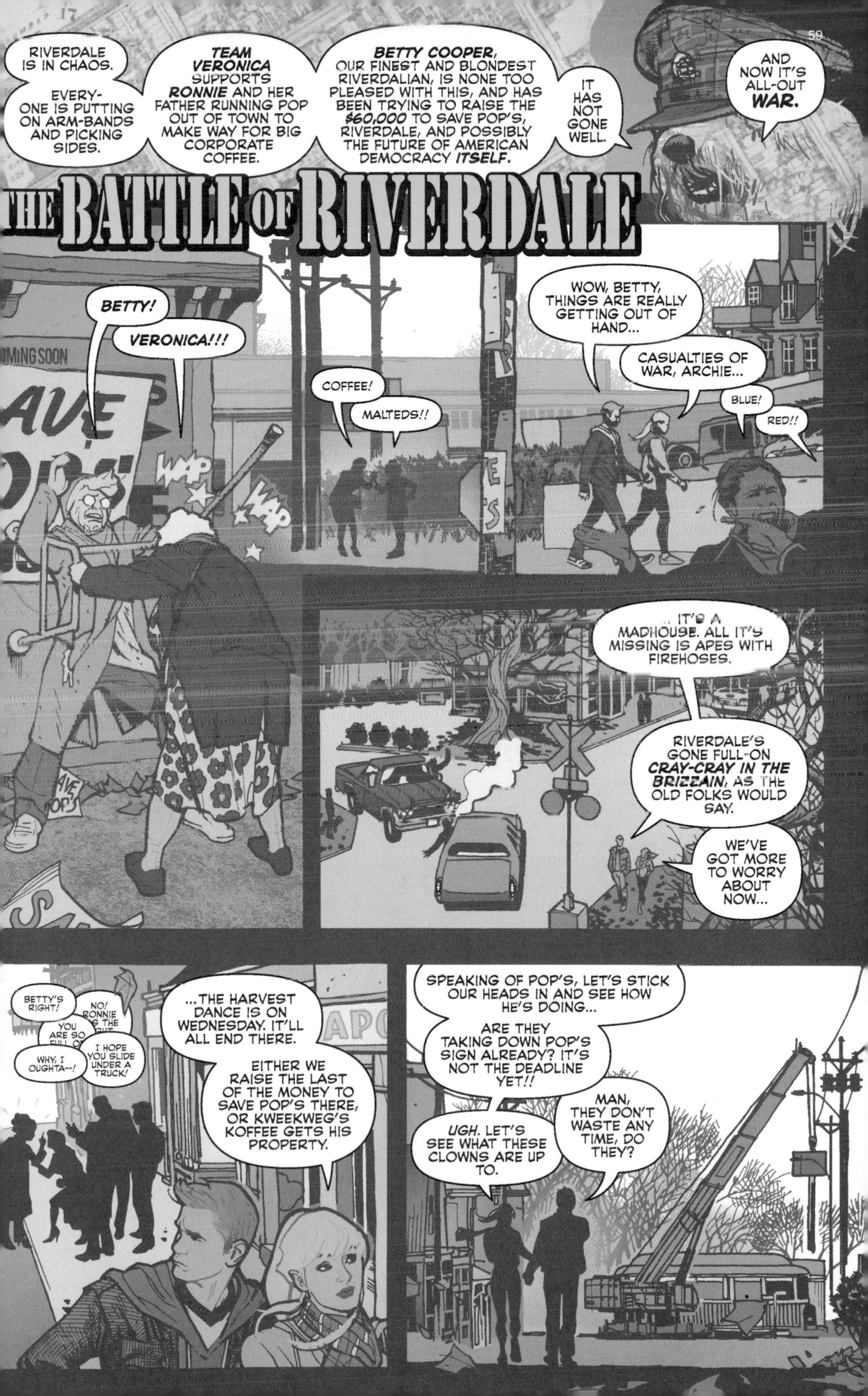
RIVERDALE IS IN CHAOS.
EVERY-ONE IS PUTTING ON ARM-BANDS AND PICKING SIDES.
TEAM VERONICA SUPPORTS RONNIE AND HER FATHER RUNNING POP OUT OF TOWN TO MAKE WAY FOR BIG CORPORATE COFFEE.
BETTY COOPER, OUR FINEST AND BLONDEST RIVERDALIAN, IS NONE TOO PLEASED WITH THIS, AND HAS BEEN TRYING TO RAISE THE $60,000 TO SAVE POP'S, RIVERDALE, AND POSSIBLY THE FUTURE OF AMERICAN DEMOCRACY ITSELF.
IT HAS NOT GONE WELL.
AND NOW IT'S ALL-OUT WAR.
THE BATTLE OF RIVERDALE
BETTY!
VERONICA!!!
WAP
WAP
COFFEE!
MALTEDS!!
WOW, BETTY, THINGS ARE REALLY GETTING OUT OF HAND...
CASUALTIES OF WAR, ARCHIE...
BLUE!
RED!!
... IT'S A MADHOUSE. ALL IT'S MISSING IS APES WITH FIREHOSES.
RIVERDALE'S GONE FULL-ON CRAY-CRAY IN THE BRIZZAIN, AS THE OLD FOLKS WOULD SAY.
WE'VE GOT MORE TO WORRY ABOUT NOW...
BETTY'S RIGHT!
NO! RONNIE
YOU ARE SO
WHY, I OUGHTA--!
I HOPE YOU SLIDE UNDER A TRUCK!
...THE HARVEST DANCE IS ON WEDNESDAY. IT'LL ALL END THERE.
EITHER WE RAISE THE LAST OF THE MONEY TO SAVE POP'S THERE, OR KWEEKWEG'S KOFFEE GETS HIS PROPERTY.
SPEAKING OF POP'S, LET'S STICK OUR HEADS IN AND SEE HOW HE'S DOING...
ARE THEY TAKING DOWN POP'S SIGN ALREADY? IT'S NOT THE DEADLINE YET!!
UGH. LET'S SEE WHAT THESE CLOWNS ARE UP TO.
MAN, THEY DON'T WASTE ANY TIME, DO THEY?

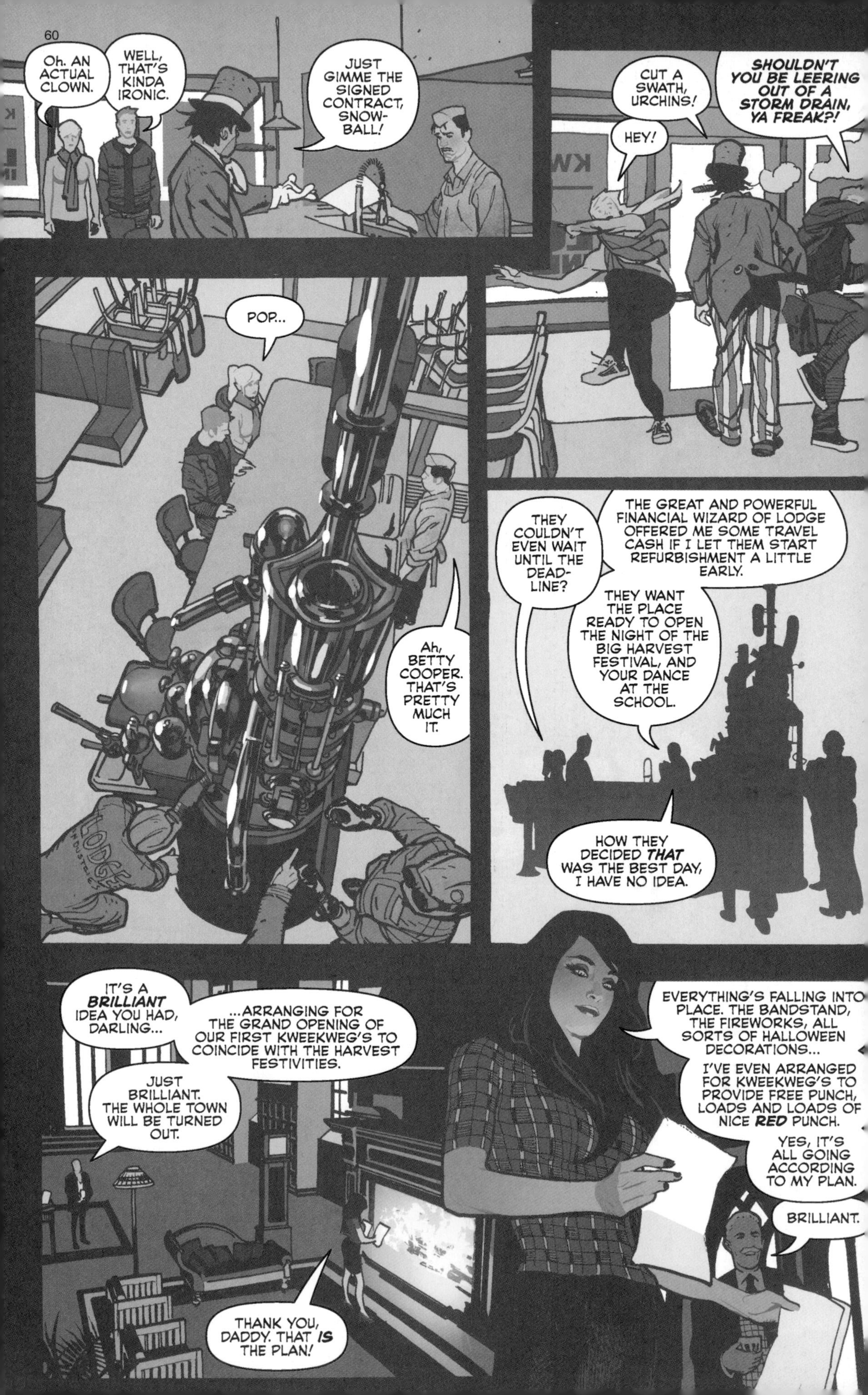
Oh. AN ACTUAL CLOWN.
WELL, THAT'S KINDA IRONIC.
JUST GIMME THE SIGNED CONTRACT, SNOW-BALL!
CUT A SWATH, URCHINS!
HEY!
SHOULDN'T YOU BE LEERING OUT OF A STORM DRAIN, YA FREAK?!
POP...
Ah, BETTY COOPER. THAT'S PRETTY MUCH IT.
THEY COULDN'T EVEN WAIT UNTIL THE DEAD-LINE?
THE GREAT AND POWERFUL FINANCIAL WIZARD OF LODGE OFFERED ME SOME TRAVEL CASH IF I LET THEM START REFURBISHMENT A LITTLE EARLY.
THEY WANT THE PLACE READY TO OPEN THE NIGHT OF THE BIG HARVEST FESTIVAL, AND YOUR DANCE AT THE SCHOOL.
HOW THEY DECIDED THAT WAS THE BEST DAY, I HAVE NO IDEA.
IT'S A BRILLIANT IDEA YOU HAD, DARLING...
...ARRANGING FOR THE GRAND OPENING OF OUR FIRST KWEEKWEG'S TO COINCIDE WITH THE HARVEST FESTIVITIES.
JUST BRILLIANT. THE WHOLE TOWN WILL BE TURNED OUT.
THANK YOU, DADDY. THAT IS THE PLAN!
EVERYTHING'S FALLING INTO PLACE. THE BANDSTAND, THE FIREWORKS, ALL SORTS OF HALLOWEEN DECORATIONS...
I'VE EVEN ARRANGED FOR KWEEKWEG'S TO PROVIDE FREE PUNCH, LOADS AND LOADS OF NICE RED PUNCH.
YES, IT'S ALL GOING ACCORDING TO MY PLAN.
BRILLIANT.

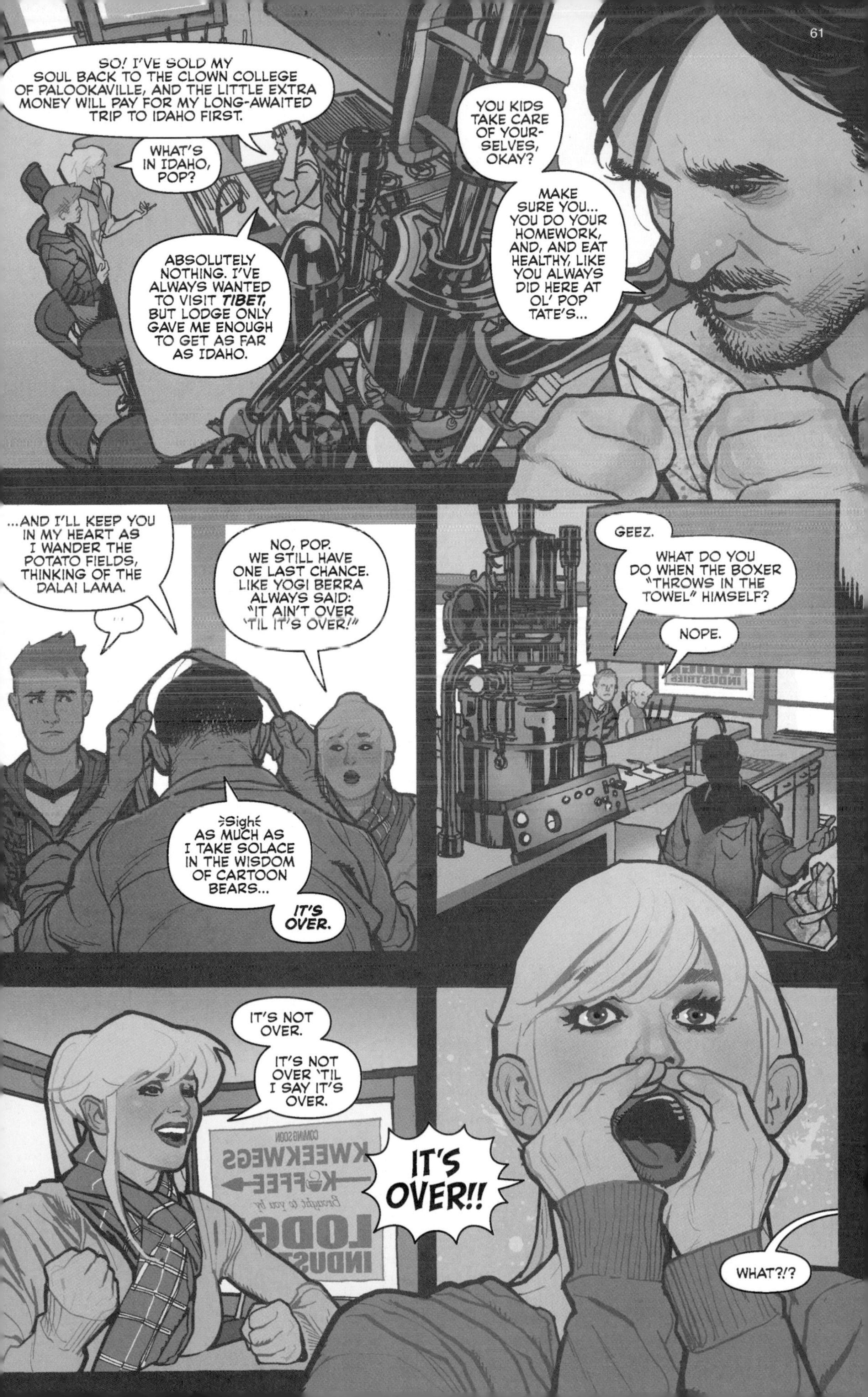
SO! I'VE SOLD MY SOUL BACK TO THE CLOWN COLLEGE OF PALOOKAVILLE, AND THE LITTLE EXTRA MONEY WILL PAY FOR MY LONG-AWAITED TRIP TO IDAHO FIRST.
WHAT'S IN IDAHO, POP?
ABSOLUTELY NOTHING. I'VE ALWAYS WANTED TO VISIT *TIBET*, BUT LODGE ONLY GAVE ME ENOUGH TO GET AS FAR AS IDAHO.
YOU KIDS TAKE CARE OF YOUR-SELVES, OKAY?
MAKE SURE YOU... YOU DO YOUR HOMEWORK, AND, AND EAT HEALTHY, LIKE YOU ALWAYS DID HERE AT OL' POP TATE'S...
...AND I'LL KEEP YOU IN MY HEART AS I WANDER THE POTATO FIELDS, THINKING OF THE DALAI LAMA.
NO, POP. WE STILL HAVE ONE LAST CHANCE. LIKE YOGI BERRA ALWAYS SAID: "IT AIN'T OVER 'TIL IT'S OVER!"
Sigh AS MUCH AS I TAKE SOLACE IN THE WISDOM OF CARTOON BEARS...
IT'S OVER.
GEEZ.
WHAT DO YOU DO WHEN THE BOXER "THROWS IN THE TOWEL" HIMSELF?
NOPE.
IT'S NOT OVER.
IT'S NOT OVER 'TIL I SAY IT'S OVER.
IT'S OVER!!
WHAT?!?

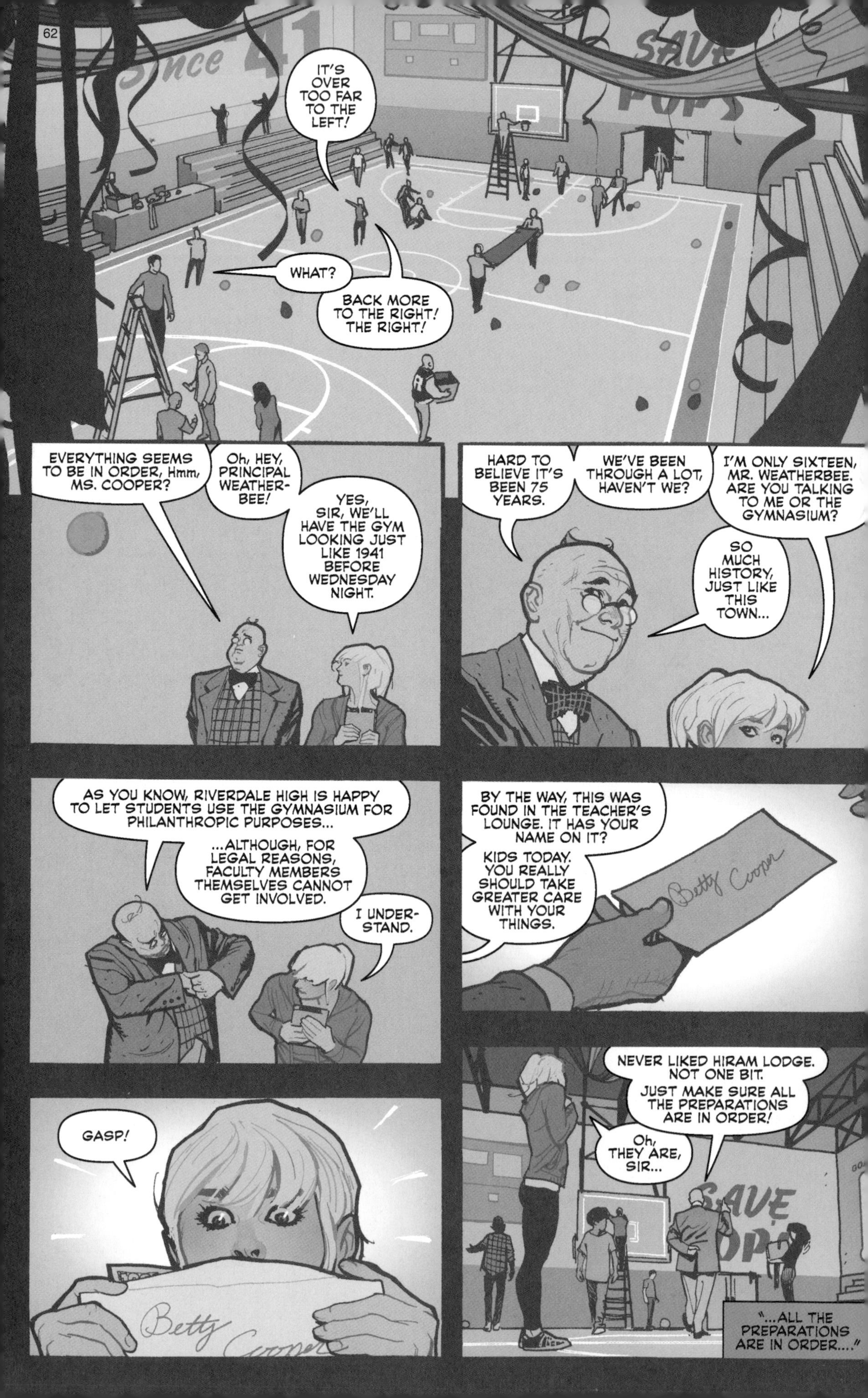
Since 41
SAVE POPS
IT'S OVER TOO FAR TO THE LEFT!
WHAT?
BACK MORE TO THE RIGHT! THE RIGHT!
EVERYTHING SEEMS TO BE IN ORDER, Hmm, MS. COOPER?
Oh, HEY, PRINCIPAL WEATHER-BEE!
YES, SIR, WE'LL HAVE THE GYM LOOKING JUST LIKE 1941 BEFORE WEDNESDAY NIGHT.
HARD TO BELIEVE IT'S BEEN 75 YEARS.
WE'VE BEEN THROUGH A LOT, HAVEN'T WE?
I'M ONLY SIXTEEN, MR. WEATHERBEE. ARE YOU TALKING TO ME OR THE GYMNASIUM?
SO MUCH HISTORY, JUST LIKE THIS TOWN...
AS YOU KNOW, RIVERDALE HIGH IS HAPPY TO LET STUDENTS USE THE GYMNASIUM FOR PHILANTHROPIC PURPOSES...
...ALTHOUGH, FOR LEGAL REASONS, FACULTY MEMBERS THEMSELVES CANNOT GET INVOLVED.
I UNDER-STAND.
BY THE WAY, THIS WAS FOUND IN THE TEACHER'S LOUNGE. IT HAS YOUR NAME ON IT?
KIDS TODAY. YOU REALLY SHOULD TAKE GREATER CARE WITH YOUR THINGS.
Betty Cooper
GASP!
Betty Cooper
NEVER LIKED HIRAM LODGE. NOT ONE BIT.
JUST MAKE SURE ALL THE PREPARATIONS ARE IN ORDER!
Oh, THEY ARE, SIR...
"...ALL THE PREPARATIONS ARE IN ORDER...."

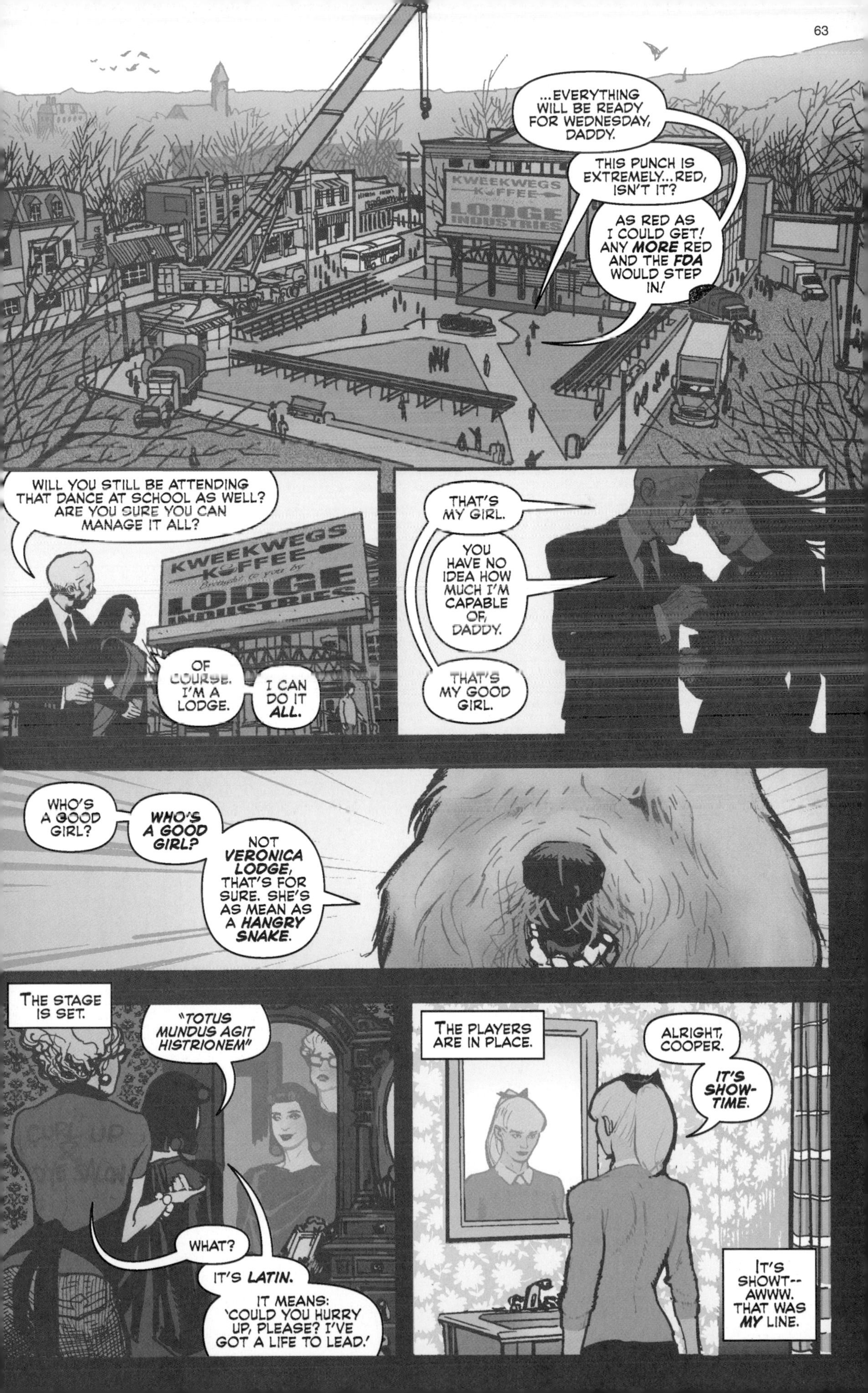
...EVERYTHING WILL BE READY FOR WEDNESDAY, DADDY.
THIS PUNCH IS EXTREMELY...RED, ISN'T IT?
AS RED AS I COULD GET! ANY MORE RED AND THE FDA WOULD STEP IN!
KWEEKWEGS KOFFEE
LODGE INDUSTRIES
WILL YOU STILL BE ATTENDING THAT DANCE AT SCHOOL AS WELL? ARE YOU SURE YOU CAN MANAGE IT ALL?
OF COURSE. I'M A LODGE.
I CAN DO IT ALL.
THAT'S MY GIRL.
YOU HAVE NO IDEA HOW MUCH I'M CAPABLE OF, DADDY.
THAT'S MY GOOD GIRL.
WHO'S A GOOD GIRL?
WHO'S A GOOD GIRL?
NOT VERONICA LODGE, THAT'S FOR SURE. SHE'S AS MEAN AS A HANGRY SNAKE.
THE STAGE IS SET.
"TOTUS MUNDUS AGIT HISTRIONEM"
WHAT?
IT'S LATIN.
IT MEANS: 'COULD YOU HURRY UP, PLEASE? I'VE GOT A LIFE TO LEAD.'
THE PLAYERS ARE IN PLACE.
ALRIGHT, COOPER.
IT'S SHOW-TIME.
IT'S SHOWT-- AWWW. THAT WAS MY LINE.

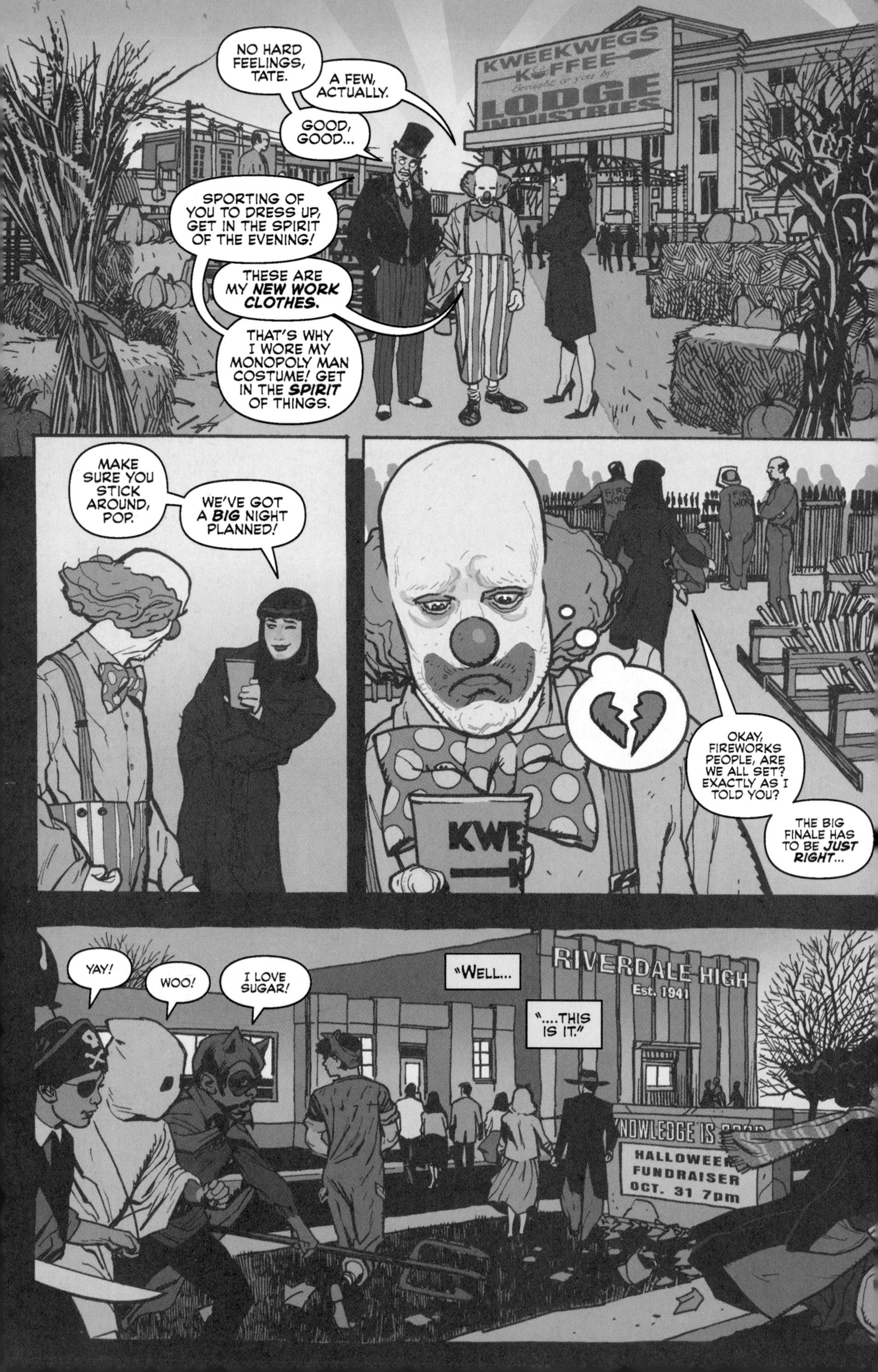
KWEEKWEGS KOFFEE Brought to you by LODGE INDUSTRIES
NO HARD FEELINGS, TATE.
A FEW, ACTUALLY.
GOOD, GOOD...
SPORTING OF YOU TO DRESS UP, GET IN THE SPIRIT OF THE EVENING!
THESE ARE MY NEW WORK CLOTHES.
THAT'S WHY I WORE MY MONOPOLY MAN COSTUME! GET IN THE SPIRIT OF THINGS.
MAKE SURE YOU STICK AROUND, POP.
WE'VE GOT A BIG NIGHT PLANNED!
KWE
OKAY, FIREWORKS PEOPLE, ARE WE ALL SET? EXACTLY AS I TOLD YOU?
THE BIG FINALE HAS TO BE JUST RIGHT...
YAY!
WOO!
I LOVE SUGAR!
"WELL...
"...THIS IS IT."
RIVERDALE HIGH Est. 1941
KNOWLEDGE IS
HALLOWEEN FUNDRAISER OCT. 31 7pm

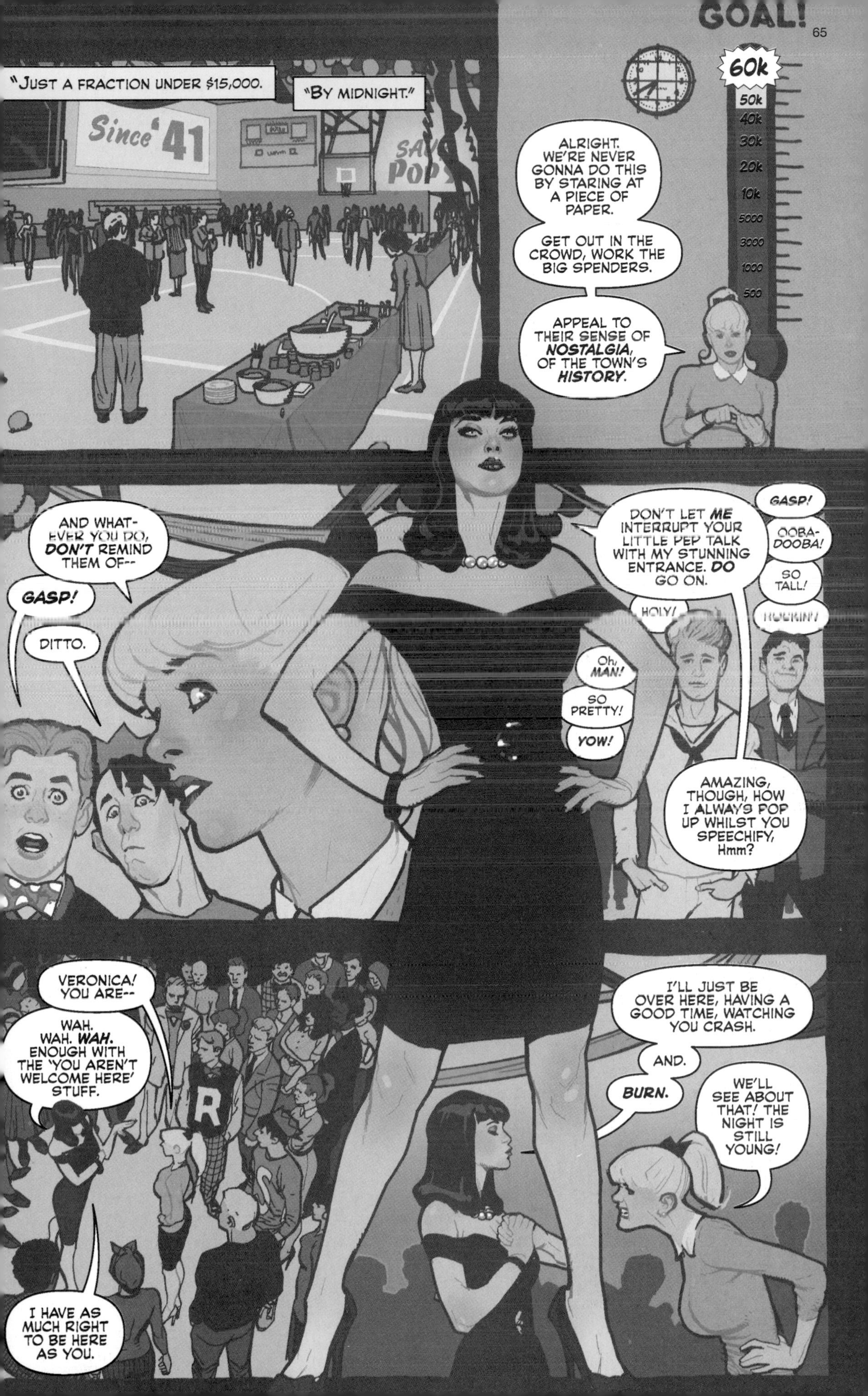
"JUST A FRACTION UNDER $15,000.
"BY MIDNIGHT."
Since '41
SAVE POP'S
GOAL!
60k
50k
40k
30k
20k
10k
5000
3000
1000
500
ALRIGHT. WE'RE NEVER GONNA DO THIS BY STARING AT A PIECE OF PAPER.
GET OUT IN THE CROWD, WORK THE BIG SPENDERS.
APPEAL TO THEIR SENSE OF ***NOSTALGIA***, OF THE TOWN'S ***HISTORY***.
AND WHATEVER YOU DO, ***DON'T*** REMIND THEM OF--
GASP!
DITTO.
DON'T LET ***ME*** INTERRUPT YOUR LITTLE PEP TALK WITH MY STUNNING ENTRANCE. ***DO*** GO ON.
GASP!
OOBA-DOOBA!
SO TALL!
ROCKIN'!
HOLY!
Oh, ***MAN!***
SO PRETTY!
YOW!
AMAZING, THOUGH, HOW I ALWAYS POP UP WHILST YOU SPEECHIFY, Hmm?
VERONICA! YOU ARE--
WAH. WAH. ***WAH.*** ENOUGH WITH THE 'YOU AREN'T WELCOME HERE' STUFF.
I HAVE AS MUCH RIGHT TO BE HERE AS YOU.
I'LL JUST BE OVER HERE, HAVING A GOOD TIME, WATCHING YOU CRASH.
AND.
BURN.
WE'LL SEE ABOUT THAT! THE NIGHT IS STILL YOUNG!

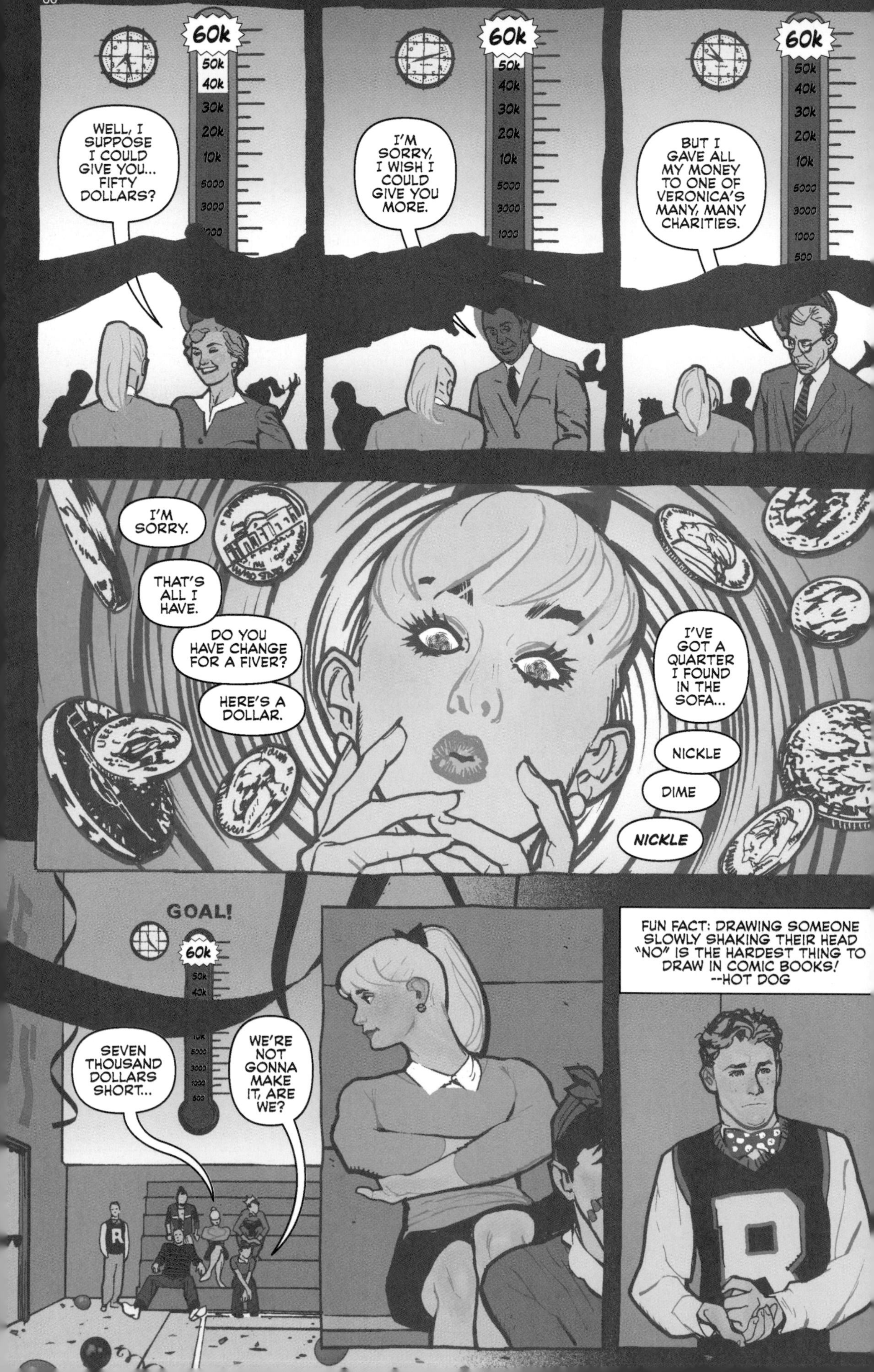
60k
WELL, I SUPPOSE I COULD GIVE YOU... FIFTY DOLLARS?
60k
I'M SORRY, I WISH I COULD GIVE YOU MORE.
60k
BUT I GAVE ALL MY MONEY TO ONE OF VERONICA'S MANY, MANY CHARITIES.
I'M SORRY.
THAT'S ALL I HAVE.
DO YOU HAVE CHANGE FOR A FIVER?
HERE'S A DOLLAR.
I'VE GOT A QUARTER I FOUND IN THE SOFA...
NICKLE
DIME
NICKLE
GOAL!
60k
SEVEN THOUSAND DOLLARS SHORT...
WE'RE NOT GONNA MAKE IT, ARE WE?
FUN FACT: DRAWING SOMEONE SLOWLY SHAKING THEIR HEAD "NO" IS THE HARDEST THING TO DRAW IN COMIC BOOKS! --HOT DOG

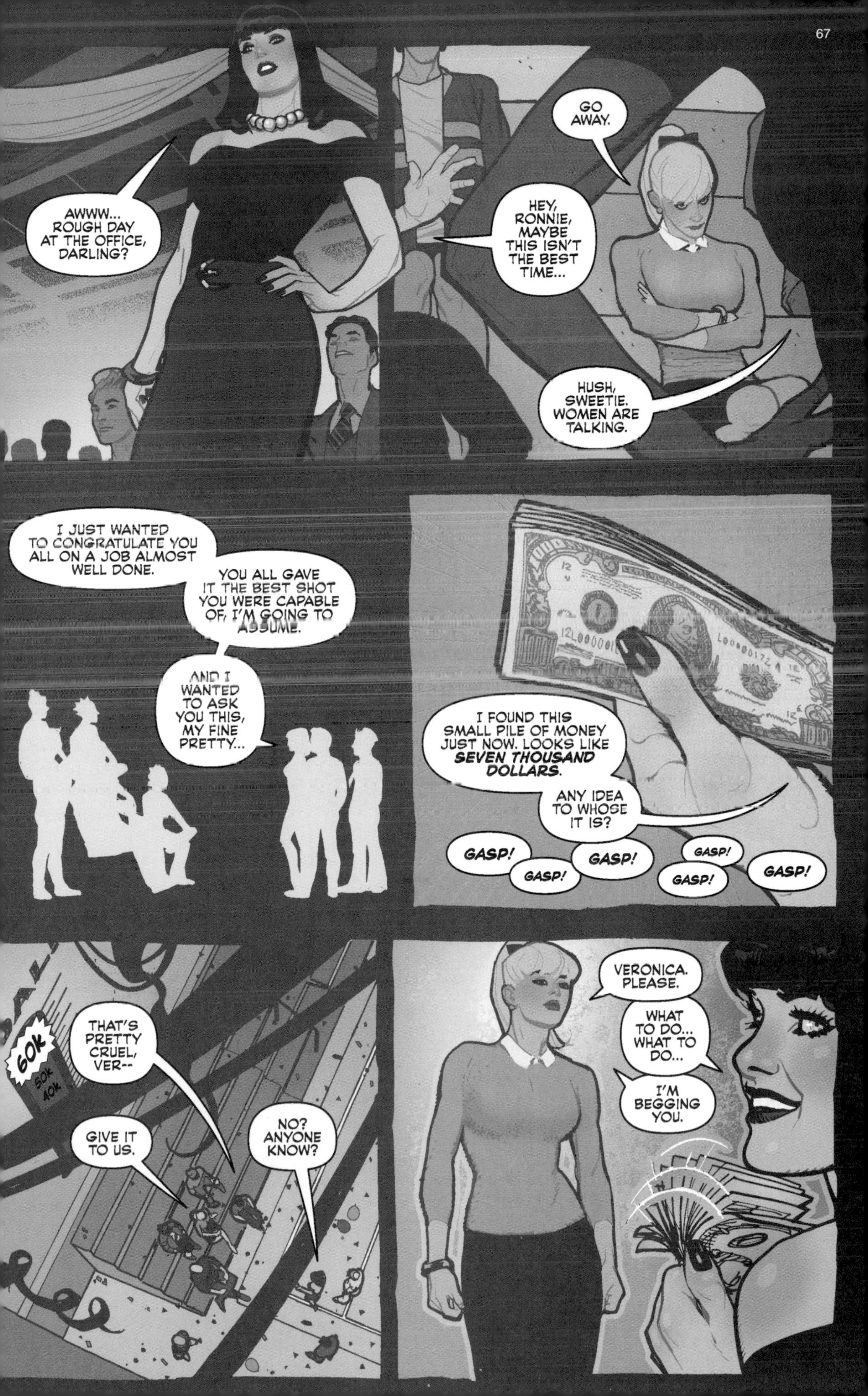
AWWW... ROUGH DAY AT THE OFFICE, DARLING?
GO AWAY.
HEY, RONNIE, MAYBE THIS ISN'T THE BEST TIME...
HUSH, SWEETIE. WOMEN ARE TALKING.
I JUST WANTED TO CONGRATULATE YOU ALL ON A JOB ALMOST WELL DONE.
YOU ALL GAVE IT THE BEST SHOT YOU WERE CAPABLE OF, I'M GOING TO ASSUME.
AND I WANTED TO ASK YOU THIS, MY FINE PRETTY...
I FOUND THIS SMALL PILE OF MONEY JUST NOW. LOOKS LIKE ***SEVEN THOUSAND DOLLARS***.
ANY IDEA TO WHOSE IT IS?
GASP!
GASP!
GASP!
GASP!
GASP!
GASP!
60K
50K
40K
THAT'S PRETTY CRUEL, VER--
GIVE IT TO US.
NO? ANYONE KNOW?
VERONICA. PLEASE.
WHAT TO DO... WHAT TO DO...
I'M BEGGING YOU.

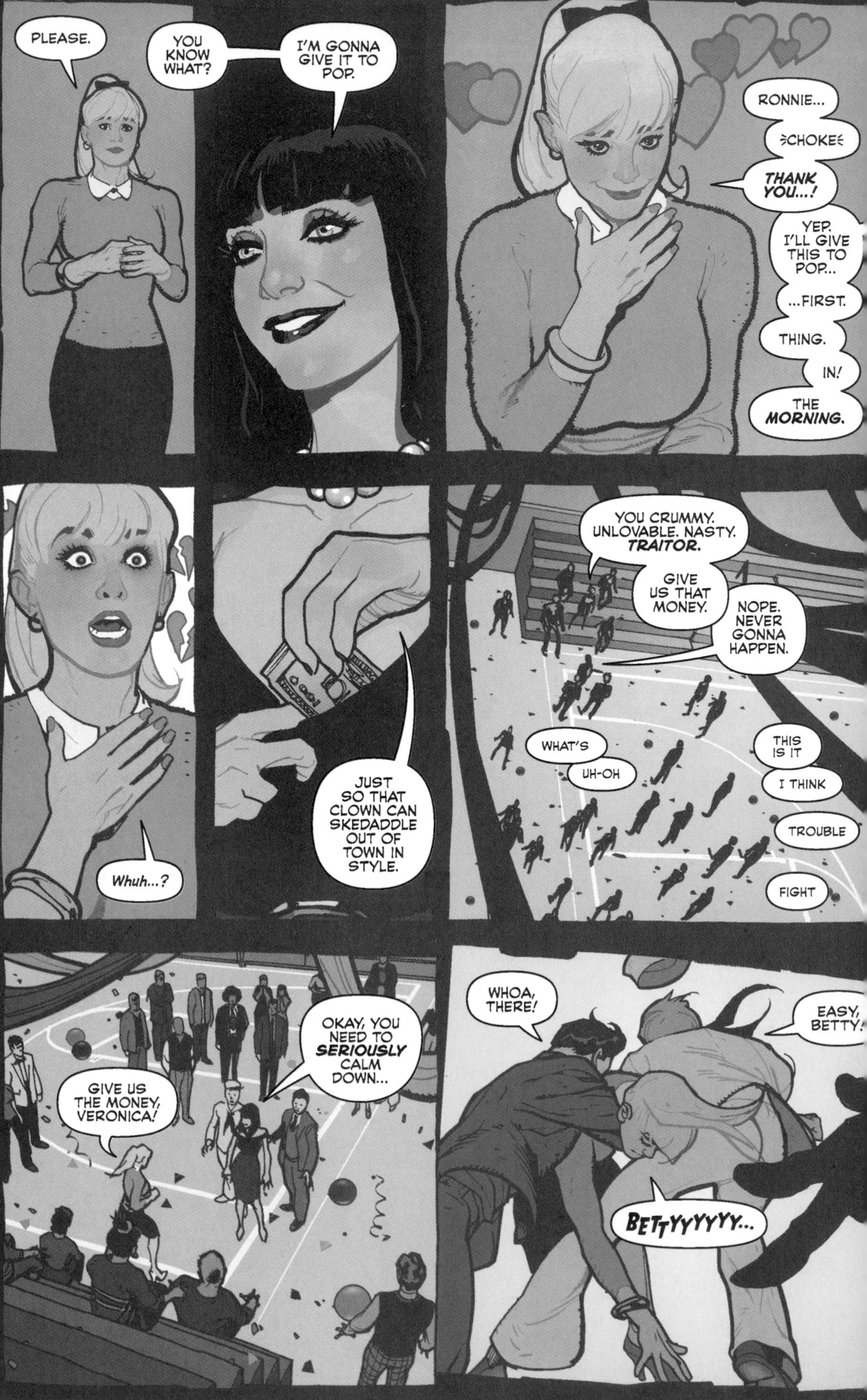
PLEASE.
YOU KNOW WHAT?
I'M GONNA GIVE IT TO POP.
RONNIE...
CHOKE
THANK YOU...!
YEP. I'LL GIVE THIS TO POP...
...FIRST.
THING.
IN!
THE *MORNING.*
Whuh...?
JUST SO THAT CLOWN CAN SKEDADDLE OUT OF TOWN IN STYLE.
YOU CRUMMY. UNLOVABLE. NASTY. *TRAITOR.*
GIVE US THAT MONEY.
NOPE. NEVER GONNA HAPPEN.
WHAT'S
UH-OH
THIS IS IT
I THINK
TROUBLE
FIGHT
GIVE US THE MONEY, VERONICA!
OKAY, YOU NEED TO *SERIOUSLY* CALM DOWN...
WHOA, THERE!
EASY, BETTY!
BETTYYYYYY...

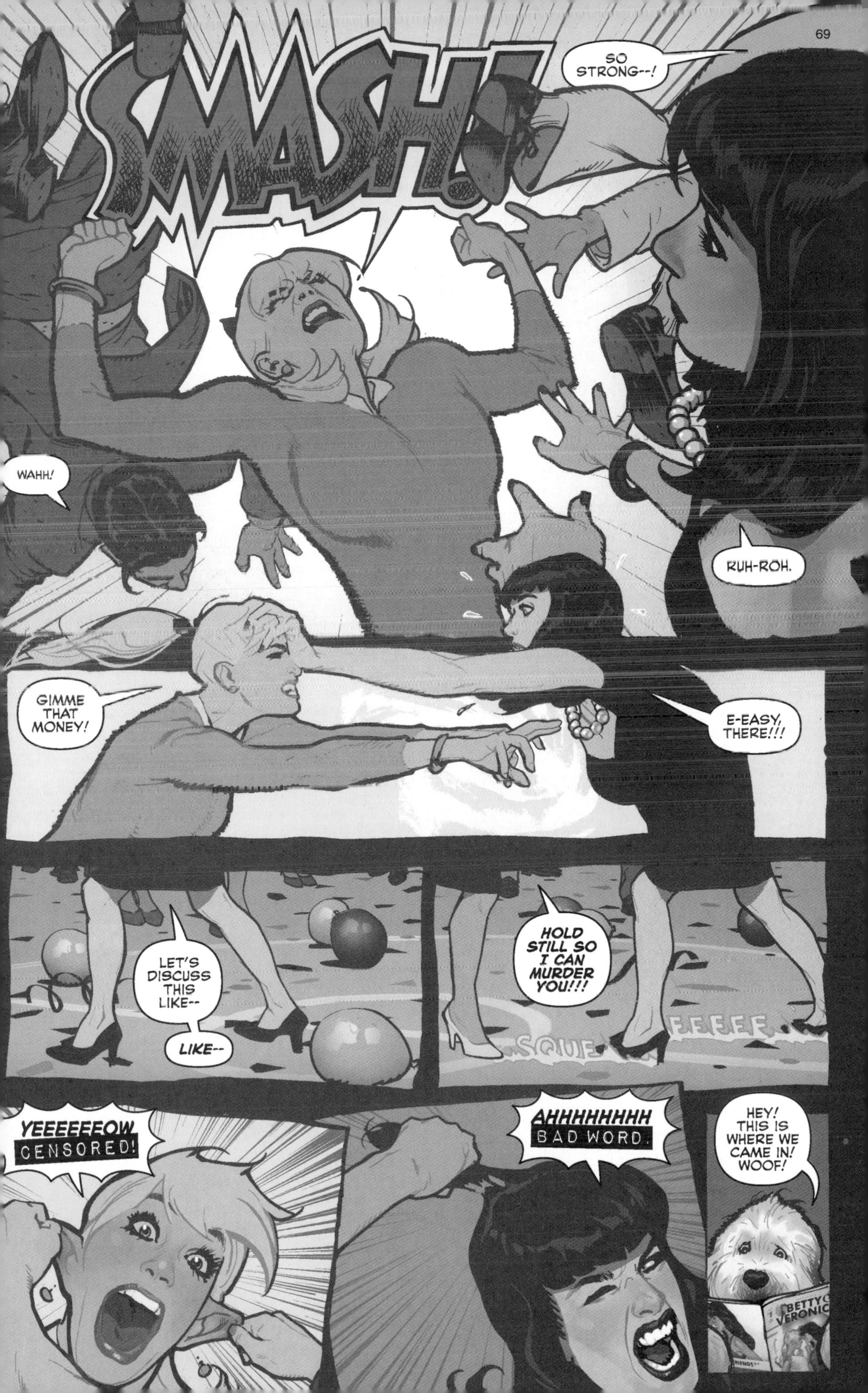
SMASH!
SO STRONG--!
WAHH!
RUH-ROH.
GIMME THAT MONEY!
E-EASY, THERE!!!
LET'S DISCUSS THIS LIKE--
LIKE--
HOLD STILL SO I CAN MURDER YOU!!!
SQUE EEEEE
YEEEEEEOW
CENSORED!
AHHHHHHHHH
BAD WORD.
HEY! THIS IS WHERE WE CAME IN! WOOF!
BETTY
VERONIC

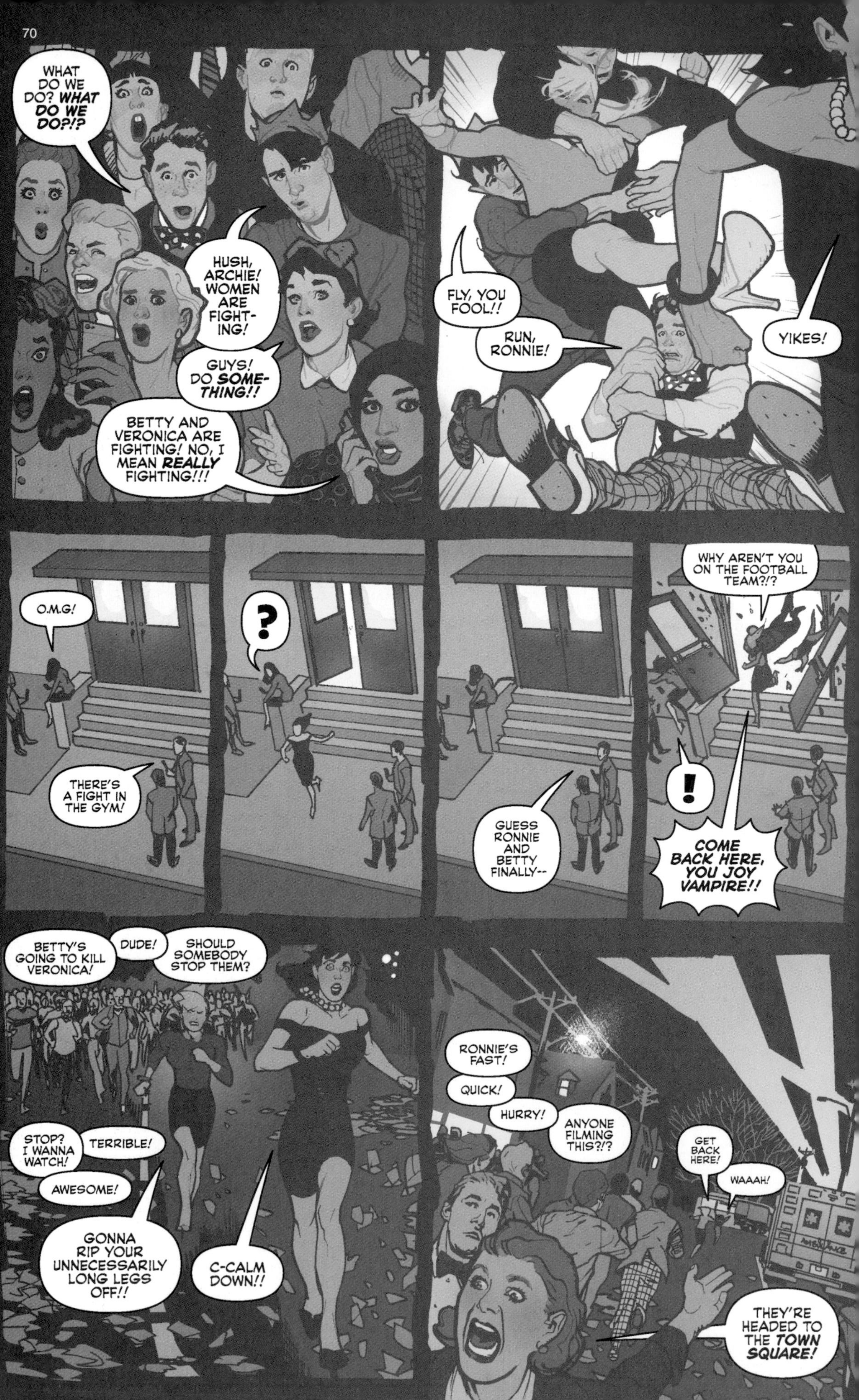
WHAT DO WE DO? WHAT DO WE DO?!?
HUSH, ARCHIE! WOMEN ARE FIGHTING!
GUYS! DO SOMETHING!!
BETTY AND VERONICA ARE FIGHTING! NO, I MEAN REALLY FIGHTING!!!
FLY, YOU FOOL!!
RUN, RONNIE!
YIKES!
O.M.G!
THERE'S A FIGHT IN THE GYM!
?
GUESS RONNIE AND BETTY FINALLY--
WHY AREN'T YOU ON THE FOOTBALL TEAM?!?
!
COME BACK HERE, YOU JOY VAMPIRE!!
BETTY'S GOING TO KILL VERONICA!
DUDE!
SHOULD SOMEBODY STOP THEM?
STOP? I WANNA WATCH!
TERRIBLE!
AWESOME!
GONNA RIP YOUR UNNECESSARILY LONG LEGS OFF!!
C-CALM DOWN!!
RONNIE'S FAST!
QUICK!
HURRY!
ANYONE FILMING THIS?!?
GET BACK HERE!
WAAAH!
THEY'RE HEADED TO THE TOWN SQUARE!

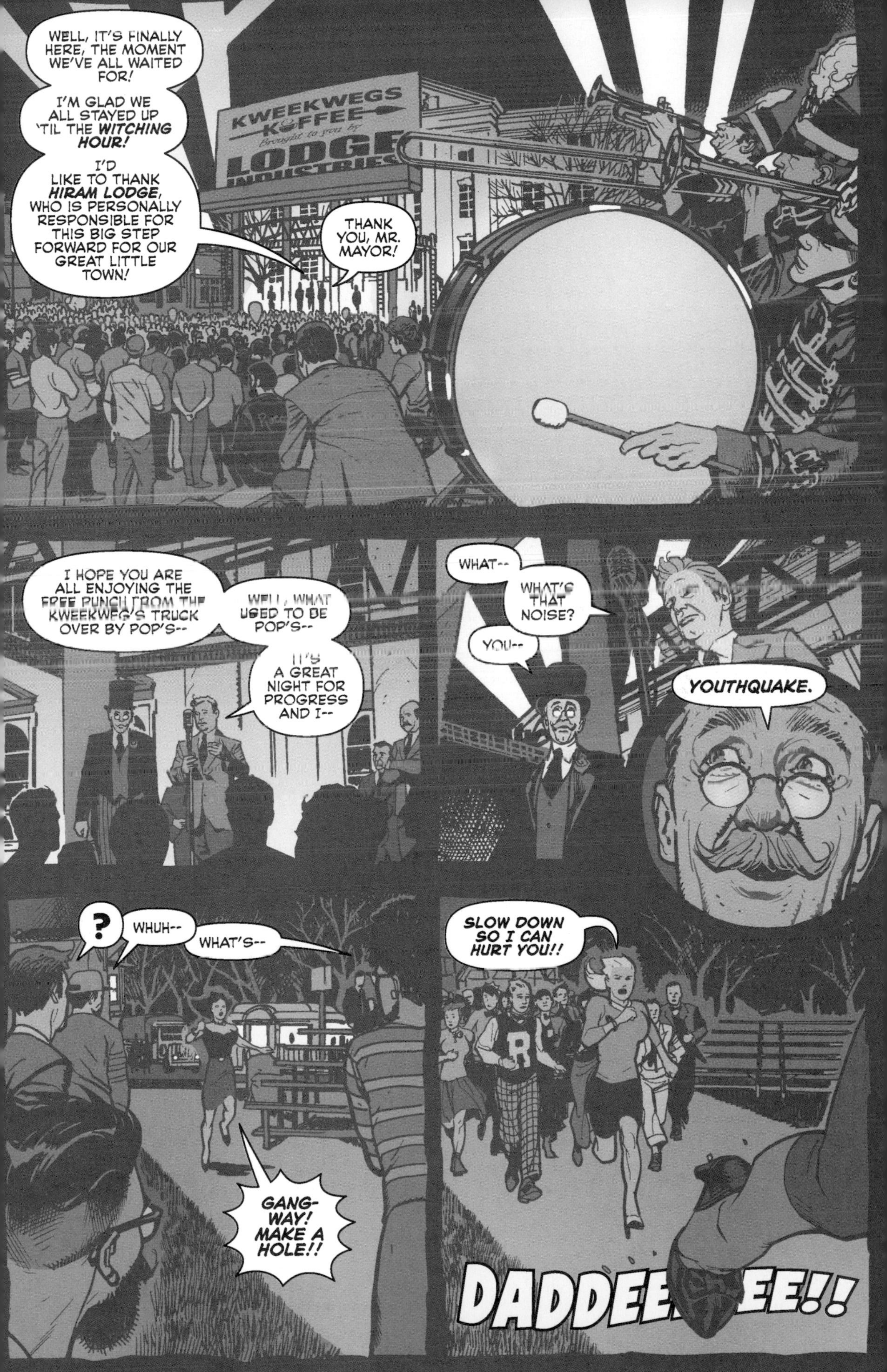
WELL, IT'S FINALLY HERE, THE MOMENT WE'VE ALL WAITED FOR!
I'M GLAD WE ALL STAYED UP 'TIL THE WITCHING HOUR!
I'D LIKE TO THANK HIRAM LODGE, WHO IS PERSONALLY RESPONSIBLE FOR THIS BIG STEP FORWARD FOR OUR GREAT LITTLE TOWN!
KWEEKWEGS KOFFEE
Brought to you by
LODGE INDUSTRIES
THANK YOU, MR. MAYOR!
I HOPE YOU ARE ALL ENJOYING THE FREE PUNCH FROM THE KWEEKWEG'S TRUCK OVER BY POP'S--
WELL, WHAT USED TO BE POP'S--
IT'S A GREAT NIGHT FOR PROGRESS AND I--
WHAT--
WHAT'S THAT NOISE?
YOU--
YOUTHQUAKE.
?
WHUH--
WHAT'S--
GANG-WAY! MAKE A HOLE!!
SLOW DOWN SO I CAN HURT YOU!!
DADDEE
EE!!

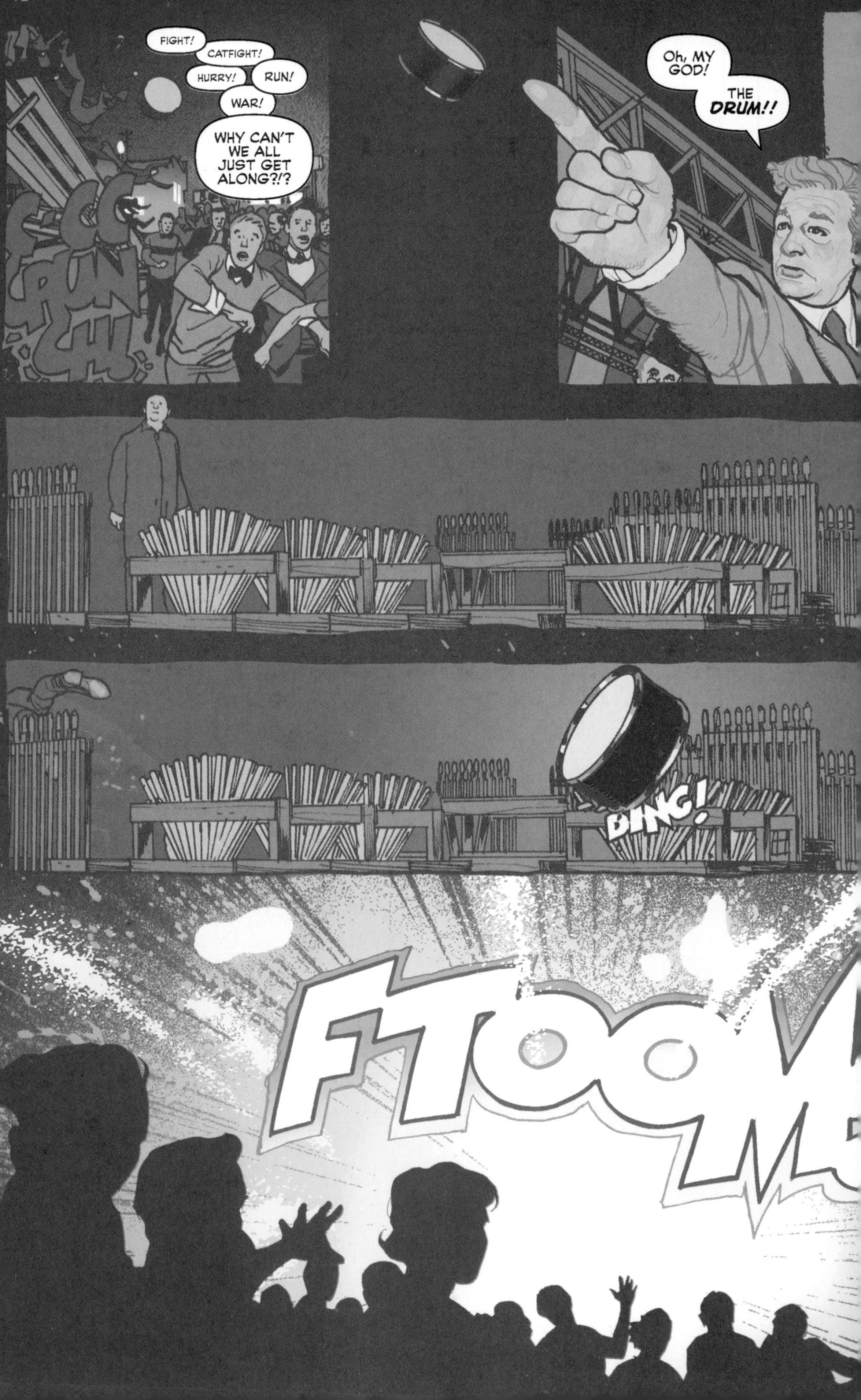
FIGHT!
CATFIGHT!
HURRY!
RUN!
WAR!
WHY CAN'T WE ALL JUST GET ALONG?!?
Oh, MY GOD!
THE DRUM!!
DING!

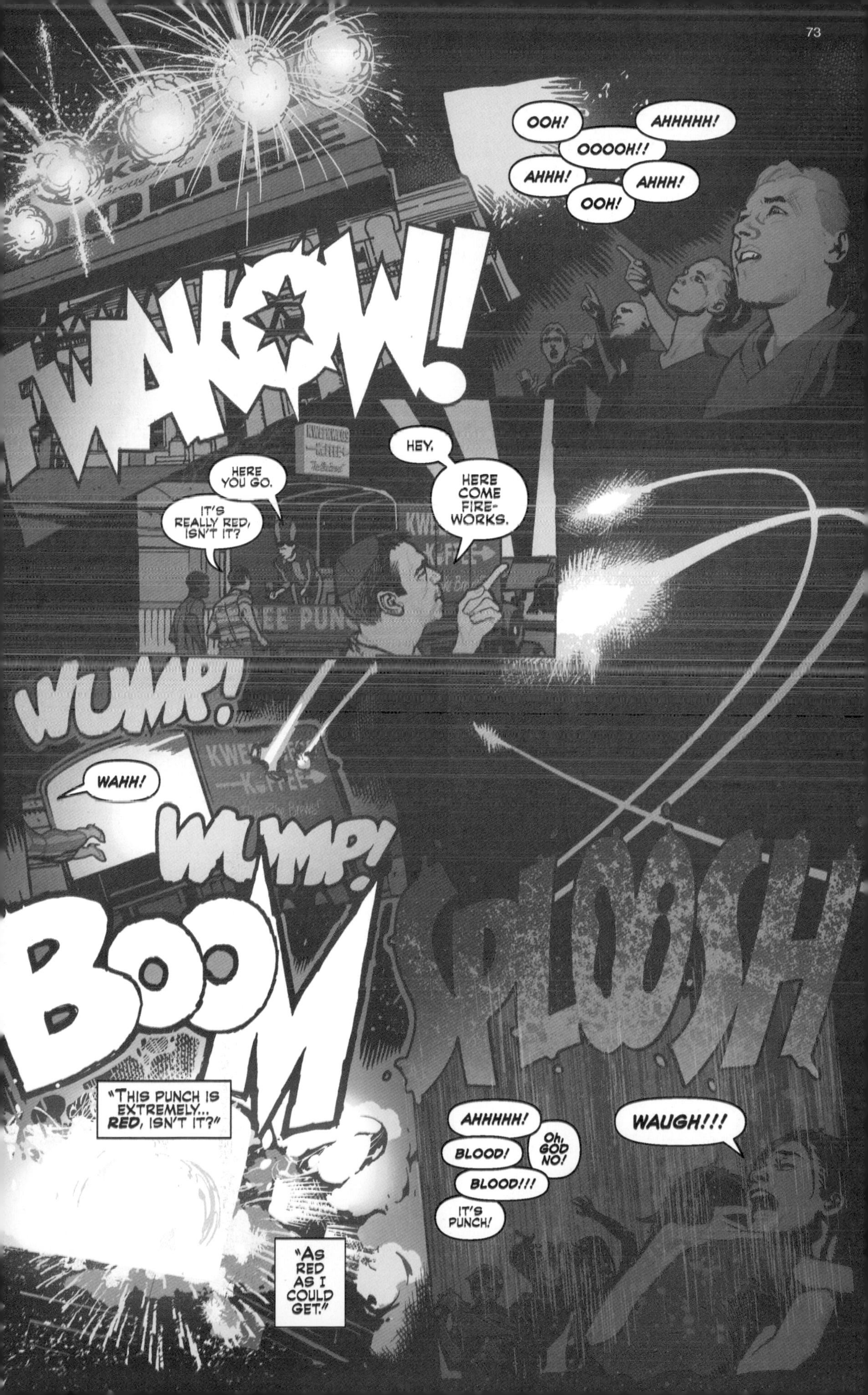
OOH!
AHHHHH!
OOOOH!!
AHHH!
AHHH!
OOH!
HEY.
HERE COME FIRE-WORKS.
HERE YOU GO.
IT'S REALLY RED, ISN'T IT?
WUMP!
WAHH!
WUMP!
BOOM
SPLOOSH
"THIS PUNCH IS EXTREMELY... RED, ISN'T IT?"
AHHHHH!
BLOOD!
Oh, GOD NO!
BLOOD!!!
IT'S PUNCH!
WAUGH!!!
"AS RED AS I COULD GET."

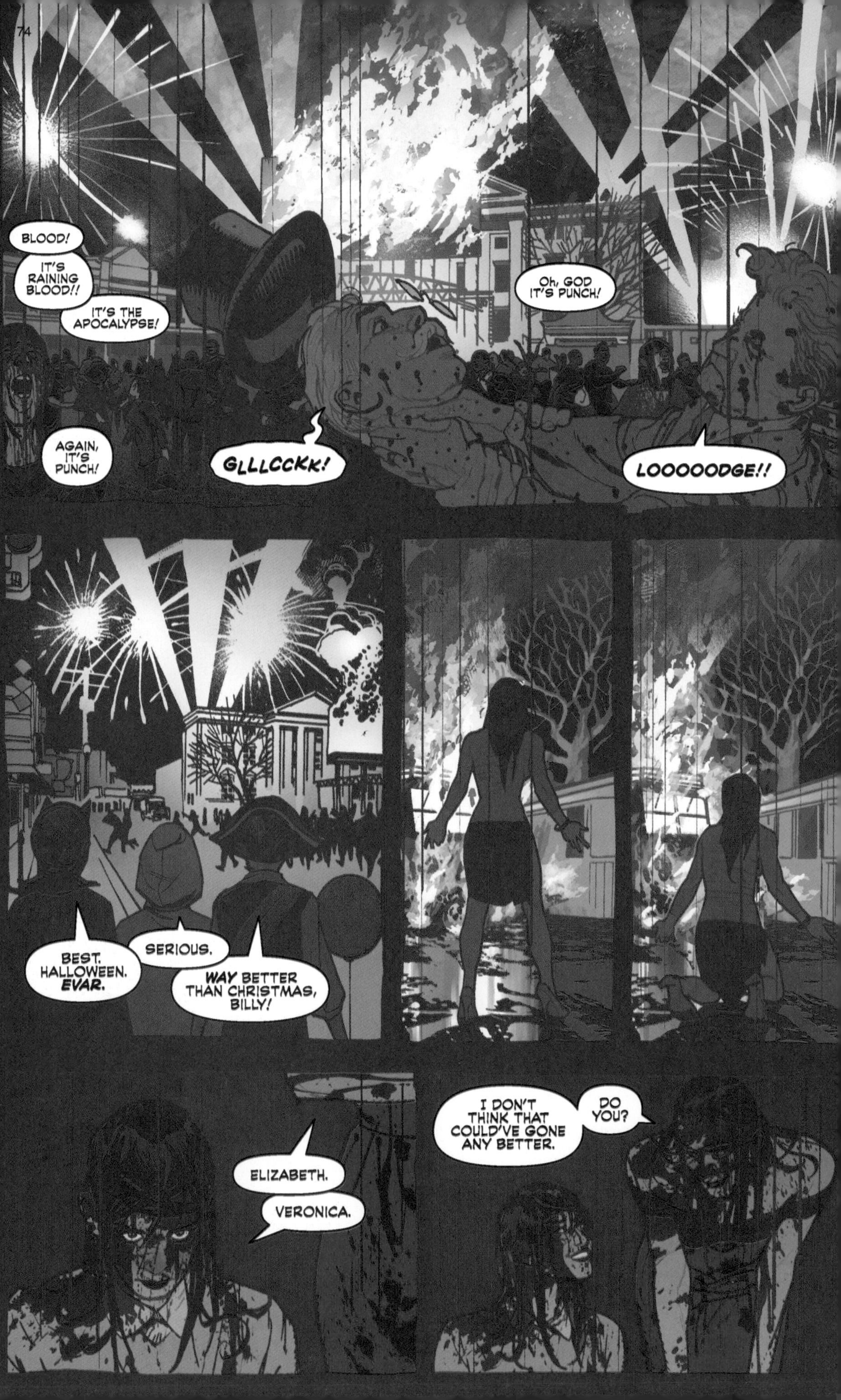
BLOOD!
IT'S RAINING BLOOD!!
IT'S THE APOCALYPSE!
Oh, GOD IT'S PUNCH!
AGAIN, IT'S PUNCH!
GLLLCCKK!
LOOOOODGE!!
BEST. HALLOWEEN. EVAR.
SERIOUS.
WAY BETTER THAN CHRISTMAS, BILLY!
ELIZABETH.
VERONICA.
I DON'T THINK THAT COULD'VE GONE ANY BETTER.
DO YOU?

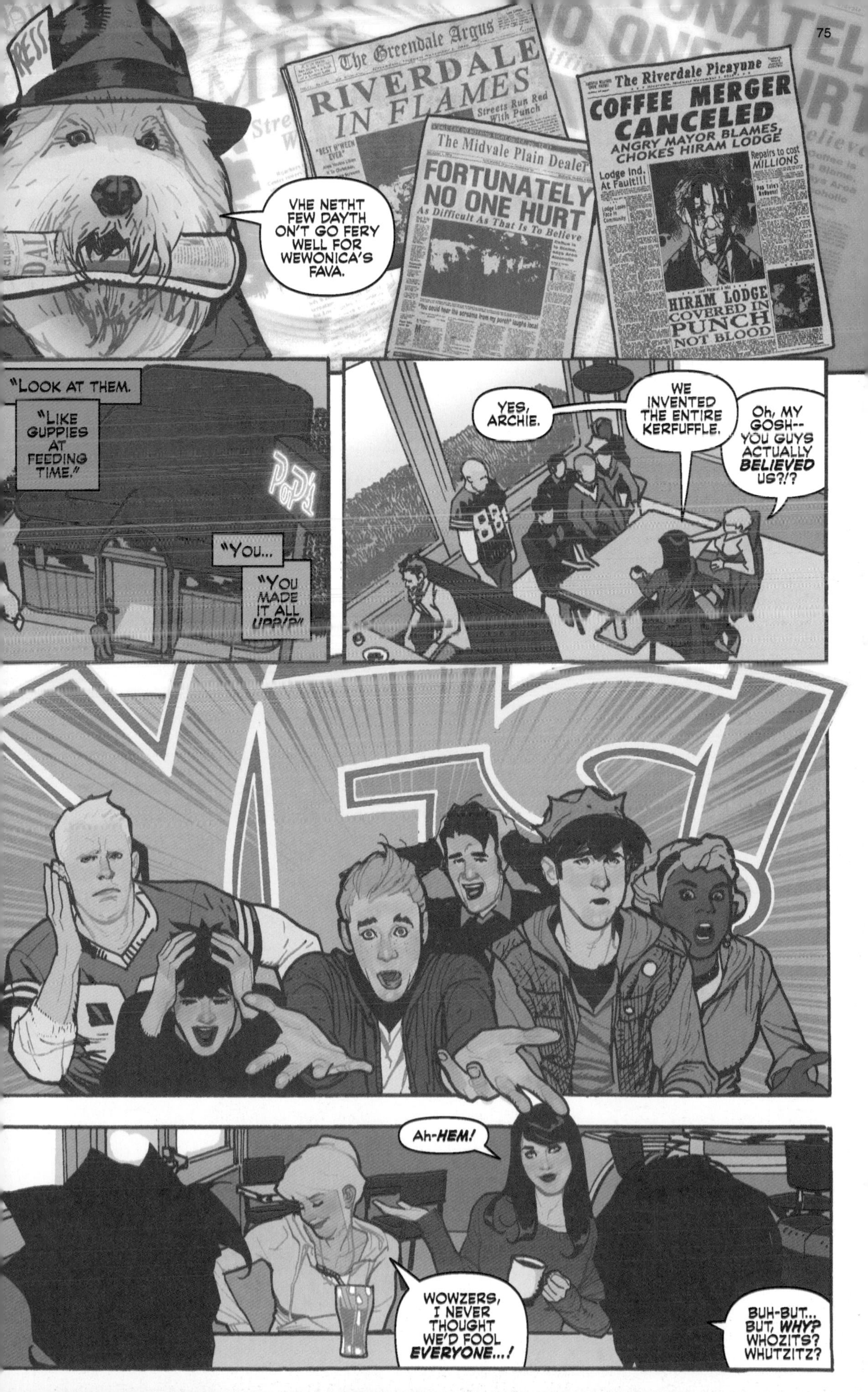
The Greendale Argus
RIVERDALE IN FLAMES
Streets Run Red With Punch
The Midvale Plain Dealer
FORTUNATELY NO ONE HURT
As Difficult As That Is To Believe
The Riverdale Picayune
COFFEE MERGER CANCELED
ANGRY MAYOR BLAMES, CHOKES HIRAM LODGE
Lodge Ind. At Fault!!!
Repairs to cost MILLIONS
HIRAM LODGE COVERED IN PUNCH NOT BLOOD
VHE NETHT FEW DAYTH ON'T GO FERY WELL FOR WEWONICA'S FAVA.
"LOOK AT THEM.
"LIKE GUPPIES AT FEEDING TIME."
POP'S
"YOU...
"YOU MADE IT ALL UP?!?"
YES, ARCHIE.
WE INVENTED THE ENTIRE KERFUFFLE.
Oh, MY GOSH-- YOU GUYS ACTUALLY BELIEVED US?!?
Ah-HEM!
WOWZERS, I NEVER THOUGHT WE'D FOOL EVERYONE...!
BUH-BUT... BUT, WHY? WHOZITS? WHUTZITZ?

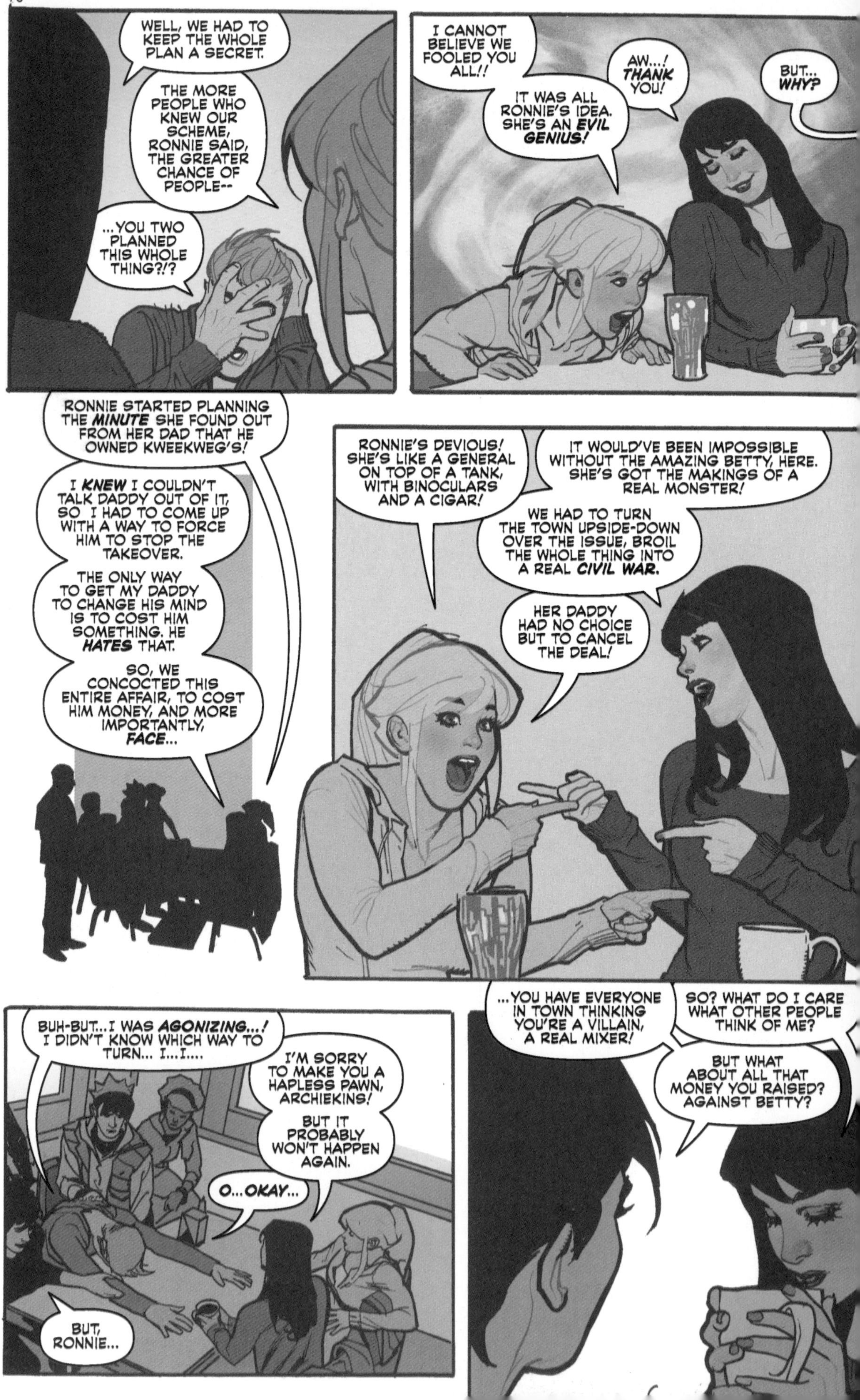
WELL, WE HAD TO KEEP THE WHOLE PLAN A SECRET.
THE MORE PEOPLE WHO KNEW OUR SCHEME, RONNIE SAID, THE GREATER CHANCE OF PEOPLE--
...YOU TWO PLANNED THIS WHOLE THING?!?
I CANNOT BELIEVE WE FOOLED YOU ALL!!
IT WAS ALL RONNIE'S IDEA. SHE'S AN EVIL GENIUS!
AW...! THANK YOU!
BUT... WHY?
RONNIE STARTED PLANNING THE MINUTE SHE FOUND OUT FROM HER DAD THAT HE OWNED KWEEKWEG'S!
I KNEW I COULDN'T TALK DADDY OUT OF IT, SO I HAD TO COME UP WITH A WAY TO FORCE HIM TO STOP THE TAKEOVER.
THE ONLY WAY TO GET MY DADDY TO CHANGE HIS MIND IS TO COST HIM SOMETHING. HE HATES THAT.
SO, WE CONCOCTED THIS ENTIRE AFFAIR, TO COST HIM MONEY, AND MORE IMPORTANTLY, FACE...
RONNIE'S DEVIOUS! SHE'S LIKE A GENERAL ON TOP OF A TANK, WITH BINOCULARS AND A CIGAR!
IT WOULD'VE BEEN IMPOSSIBLE WITHOUT THE AMAZING BETTY, HERE. SHE'S GOT THE MAKINGS OF A REAL MONSTER!
WE HAD TO TURN THE TOWN UPSIDE-DOWN OVER THE ISSUE, BROIL THE WHOLE THING INTO A REAL CIVIL WAR.
HER DADDY HAD NO CHOICE BUT TO CANCEL THE DEAL!
BUH-BUT...I WAS AGONIZING...! I DIDN'T KNOW WHICH WAY TO TURN... I...I....
I'M SORRY TO MAKE YOU A HAPLESS PAWN, ARCHIEKINS!
BUT IT PROBABLY WON'T HAPPEN AGAIN.
O...OKAY...
BUT, RONNIE...
...YOU HAVE EVERYONE IN TOWN THINKING YOU'RE A VILLAIN, A REAL MIXER!
SO? WHAT DO I CARE WHAT OTHER PEOPLE THINK OF ME?
BUT WHAT ABOUT ALL THAT MONEY YOU RAISED? AGAINST BETTY?

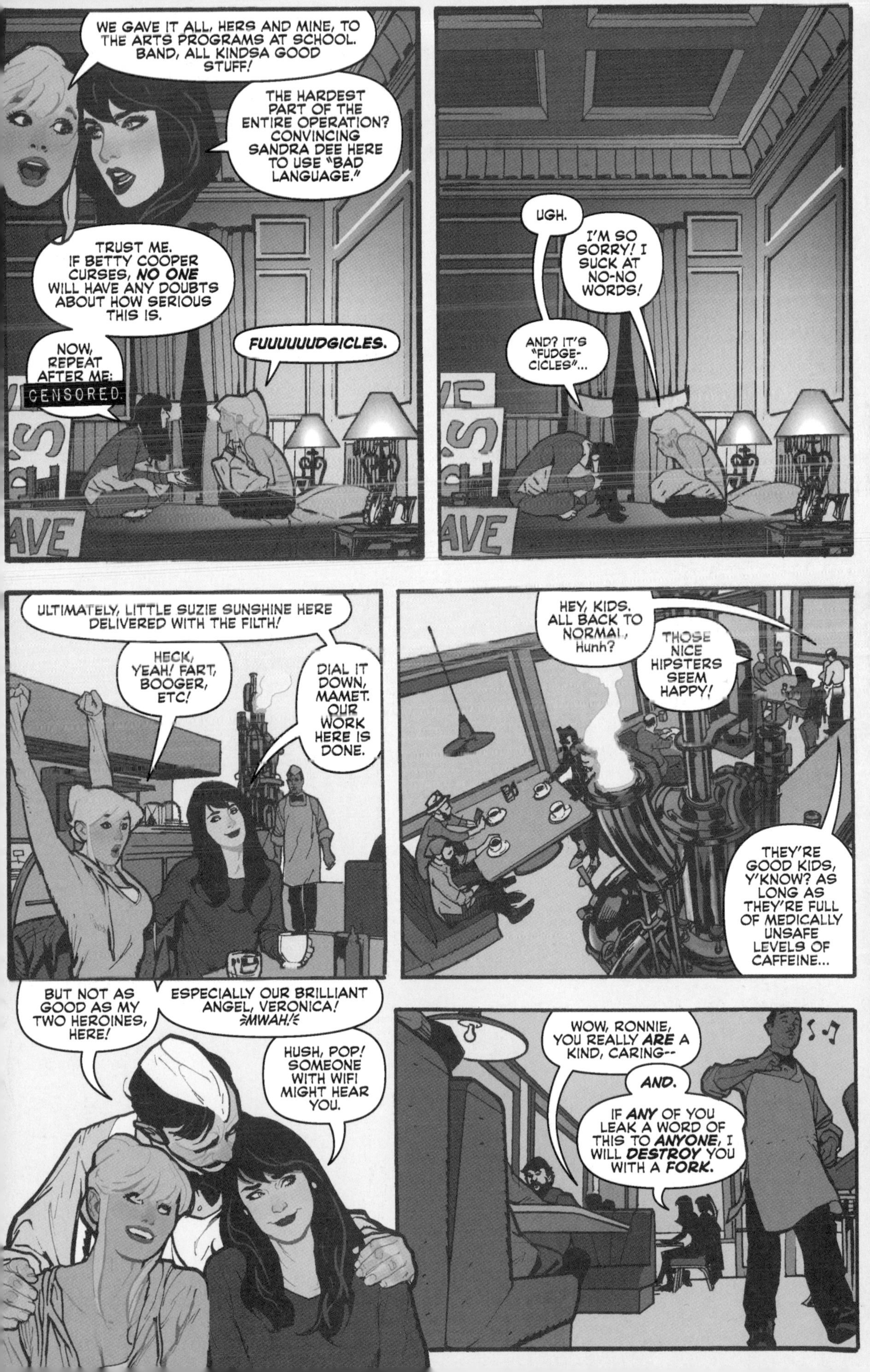
WE GAVE IT ALL, HERS AND MINE, TO THE ARTS PROGRAMS AT SCHOOL. BAND, ALL KINDSA GOOD STUFF!
THE HARDEST PART OF THE ENTIRE OPERATION? CONVINCING SANDRA DEE HERE TO USE "BAD LANGUAGE."
TRUST ME. IF BETTY COOPER CURSES, NO ONE WILL HAVE ANY DOUBTS ABOUT HOW SERIOUS THIS IS.
NOW, REPEAT AFTER ME:
CENSORED
FUUUUUUDGICLES.
UGH.
I'M SO SORRY! I SUCK AT NO-NO WORDS!
AND? IT'S "FUDGE-CICLES"...
ULTIMATELY, LITTLE SUZIE SUNSHINE HERE DELIVERED WITH THE FILTH!
HECK, YEAH! FART, BOOGER, ETC!
DIAL IT DOWN, MAMET. OUR WORK HERE IS DONE.
HEY, KIDS. ALL BACK TO NORMAL, Hunh?
THOSE NICE HIPSTERS SEEM HAPPY!
THEY'RE GOOD KIDS, Y'KNOW? AS LONG AS THEY'RE FULL OF MEDICALLY UNSAFE LEVELS OF CAFFEINE...
BUT NOT AS GOOD AS MY TWO HEROINES, HERE!
ESPECIALLY OUR BRILLIANT ANGEL, VERONICA! MWAH!
HUSH, POP! SOMEONE WITH WIFI MIGHT HEAR YOU.
WOW, RONNIE, YOU REALLY ARE A KIND, CARING--
AND.
IF ANY OF YOU LEAK A WORD OF THIS TO ANYONE, I WILL DESTROY YOU WITH A FORK.

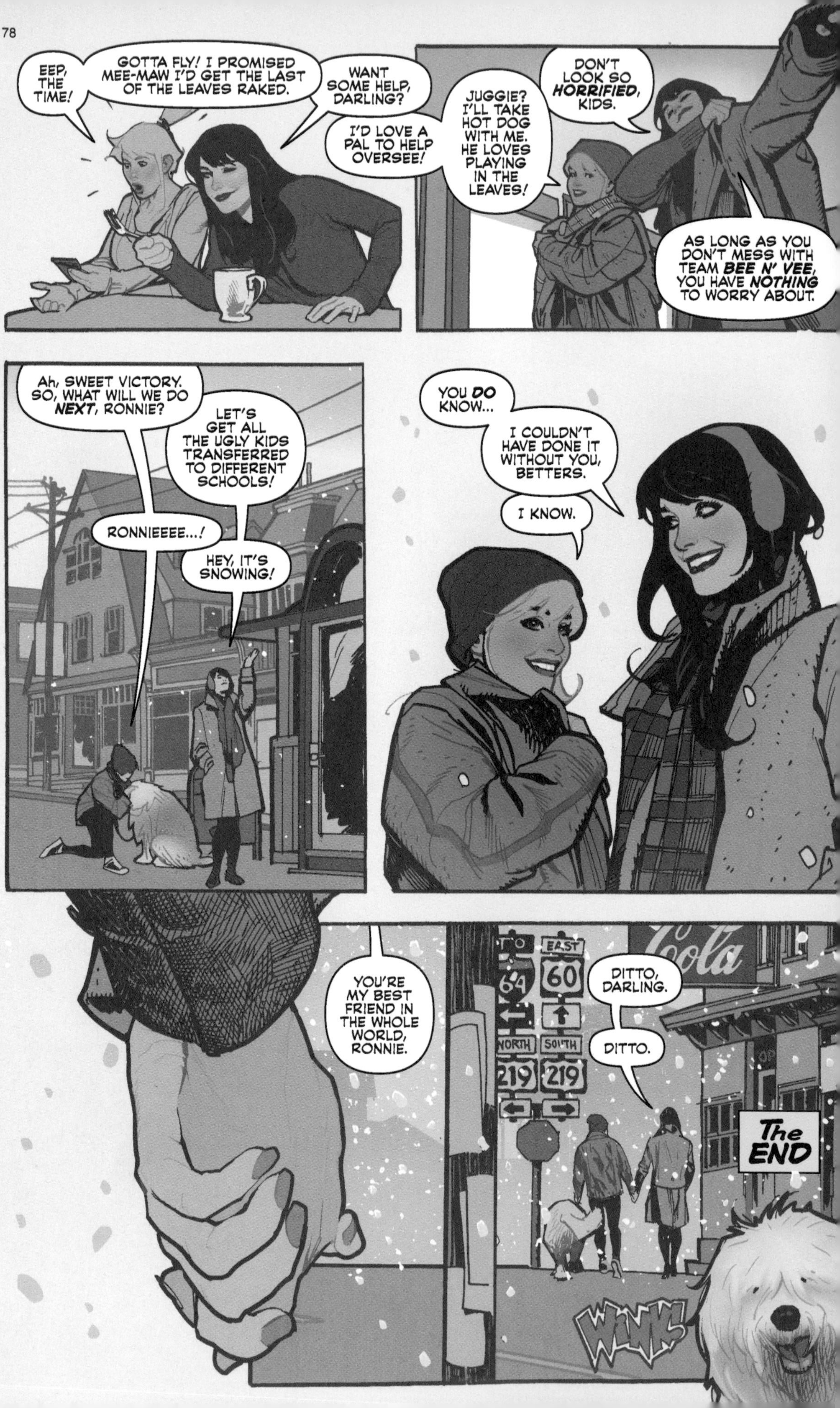
EEP, THE TIME!
GOTTA FLY! I PROMISED MEE-MAW I'D GET THE LAST OF THE LEAVES RAKED.
WANT SOME HELP, DARLING?
I'D LOVE A PAL TO HELP OVERSEE!
JUGGIE? I'LL TAKE HOT DOG WITH ME. HE LOVES PLAYING IN THE LEAVES!
DON'T LOOK SO HORRIFIED, KIDS.
AS LONG AS YOU DON'T MESS WITH TEAM BEE N' VEE, YOU HAVE NOTHING TO WORRY ABOUT.
Ah, SWEET VICTORY. SO, WHAT WILL WE DO NEXT, RONNIE?
LET'S GET ALL THE UGLY KIDS TRANSFERRED TO DIFFERENT SCHOOLS!
RONNIEEEE...!
HEY, IT'S SNOWING!
YOU DO KNOW...
I COULDN'T HAVE DONE IT WITHOUT YOU, BETTERS.
I KNOW.
YOU'RE MY BEST FRIEND IN THE WHOLE WORLD, RONNIE.
DITTO, DARLING.
DITTO.
Coola
TO
64
EAST
60
NORTH
219
SOUTH
219
WINK!
The END

Josie and the Pussycats

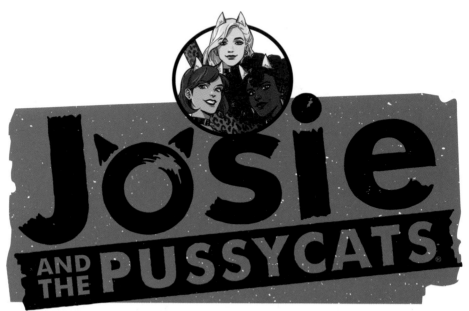

PREVIOUSLY IN THE TOWN OF RIVERDALE...

JOSIE AND THE PUSSYCATS have hit the big time and are headlining tours all across the country!

Well, not quite. They had one successful show that happened to catch the eye of the mysterious music exec Alan M., who became their band manager, got them a snazzy tour bus like something straight out of *Spice World* and hooked them up with a couple of gigs. Unfortunately, the shows were at some less-than-glamorous biker dive bars. Fortunately, their last show ended in a HIGH SPEED MOTORCYLE RACE that proved that no one can try to tell Josie, Melody and Valerie what to do.

The road to stardom may be a rocky one, but one thing's for certain—these girls know how to turn a bad night into the adventure of a lifetime!

STORY BY
MARGUERITE BENNETT
&CAMERON DeORDIO

ART BY
AUDREY MOK

COLORING BY
KELLY FITZPATRICK

LETTERING BY
JACK MORELLI

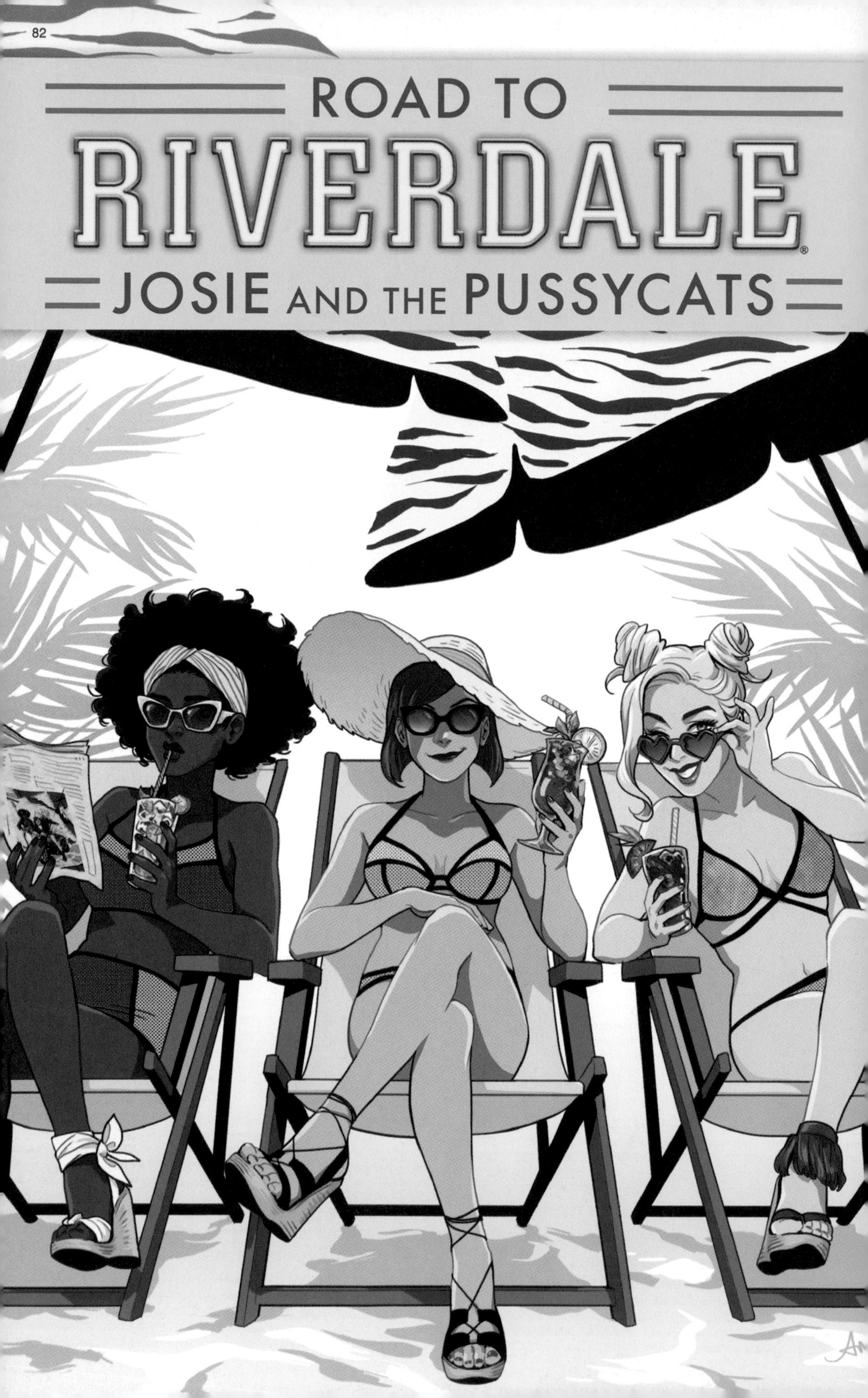
ROAD TO
RIVERDALE®
JOSIE AND THE PUSSYCATS

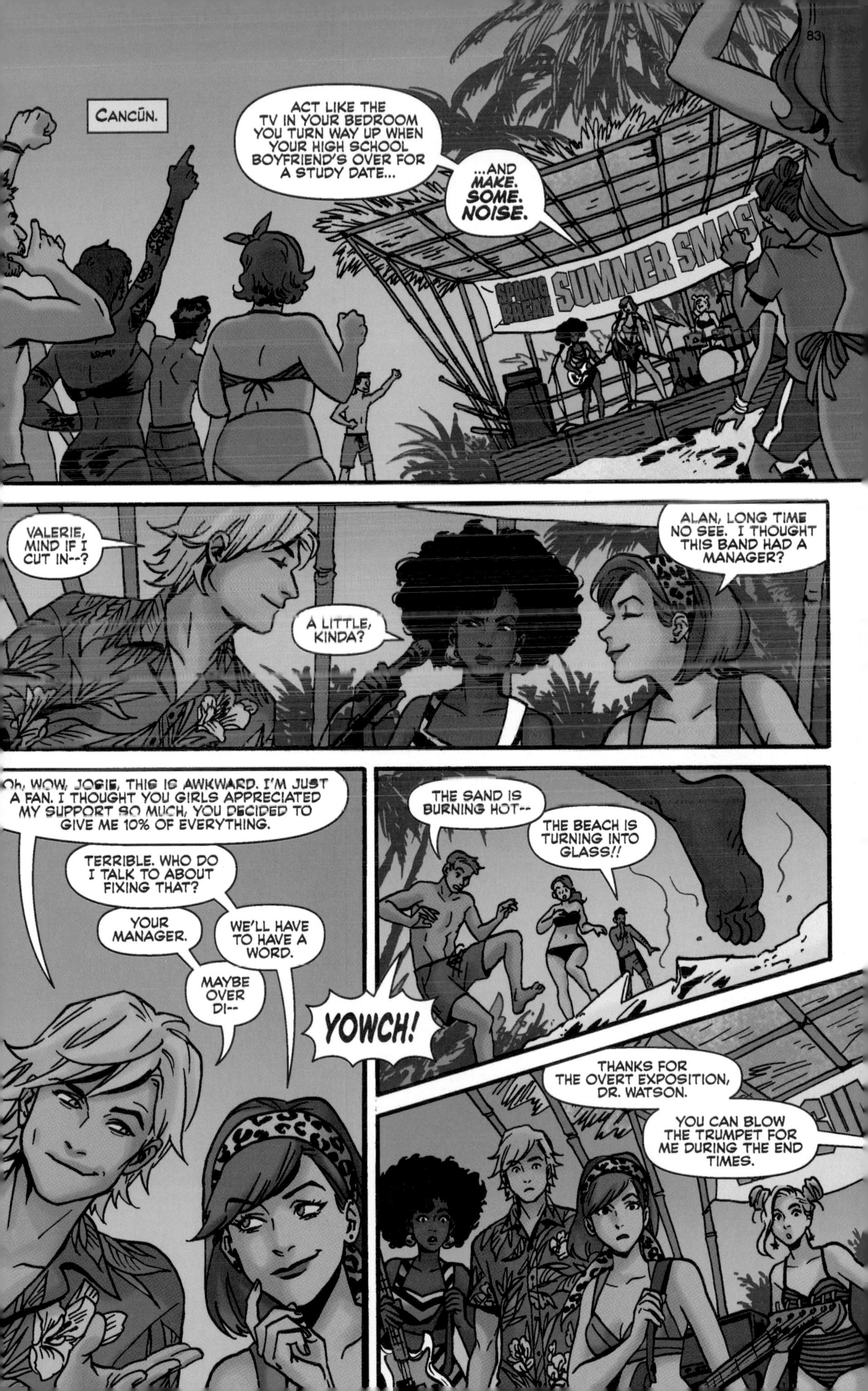
CANCÚN.
ACT LIKE THE TV IN YOUR BEDROOM YOU TURN WAY UP WHEN YOUR HIGH SCHOOL BOYFRIEND'S OVER FOR A STUDY DATE...
...AND MAKE. SOME. NOISE.
SPRING BREAK SUMMER SMAS
VALERIE, MIND IF I CUT IN--?
ALAN, LONG TIME NO SEE. I THOUGHT THIS BAND HAD A MANAGER?
A LITTLE, KINDA?
OH, WOW, JOSIE, THIS IS AWKWARD. I'M JUST A FAN. I THOUGHT YOU GIRLS APPRECIATED MY SUPPORT SO MUCH, YOU DECIDED TO GIVE ME 10% OF EVERYTHING.
TERRIBLE. WHO DO I TALK TO ABOUT FIXING THAT?
YOUR MANAGER.
WE'LL HAVE TO HAVE A WORD.
MAYBE OVER DI--
THE SAND IS BURNING HOT--
THE BEACH IS TURNING INTO GLASS!!
YOWCH!
THANKS FOR THE OVERT EXPOSITION, DR. WATSON.
YOU CAN BLOW THE TRUMPET FOR ME DURING THE END TIMES.

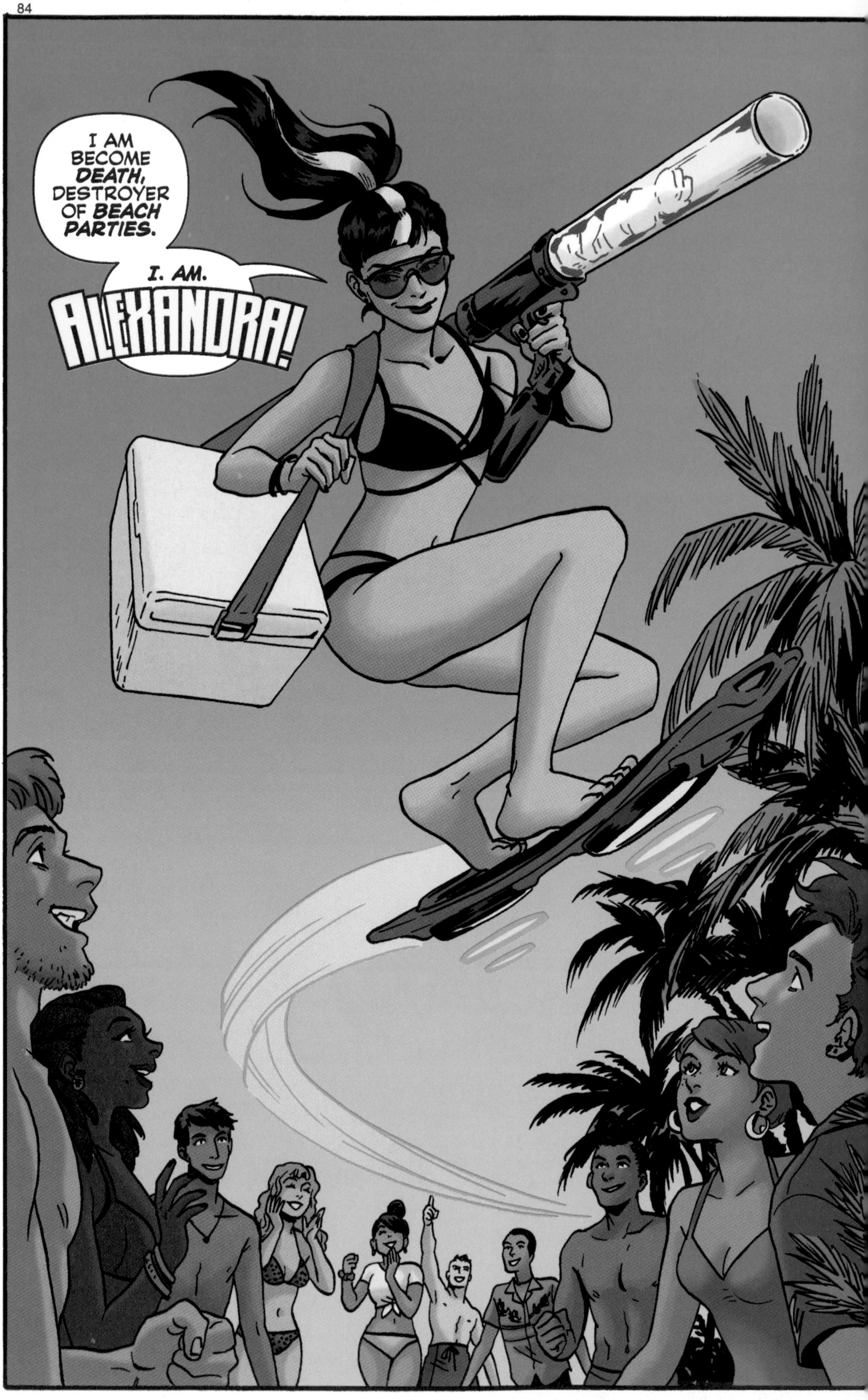
I AM BECOME *DEATH*, DESTROYER OF *BEACH PARTIES*.
I. AM.
ALEXANDRA!

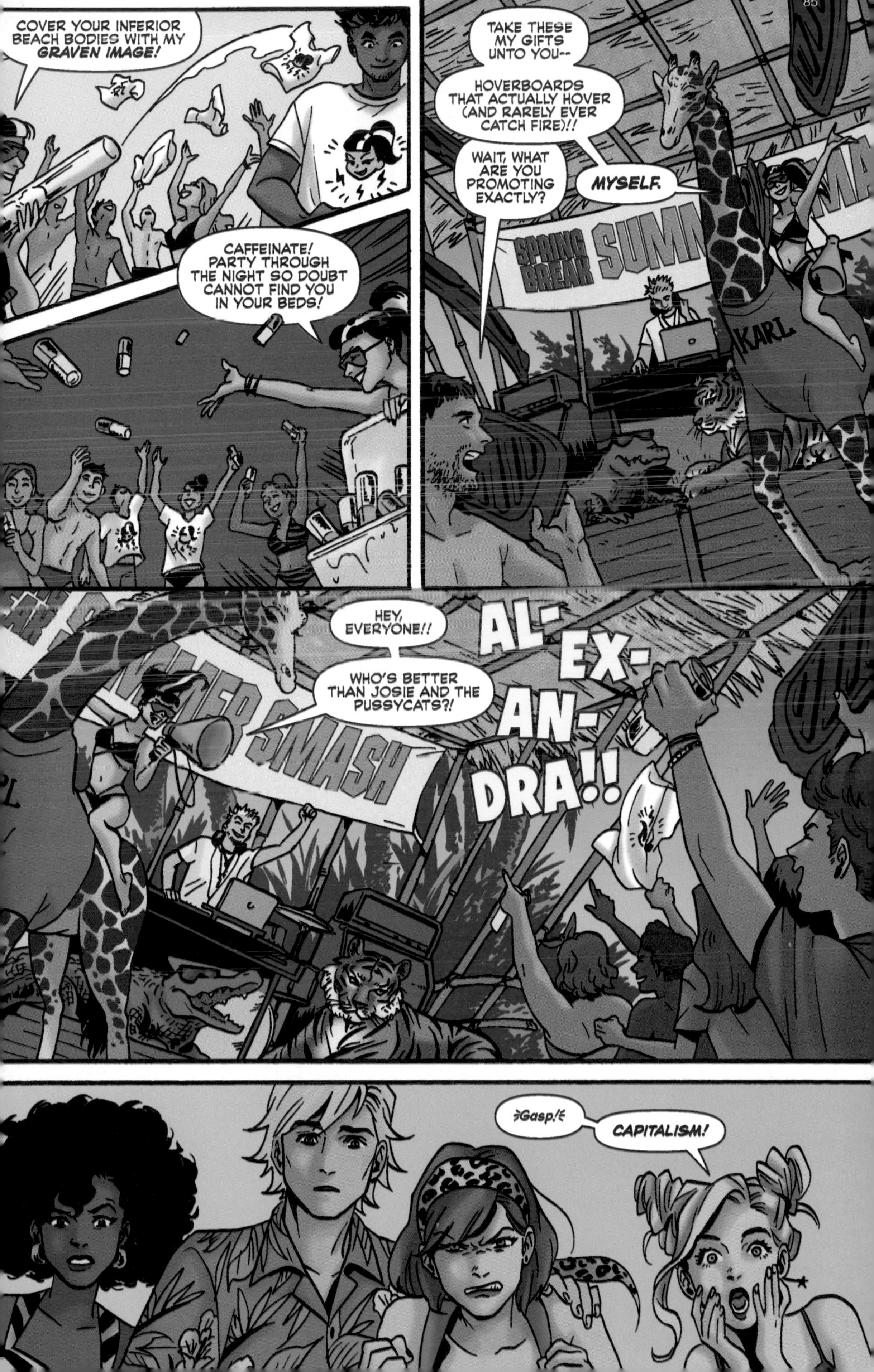
COVER YOUR INFERIOR BEACH BODIES WITH MY GRAVEN IMAGE!
CAFFEINATE! PARTY THROUGH THE NIGHT SO DOUBT CANNOT FIND YOU IN YOUR BEDS!
TAKE THESE MY GIFTS UNTO YOU--
HOVERBOARDS THAT ACTUALLY HOVER (AND RARELY EVER CATCH FIRE)!!
WAIT, WHAT ARE YOU PROMOTING EXACTLY?
MYSELF.
SPRING BREAK SUMM
KARL
HEY, EVERYONE!!
WHO'S BETTER THAN JOSIE AND THE PUSSYCATS?!
SMASH
AL-EX-AN-DRA!!
Gasp!
CAPITALISM!

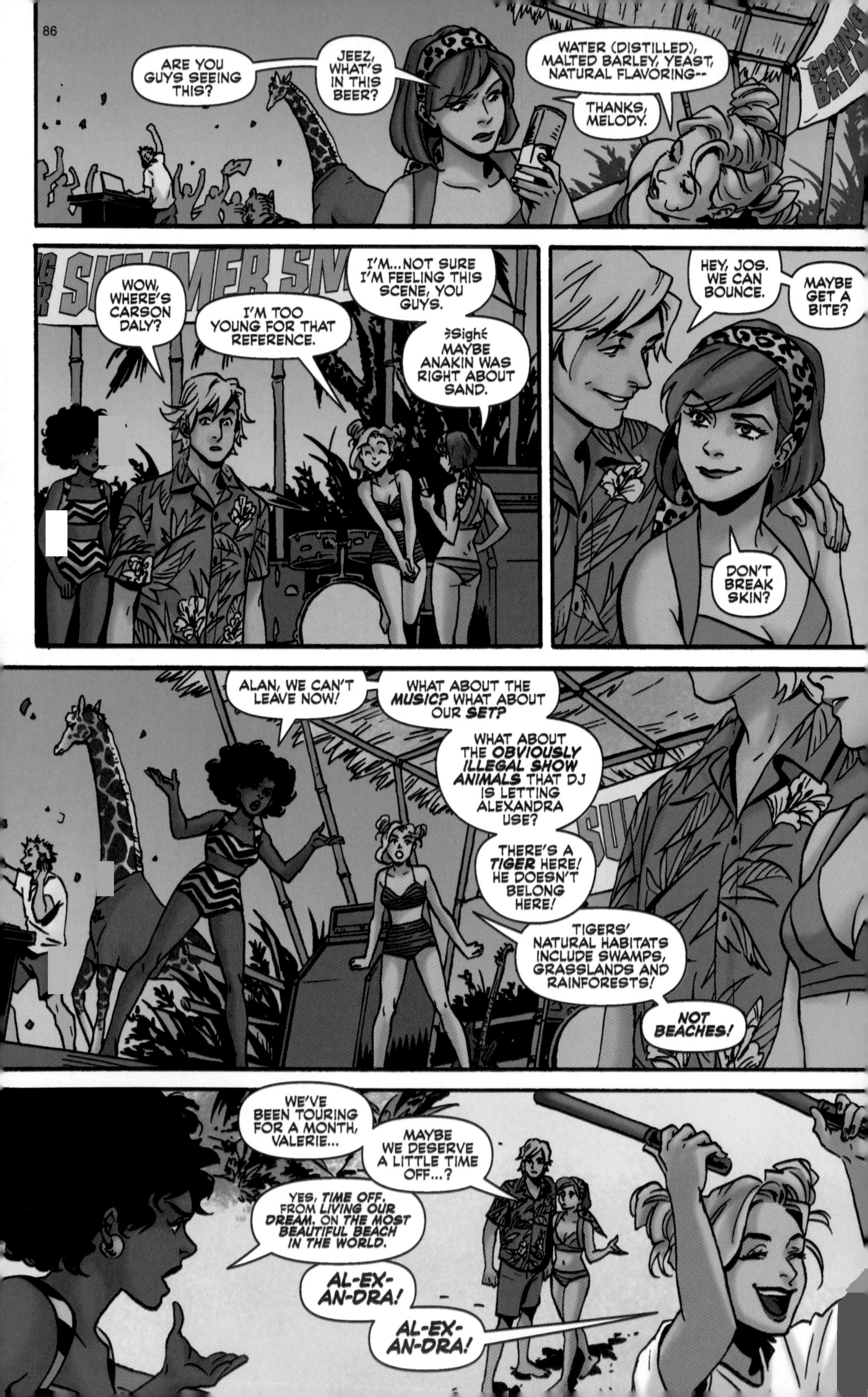
ARE YOU GUYS SEEING THIS?
JEEZ, WHAT'S IN THIS BEER?
WATER (DISTILLED), MALTED BARLEY, YEAST, NATURAL FLAVORING--
THANKS, MELODY.
SPRING BREA
SUMMER SM
WOW, WHERE'S CARSON DALY?
I'M TOO YOUNG FOR THAT REFERENCE.
I'M...NOT SURE I'M FEELING THIS SCENE, YOU GUYS.
Sigh MAYBE ANAKIN WAS RIGHT ABOUT SAND.
HEY, JOS. WE CAN BOUNCE.
MAYBE GET A BITE?
DON'T BREAK SKIN?
ALAN, WE CAN'T LEAVE NOW!
WHAT ABOUT THE *MUSIC?* WHAT ABOUT OUR *SET?*
WHAT ABOUT THE ***OBVIOUSLY ILLEGAL SHOW ANIMALS*** THAT DJ IS LETTING ALEXANDRA USE?
THERE'S A ***TIGER*** HERE! HE DOESN'T BELONG HERE!
TIGERS' NATURAL HABITATS INCLUDE SWAMPS, GRASSLANDS AND RAINFORESTS!
NOT BEACHES!
WE'VE BEEN TOURING FOR A MONTH, VALERIE...
MAYBE WE DESERVE A LITTLE TIME OFF...?
YES, *TIME OFF.* FROM *LIVING OUR DREAM.* ON *THE MOST BEAUTIFUL BEACH IN THE WORLD.*
AL-EX-AN-DRA!
AL-EX-AN-DRA!

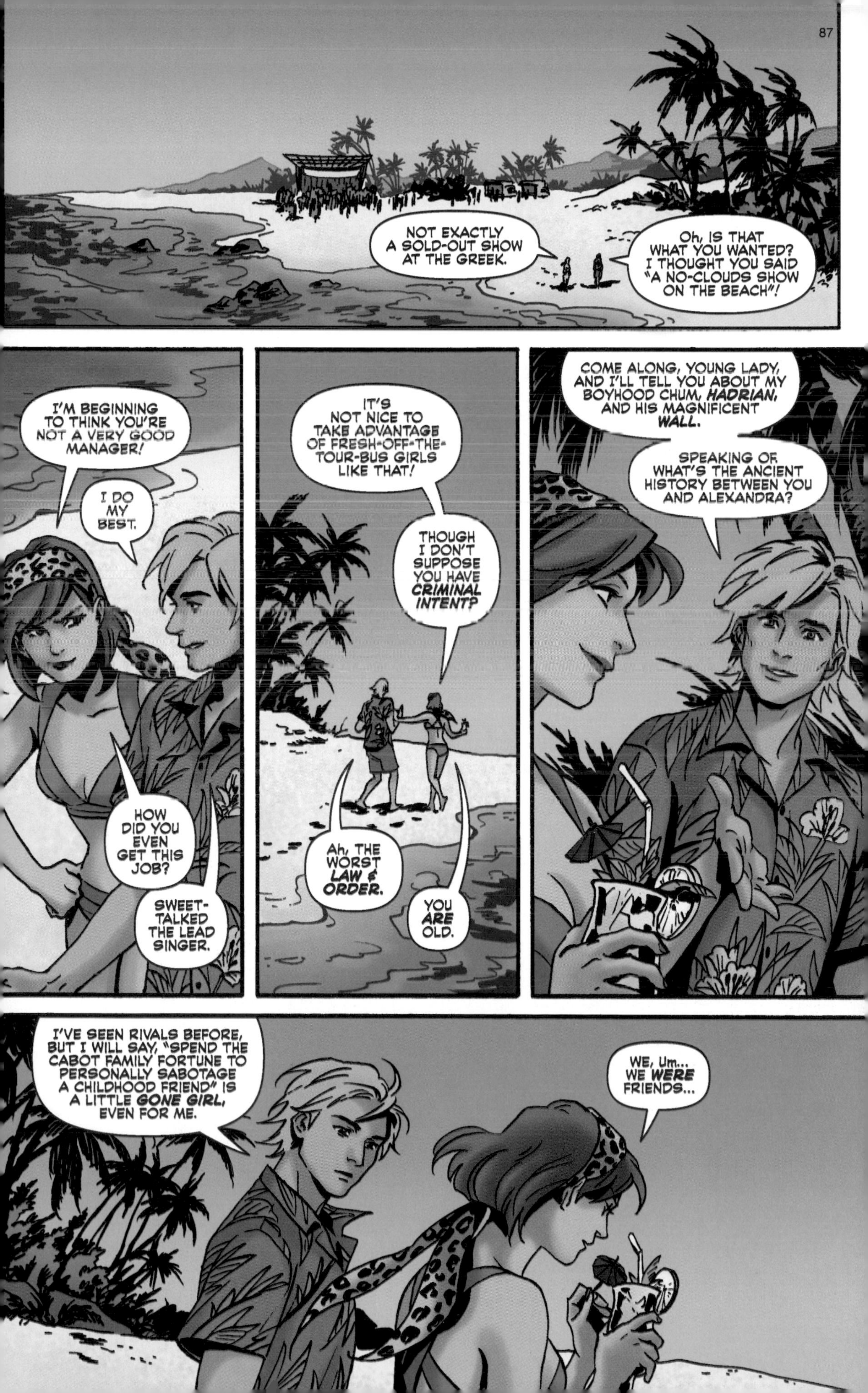
NOT EXACTLY A SOLD-OUT SHOW AT THE GREEK.
Oh, IS THAT WHAT YOU WANTED? I THOUGHT YOU SAID "A NO-CLOUDS SHOW ON THE BEACH"!
I'M BEGINNING TO THINK YOU'RE NOT A VERY GOOD MANAGER!
I DO MY BEST.
HOW DID YOU EVEN GET THIS JOB?
SWEET-TALKED THE LEAD SINGER.
IT'S NOT NICE TO TAKE ADVANTAGE OF FRESH-OFF-THE-TOUR-BUS GIRLS LIKE THAT!
THOUGH I DON'T SUPPOSE YOU HAVE CRIMINAL INTENT?
Ah, THE WORST LAW & ORDER.
YOU ARE OLD.
COME ALONG, YOUNG LADY, AND I'LL TELL YOU ABOUT MY BOYHOOD CHUM, HADRIAN, AND HIS MAGNIFICENT WALL.
SPEAKING OF. WHAT'S THE ANCIENT HISTORY BETWEEN YOU AND ALEXANDRA?
I'VE SEEN RIVALS BEFORE, BUT I WILL SAY, "SPEND THE CABOT FAMILY FORTUNE TO PERSONALLY SABOTAGE A CHILDHOOD FRIEND" IS A LITTLE GONE GIRL, EVEN FOR ME.
WE, Um... WE WERE FRIENDS...

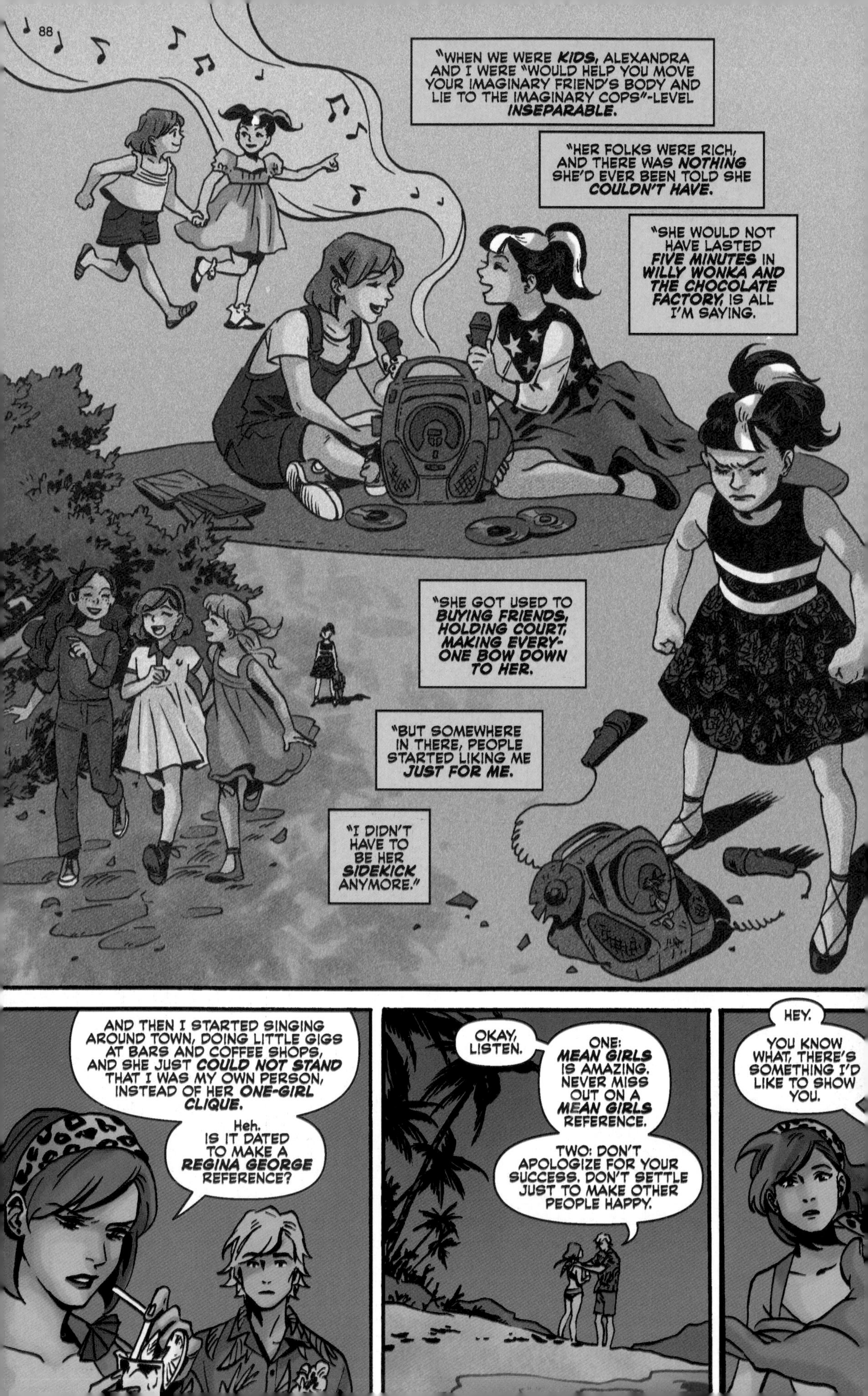
"WHEN WE WERE KIDS, ALEXANDRA AND I WERE "WOULD HELP YOU MOVE YOUR IMAGINARY FRIEND'S BODY AND LIE TO THE IMAGINARY COPS"-LEVEL INSEPARABLE.
"HER FOLKS WERE RICH, AND THERE WAS NOTHING SHE'D EVER BEEN TOLD SHE COULDN'T HAVE.
"SHE WOULD NOT HAVE LASTED FIVE MINUTES IN WILLY WONKA AND THE CHOCOLATE FACTORY, IS ALL I'M SAYING.
"SHE GOT USED TO BUYING FRIENDS, HOLDING COURT, MAKING EVERY-ONE BOW DOWN TO HER.
"BUT SOMEWHERE IN THERE, PEOPLE STARTED LIKING ME JUST FOR ME.
"I DIDN'T HAVE TO BE HER SIDEKICK ANYMORE."
AND THEN I STARTED SINGING AROUND TOWN, DOING LITTLE GIGS AT BARS AND COFFEE SHOPS, AND SHE JUST COULD NOT STAND THAT I WAS MY OWN PERSON, INSTEAD OF HER ONE-GIRL CLIQUE.
Heh. IS IT DATED TO MAKE A REGINA GEORGE REFERENCE?
OKAY, LISTEN.
ONE: MEAN GIRLS IS AMAZING. NEVER MISS OUT ON A MEAN GIRLS REFERENCE.
TWO: DON'T APOLOGIZE FOR YOUR SUCCESS. DON'T SETTLE JUST TO MAKE OTHER PEOPLE HAPPY.
HEY.
YOU KNOW WHAT, THERE'S SOMETHING I'D LIKE TO SHOW YOU.

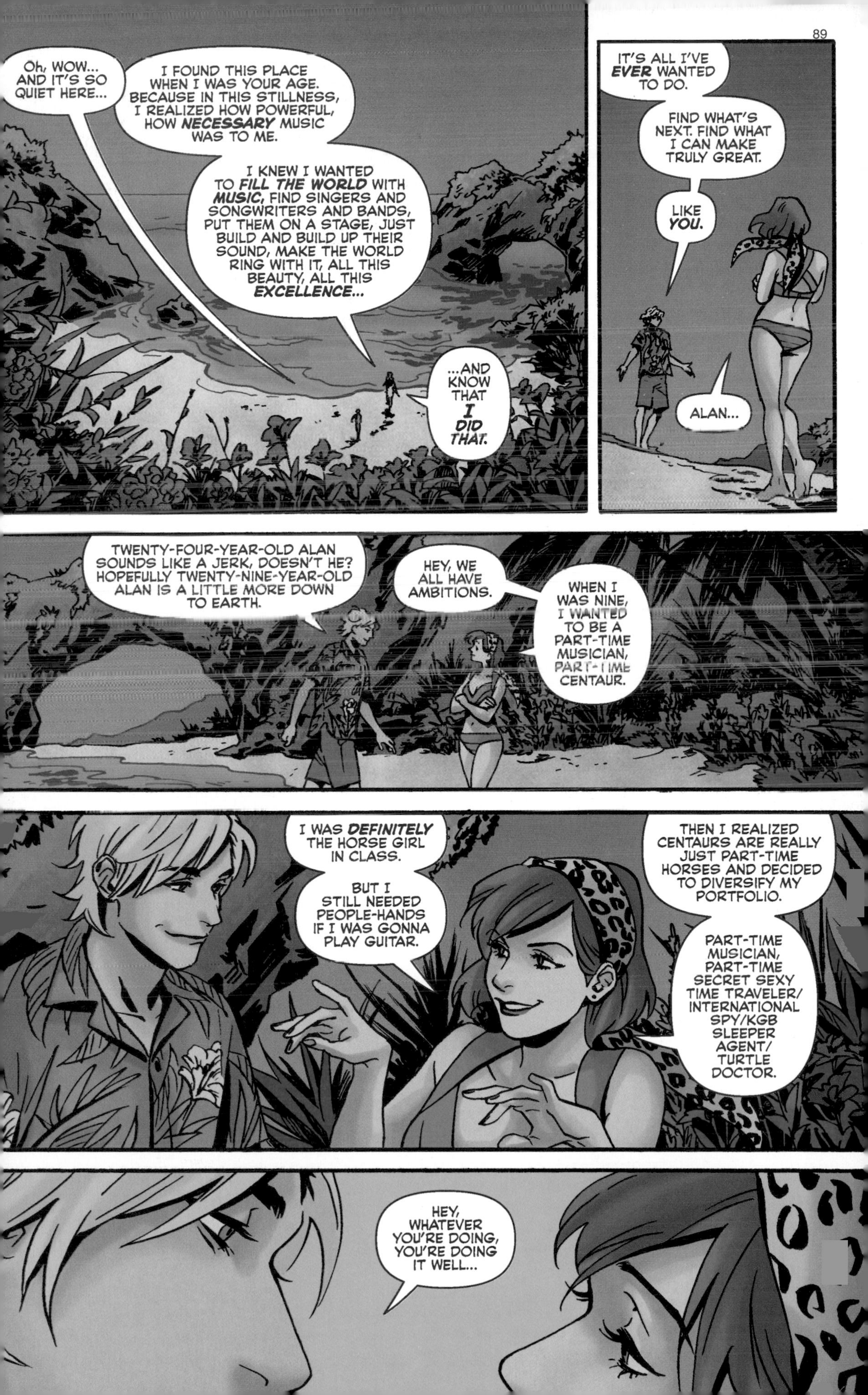
Oh, WOW... AND IT'S SO QUIET HERE...
I FOUND THIS PLACE WHEN I WAS YOUR AGE. BECAUSE IN THIS STILLNESS, I REALIZED HOW POWERFUL, HOW NECESSARY MUSIC WAS TO ME.
I KNEW I WANTED TO FILL THE WORLD WITH MUSIC, FIND SINGERS AND SONGWRITERS AND BANDS, PUT THEM ON A STAGE, JUST BUILD AND BUILD UP THEIR SOUND, MAKE THE WORLD RING WITH IT, ALL THIS BEAUTY, ALL THIS EXCELLENCE...
...AND KNOW THAT I DID THAT.
IT'S ALL I'VE EVER WANTED TO DO.
FIND WHAT'S NEXT. FIND WHAT I CAN MAKE TRULY GREAT.
LIKE YOU.
ALAN...
TWENTY-FOUR-YEAR-OLD ALAN SOUNDS LIKE A JERK, DOESN'T HE? HOPEFULLY TWENTY-NINE-YEAR-OLD ALAN IS A LITTLE MORE DOWN TO EARTH.
HEY, WE ALL HAVE AMBITIONS.
WHEN I WAS NINE, I WANTED TO BE A PART-TIME MUSICIAN, PART-TIME CENTAUR.
I WAS DEFINITELY THE HORSE GIRL IN CLASS.
BUT I STILL NEEDED PEOPLE-HANDS IF I WAS GONNA PLAY GUITAR.
THEN I REALIZED CENTAURS ARE REALLY JUST PART-TIME HORSES AND DECIDED TO DIVERSIFY MY PORTFOLIO.
PART-TIME MUSICIAN, PART-TIME SECRET SEXY TIME TRAVELER/ INTERNATIONAL SPY/KGB SLEEPER AGENT/ TURTLE DOCTOR.
HEY, WHATEVER YOU'RE DOING, YOU'RE DOING IT WELL...

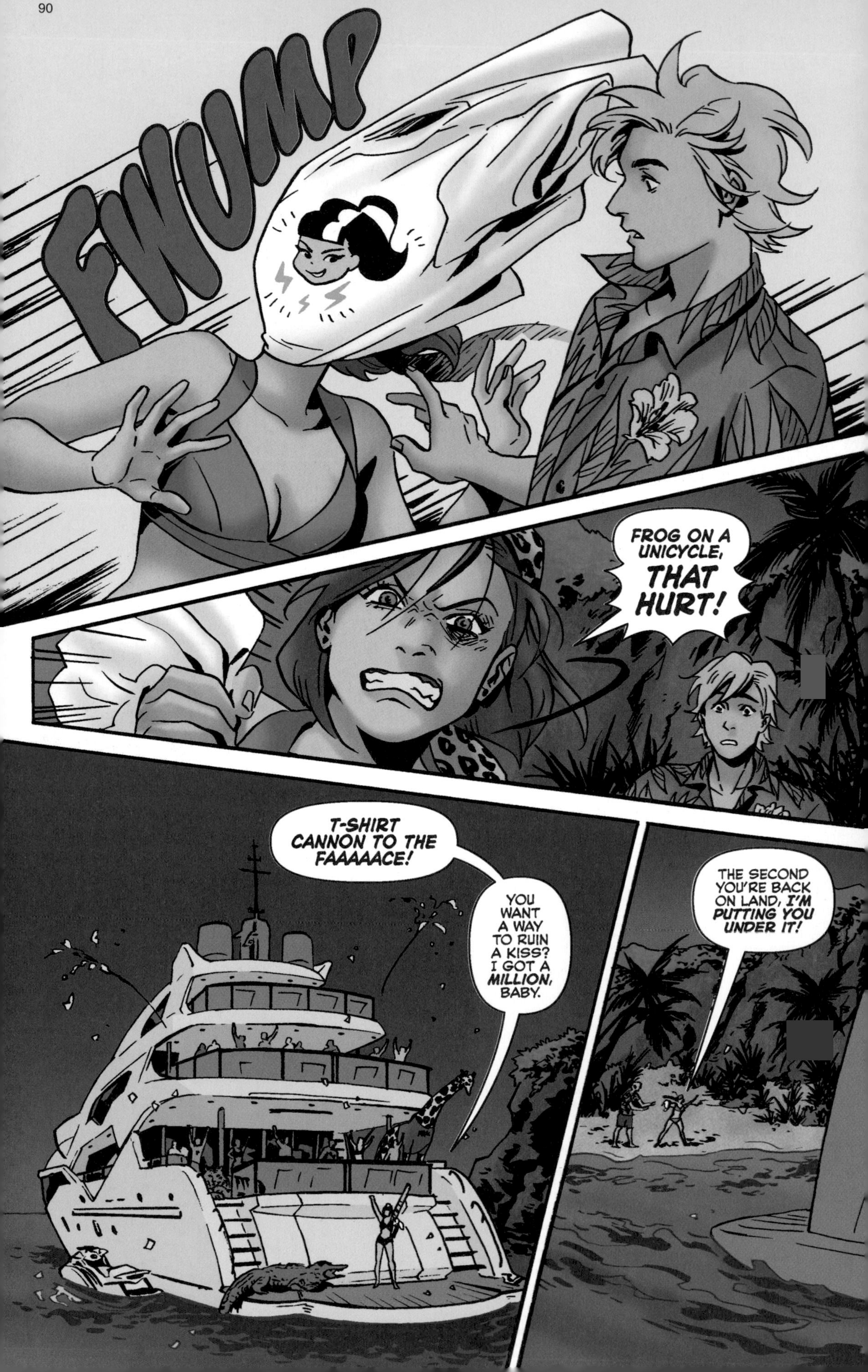
FWUMP
FROG ON A UNICYCLE, THAT HURT!
T-SHIRT CANNON TO THE FAAAAACE!
YOU WANT A WAY TO RUIN A KISS? I GOT A MILLION, BABY.
THE SECOND YOU'RE BACK ON LAND, I'M PUTTING YOU UNDER IT!

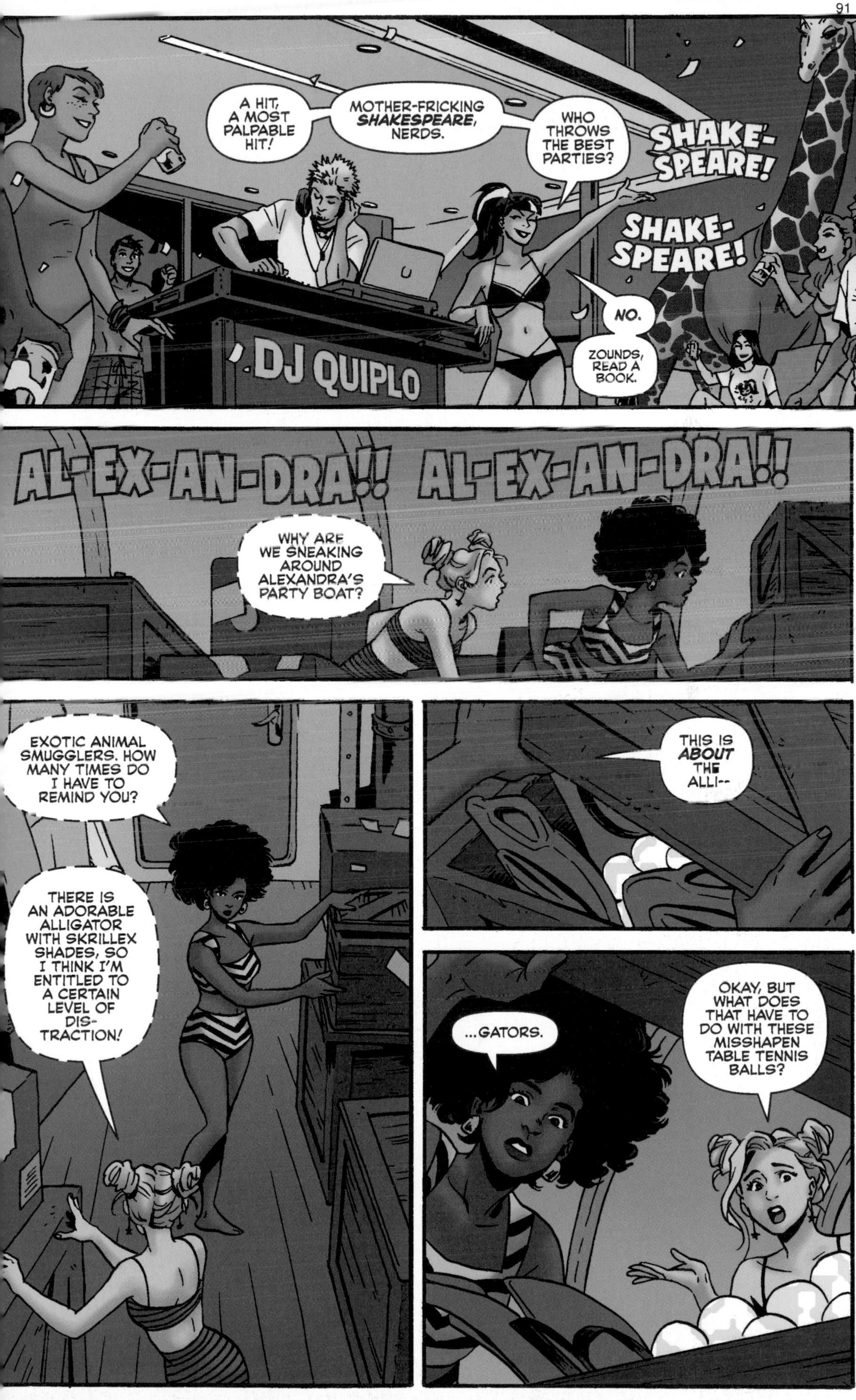
A HIT, A MOST PALPABLE HIT!
MOTHER-FRICKING SHAKESPEARE, NERDS.
WHO THROWS THE BEST PARTIES?
SHAKE-SPEARE!
SHAKE-SPEARE!
NO.
ZOUNDS, READ A BOOK.
DJ QUIPLO
AL-EX-AN-DRA!! AL-EX-AN-DRA!!
WHY ARE WE SNEAKING AROUND ALEXANDRA'S PARTY BOAT?
EXOTIC ANIMAL SMUGGLERS. HOW MANY TIMES DO I HAVE TO REMIND YOU?
THERE IS AN ADORABLE ALLIGATOR WITH SKRILLEX SHADES, SO I THINK I'M ENTITLED TO A CERTAIN LEVEL OF DIS-TRACTION!
THIS IS ABOUT THE ALLI--
...GATORS.
OKAY, BUT WHAT DOES THAT HAVE TO DO WITH THESE MISSHAPEN TABLE TENNIS BALLS?

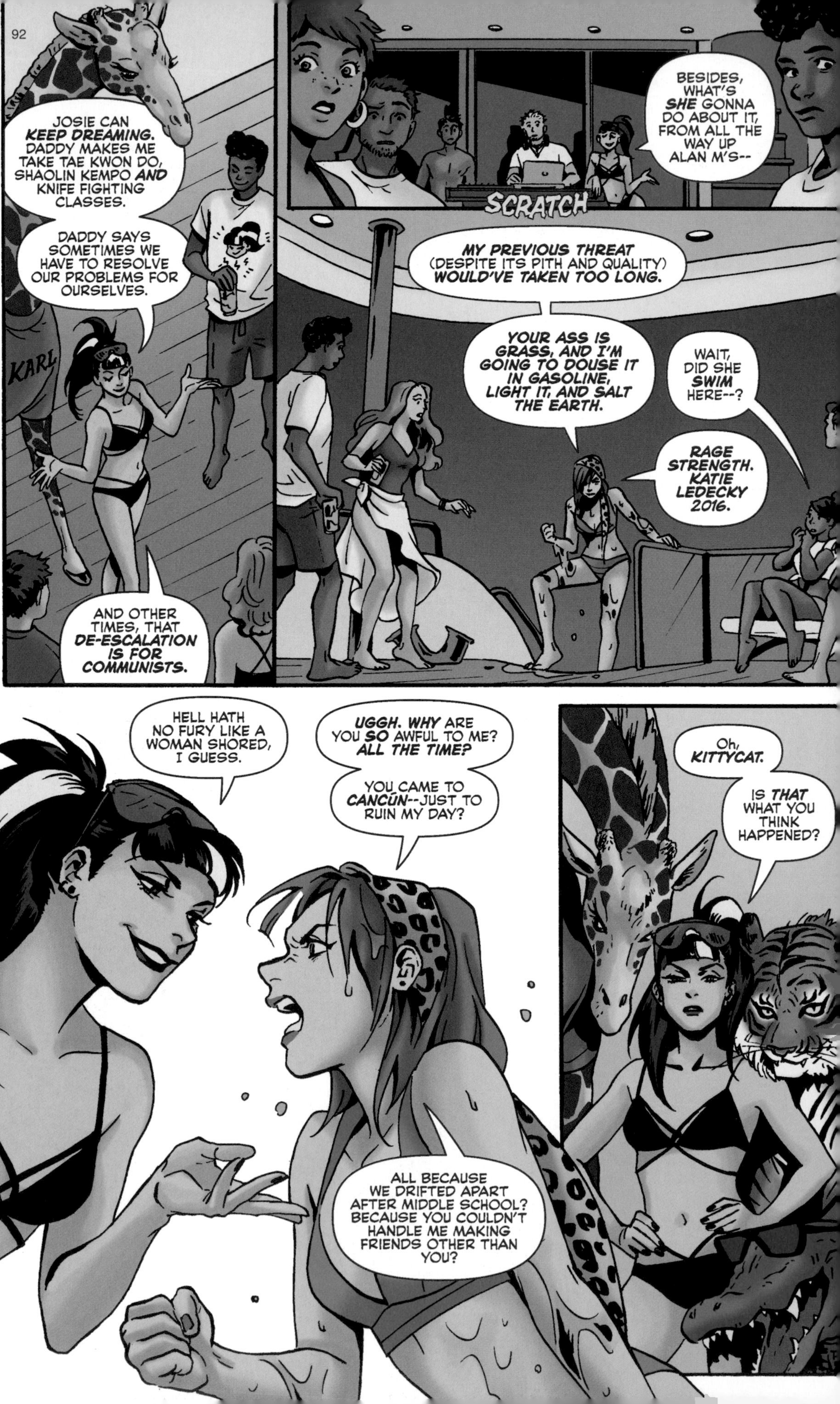
JOSIE CAN KEEP DREAMING. DADDY MAKES ME TAKE TAE KWON DO, SHAOLIN KEMPO AND KNIFE FIGHTING CLASSES.
DADDY SAYS SOMETIMES WE HAVE TO RESOLVE OUR PROBLEMS FOR OURSELVES.
KARL
AND OTHER TIMES, THAT DE-ESCALATION IS FOR COMMUNISTS.
BESIDES, WHAT'S SHE GONNA DO ABOUT IT, FROM ALL THE WAY UP ALAN M'S--
SCRATCH
MY PREVIOUS THREAT (DESPITE ITS PITH AND QUALITY) WOULD'VE TAKEN TOO LONG.
YOUR ASS IS GRASS, AND I'M GOING TO DOUSE IT IN GASOLINE, LIGHT IT, AND SALT THE EARTH.
WAIT, DID SHE SWIM HERE--?
RAGE STRENGTH. KATIE LEDECKY 2016.
HELL HATH NO FURY LIKE A WOMAN SHORED, I GUESS.
UGGH. WHY ARE YOU SO AWFUL TO ME? ALL THE TIME?
YOU CAME TO CANCÚN--JUST TO RUIN MY DAY?
ALL BECAUSE WE DRIFTED APART AFTER MIDDLE SCHOOL? BECAUSE YOU COULDN'T HANDLE ME MAKING FRIENDS OTHER THAN YOU?
Oh, KITTYCAT.
IS THAT WHAT YOU THINK HAPPENED?

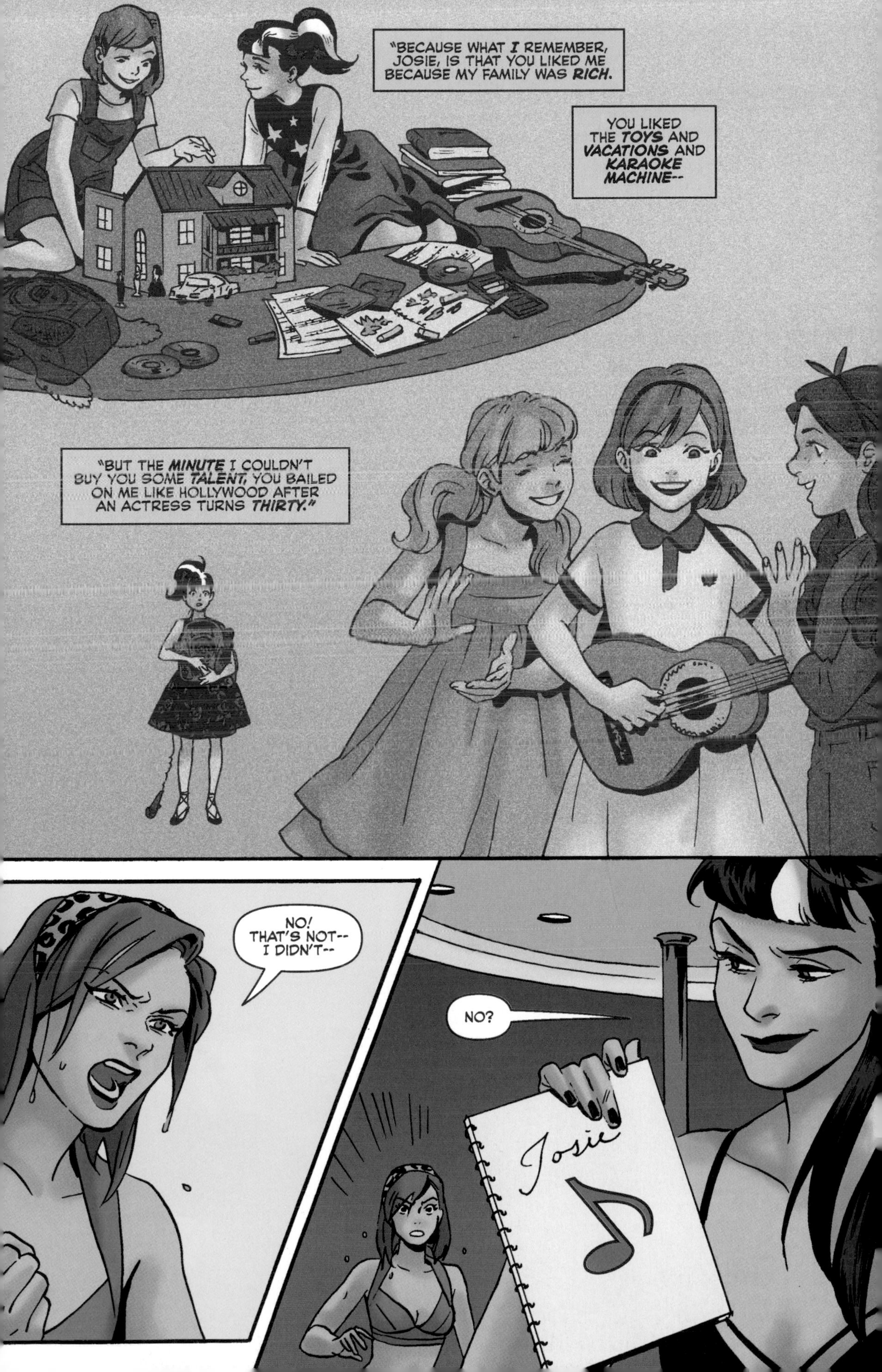
"BECAUSE WHAT I REMEMBER, JOSIE, IS THAT YOU LIKED ME BECAUSE MY FAMILY WAS RICH.
YOU LIKED THE TOYS AND VACATIONS AND KARAOKE MACHINE--
"BUT THE MINUTE I COULDN'T BUY YOU SOME TALENT, YOU BAILED ON ME LIKE HOLLYWOOD AFTER AN ACTRESS TURNS THIRTY."
NO! THAT'S NOT-- I DIDN'T--
NO?
Josie

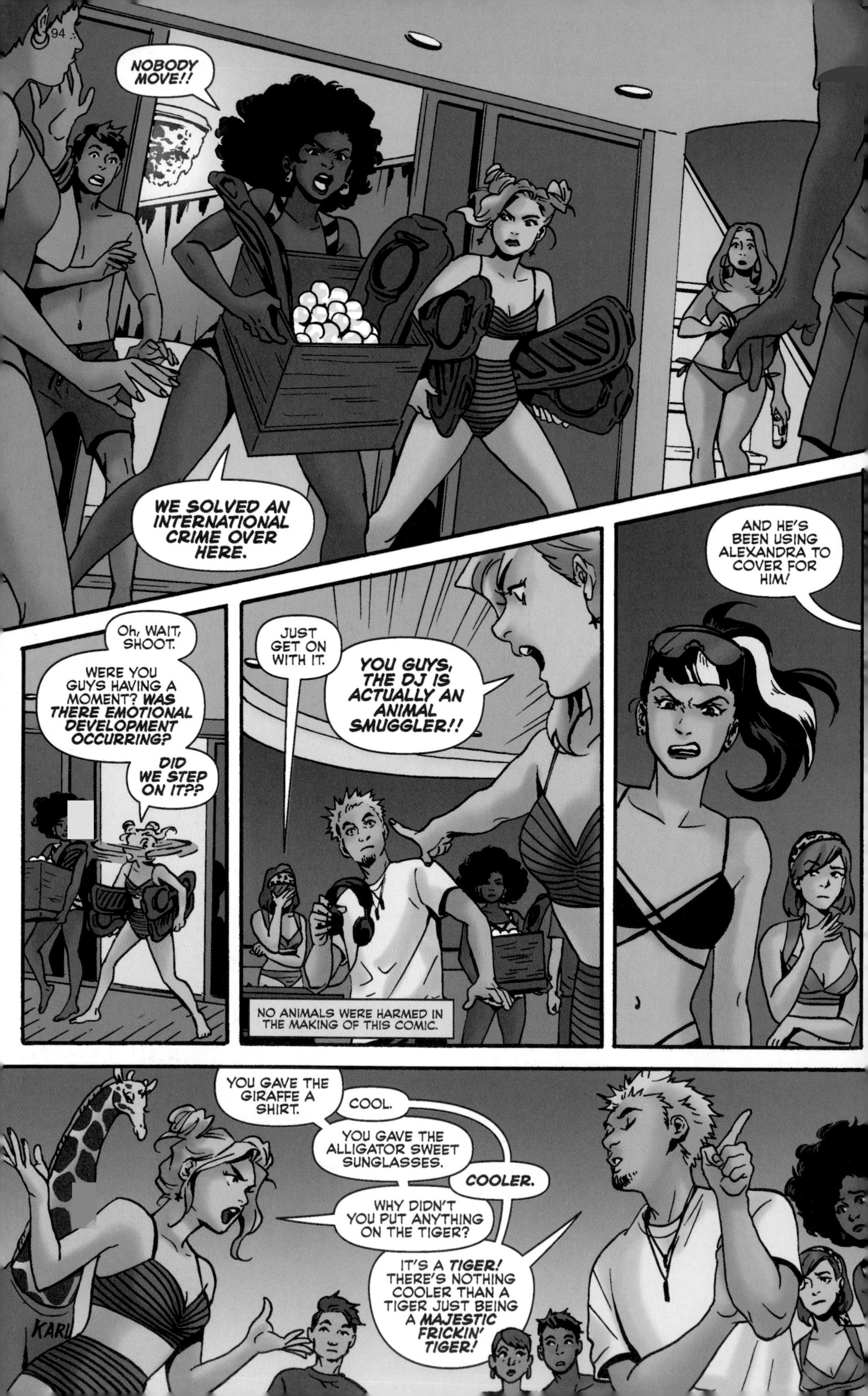
NOBODY MOVE!!
WE SOLVED AN INTERNATIONAL CRIME OVER HERE.
Oh, WAIT, SHOOT.
WERE YOU GUYS HAVING A MOMENT? WAS THERE EMOTIONAL DEVELOPMENT OCCURRING?
DID WE STEP ON IT??
JUST GET ON WITH IT.
YOU GUYS, THE DJ IS ACTUALLY AN ANIMAL SMUGGLER!!
NO ANIMALS WERE HARMED IN THE MAKING OF THIS COMIC.
AND HE'S BEEN USING ALEXANDRA TO COVER FOR HIM!
YOU GAVE THE GIRAFFE A SHIRT.
COOL.
YOU GAVE THE ALLIGATOR SWEET SUNGLASSES.
COOLER.
WHY DIDN'T YOU PUT ANYTHING ON THE TIGER?
IT'S A TIGER! THERE'S NOTHING COOLER THAN A TIGER JUST BEING A MAJESTIC FRICKIN' TIGER!
KARL

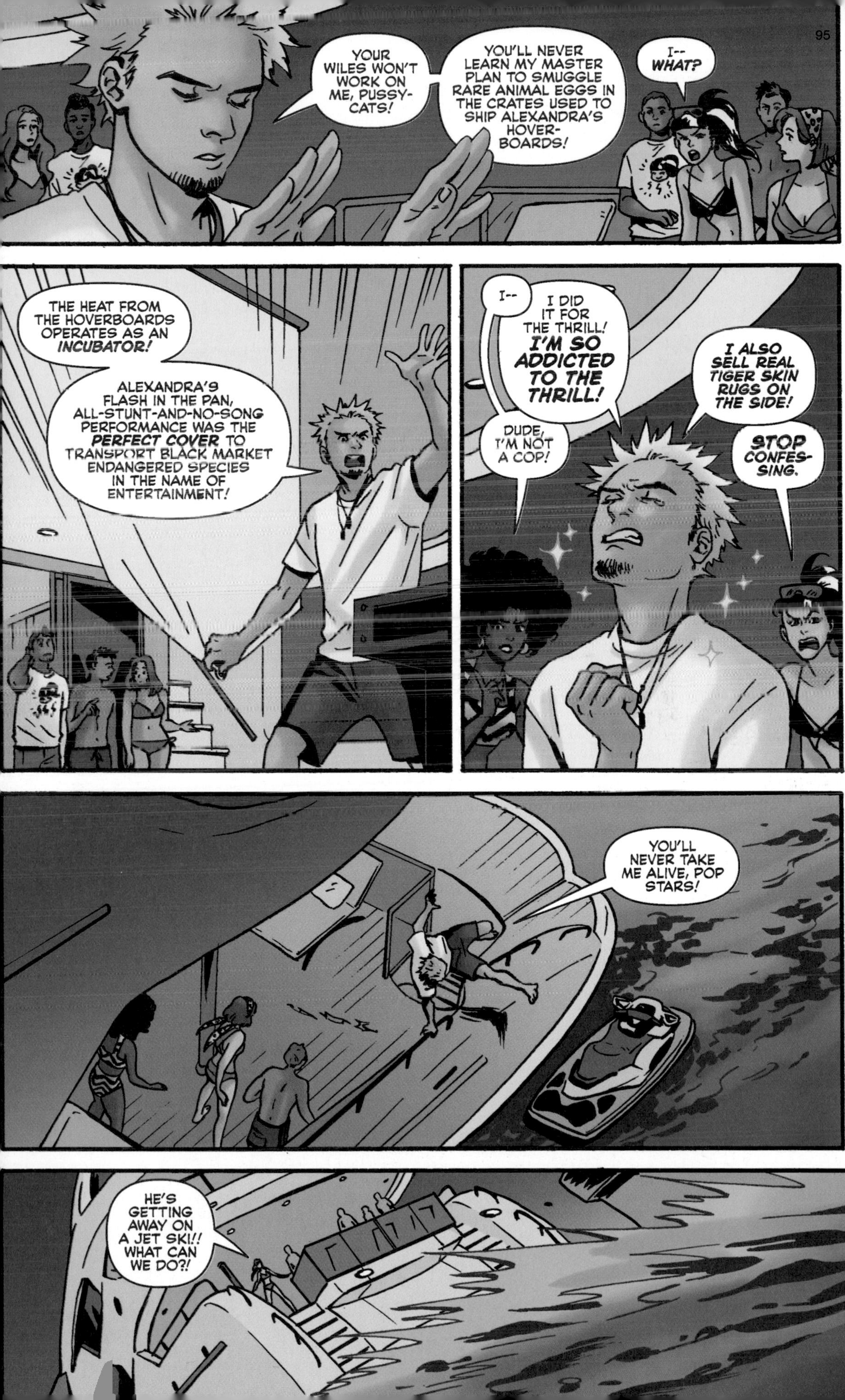
YOUR WILES WON'T WORK ON ME, PUSSY-CATS!
YOU'LL NEVER LEARN MY MASTER PLAN TO SMUGGLE RARE ANIMAL EGGS IN THE CRATES USED TO SHIP ALEXANDRA'S HOVER-BOARDS!
I-- WHAT?
THE HEAT FROM THE HOVERBOARDS OPERATES AS AN INCUBATOR!
ALEXANDRA'S FLASH IN THE PAN, ALL-STUNT-AND-NO-SONG PERFORMANCE WAS THE PERFECT COVER TO TRANSPORT BLACK MARKET ENDANGERED SPECIES IN THE NAME OF ENTERTAINMENT!
I--
I DID IT FOR THE THRILL! I'M SO ADDICTED TO THE THRILL!
DUDE, I'M NOT A COP!
I ALSO SELL REAL TIGER SKIN RUGS ON THE SIDE!
STOP CONFES-SING.
YOU'LL NEVER TAKE ME ALIVE, POP STARS!
HE'S GETTING AWAY ON A JET SKI!! WHAT CAN WE DO?!

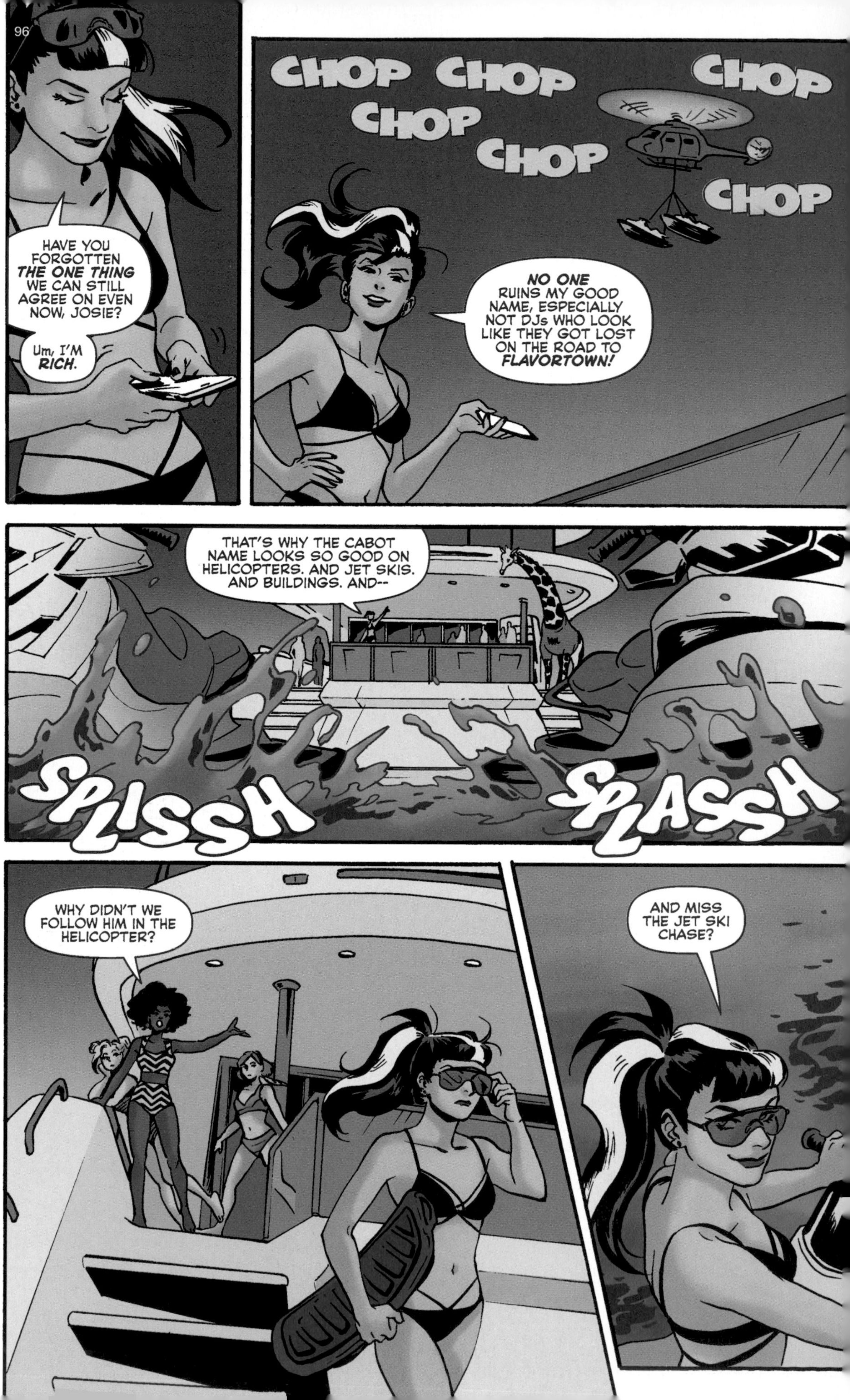
HAVE YOU FORGOTTEN THE ONE THING WE CAN STILL AGREE ON EVEN NOW, JOSIE?
Um, I'M RICH.
CHOP CHOP CHOP CHOP CHOP CHOP
NO ONE RUINS MY GOOD NAME, ESPECIALLY NOT DJs WHO LOOK LIKE THEY GOT LOST ON THE ROAD TO FLAVORTOWN!
THAT'S WHY THE CABOT NAME LOOKS SO GOOD ON HELICOPTERS. AND JET SKIS. AND BUILDINGS. AND--
SPLISSH
SPLASSH
WHY DIDN'T WE FOLLOW HIM IN THE HELICOPTER?
AND MISS THE JET SKI CHASE?

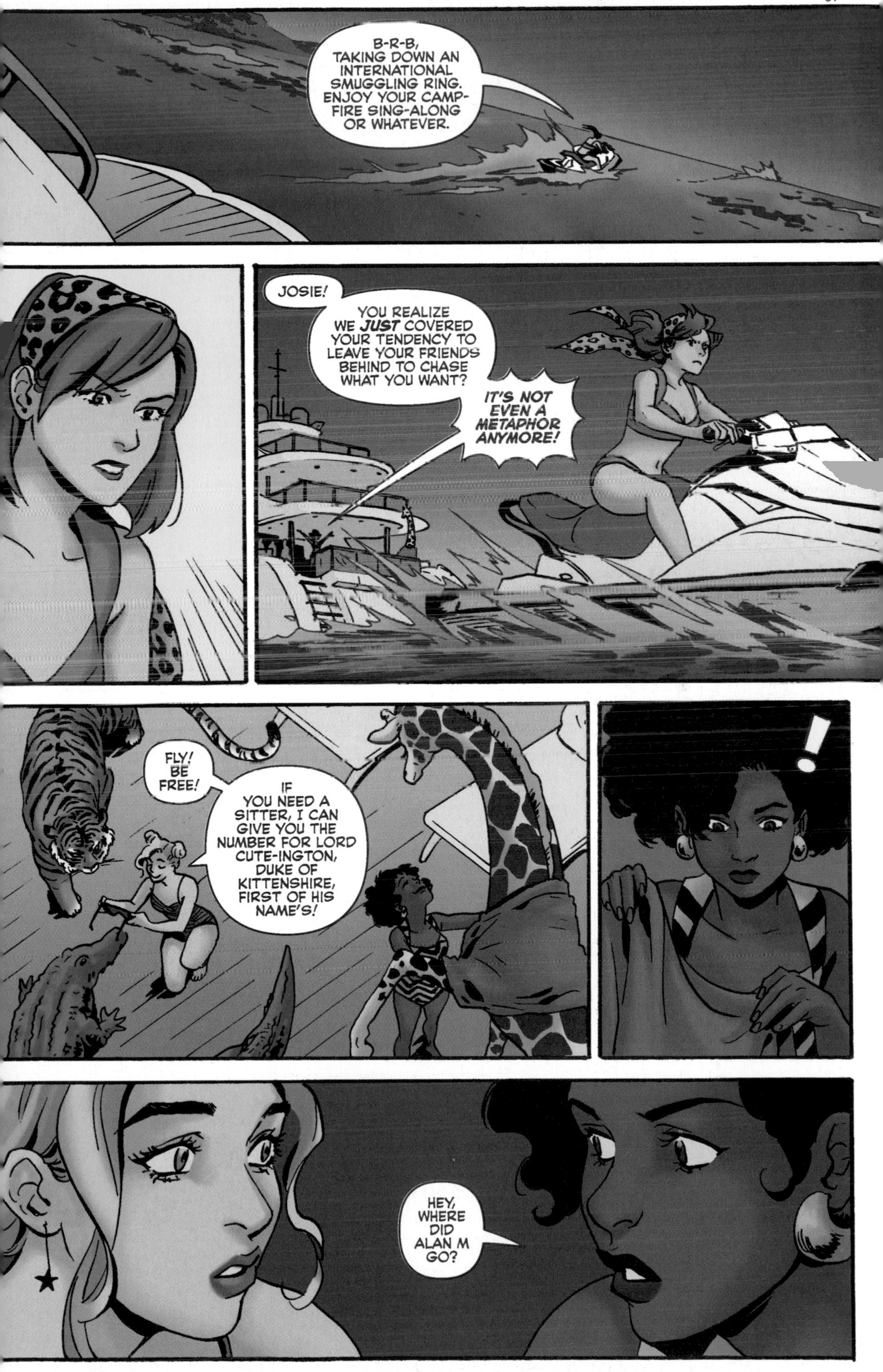
B-R-B, TAKING DOWN AN INTERNATIONAL SMUGGLING RING. ENJOY YOUR CAMP-FIRE SING-ALONG OR WHATEVER.
JOSIE!
YOU REALIZE WE JUST COVERED YOUR TENDENCY TO LEAVE YOUR FRIENDS BEHIND TO CHASE WHAT YOU WANT?
IT'S NOT EVEN A METAPHOR ANYMORE!
FLY! BE FREE!
IF YOU NEED A SITTER, I CAN GIVE YOU THE NUMBER FOR LORD CUTE-INGTON, DUKE OF KITTENSHIRE, FIRST OF HIS NAME'S!
!
HEY, WHERE DID ALAN M GO?

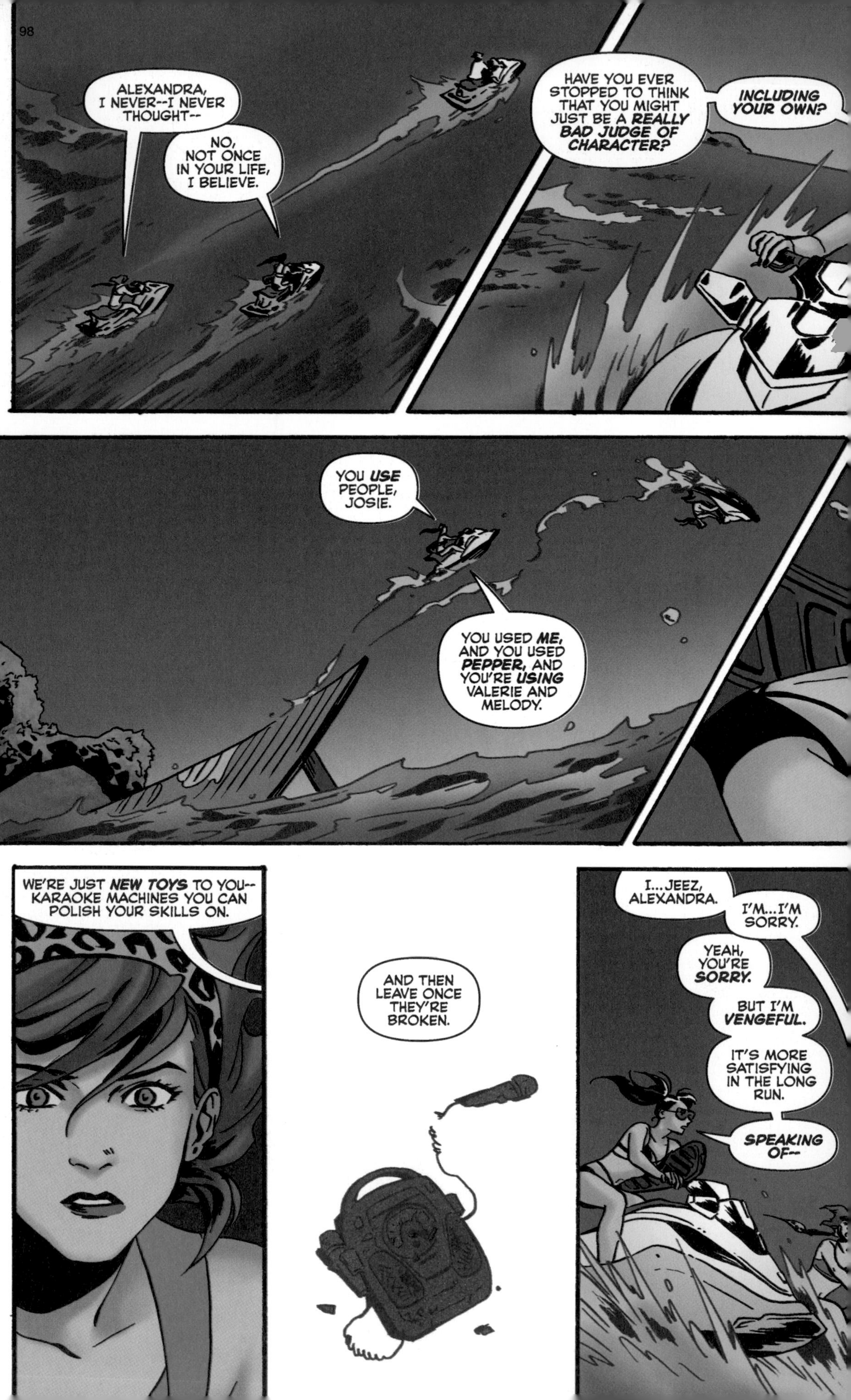
ALEXANDRA, I NEVER--I NEVER THOUGHT--
NO, NOT ONCE IN YOUR LIFE, I BELIEVE.
HAVE YOU EVER STOPPED TO THINK THAT YOU MIGHT JUST BE A REALLY BAD JUDGE OF CHARACTER?
INCLUDING YOUR OWN?
YOU USE PEOPLE, JOSIE.
YOU USED ME, AND YOU USED PEPPER, AND YOU'RE USING VALERIE AND MELODY.
WE'RE JUST NEW TOYS TO YOU--KARAOKE MACHINES YOU CAN POLISH YOUR SKILLS ON.
AND THEN LEAVE ONCE THEY'RE BROKEN.
I...JEEZ, ALEXANDRA.
I'M...I'M SORRY.
YEAH, YOU'RE SORRY.
BUT I'M VENGEFUL.
IT'S MORE SATISFYING IN THE LONG RUN.
SPEAKING OF--

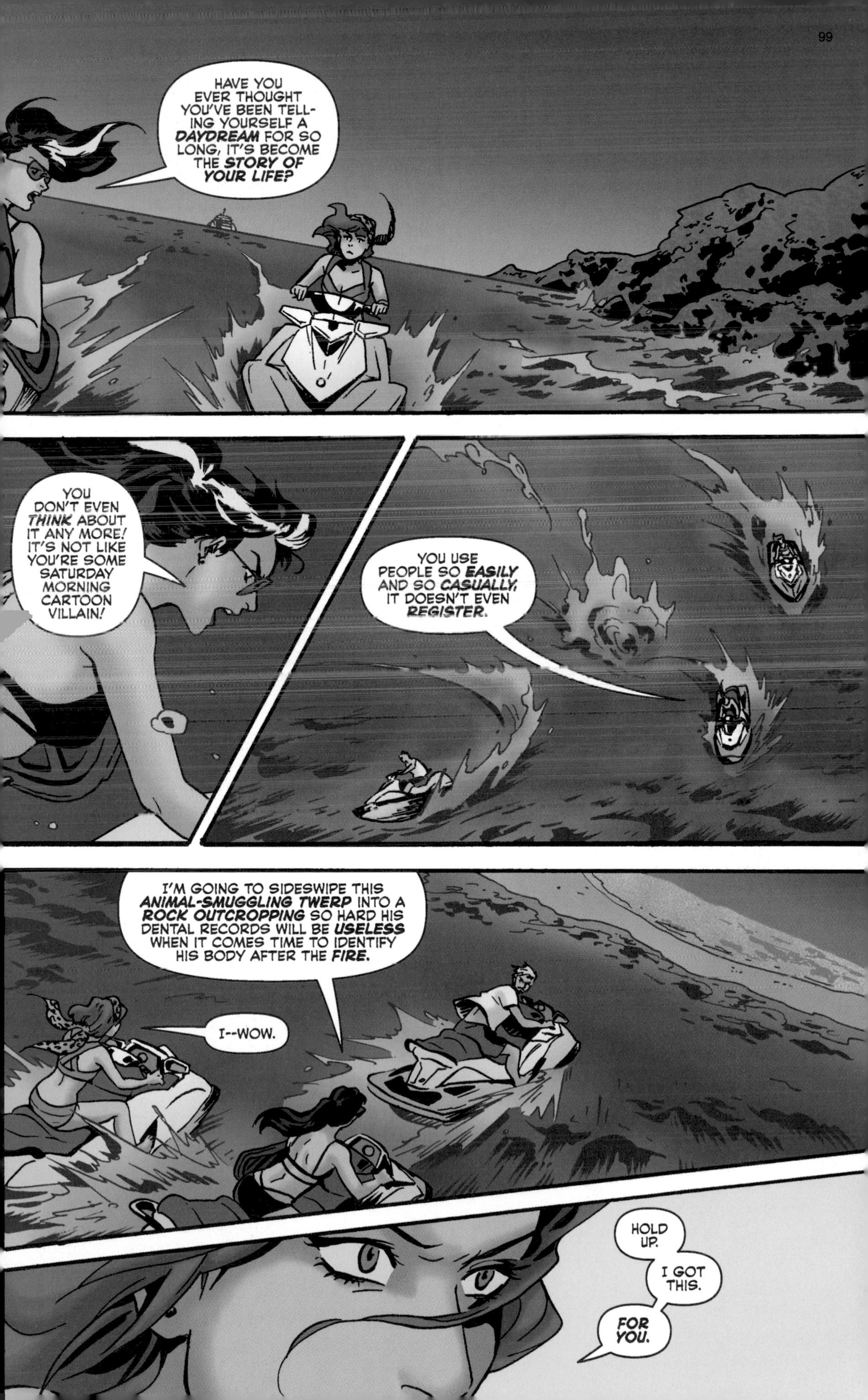
HAVE YOU EVER THOUGHT YOU'VE BEEN TELLING YOURSELF A DAYDREAM FOR SO LONG, IT'S BECOME THE STORY OF YOUR LIFE?
YOU DON'T EVEN THINK ABOUT IT ANY MORE! IT'S NOT LIKE YOU'RE SOME SATURDAY MORNING CARTOON VILLAIN!
YOU USE PEOPLE SO EASILY AND SO CASUALLY, IT DOESN'T EVEN REGISTER.
I'M GOING TO SIDESWIPE THIS ANIMAL-SMUGGLING TWERP INTO A ROCK OUTCROPPING SO HARD HIS DENTAL RECORDS WILL BE USELESS WHEN IT COMES TIME TO IDENTIFY HIS BODY AFTER THE FIRE.
I--WOW.
HOLD UP.
I GOT THIS.
FOR YOU.

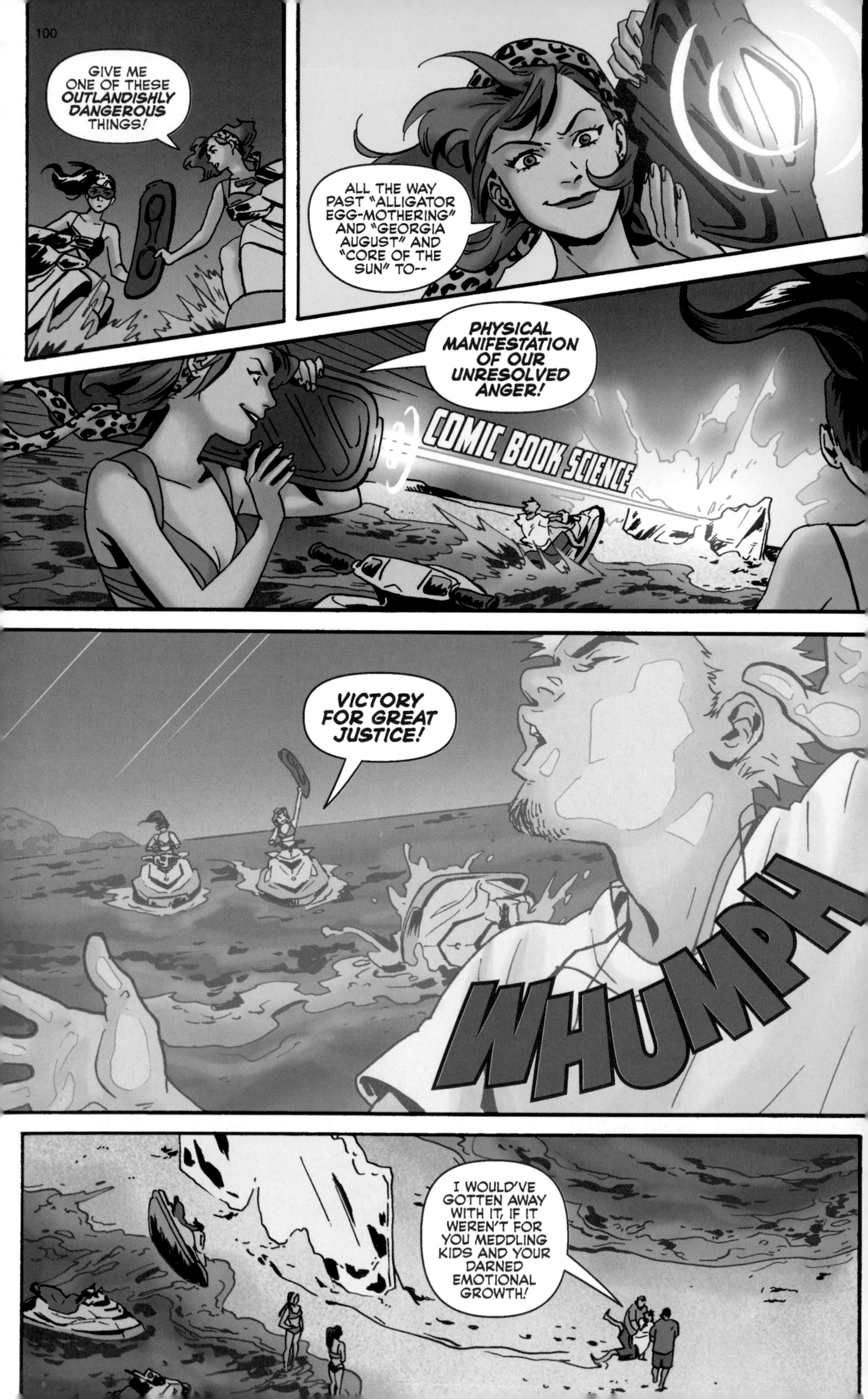
GIVE ME ONE OF THESE OUTLANDISHLY DANGEROUS THINGS!
ALL THE WAY PAST "ALLIGATOR EGG-MOTHERING" AND "GEORGIA AUGUST" AND "CORE OF THE SUN" TO--
PHYSICAL MANIFESTATION OF OUR UNRESOLVED ANGER!
COMIC BOOK SCIENCE
VICTORY FOR GREAT JUSTICE!
WHUMPH
I WOULD'VE GOTTEN AWAY WITH IT, IF IT WEREN'T FOR YOU MEDDLING KIDS AND YOUR DARNED EMOTIONAL GROWTH!

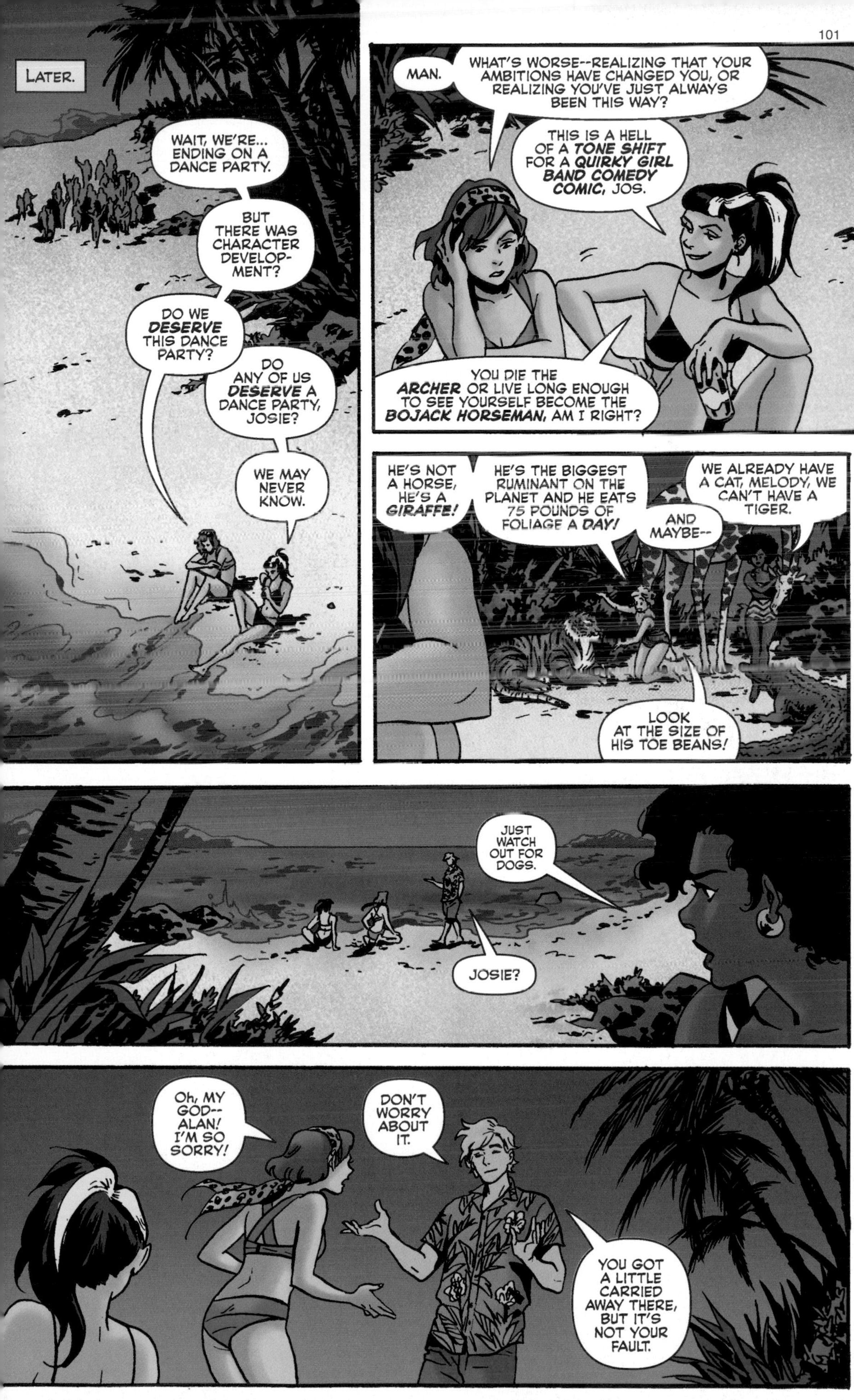
LATER.
WAIT, WE'RE... ENDING ON A DANCE PARTY.
BUT THERE WAS CHARACTER DEVELOP-MENT?
DO WE DESERVE THIS DANCE PARTY?
DO ANY OF US DESERVE A DANCE PARTY, JOSIE?
WE MAY NEVER KNOW.
MAN.
WHAT'S WORSE--REALIZING THAT YOUR AMBITIONS HAVE CHANGED YOU, OR REALIZING YOU'VE JUST ALWAYS BEEN THIS WAY?
THIS IS A HELL OF A TONE SHIFT FOR A QUIRKY GIRL BAND COMEDY COMIC, JOS.
YOU DIE THE ARCHER OR LIVE LONG ENOUGH TO SEE YOURSELF BECOME THE BOJACK HORSEMAN, AM I RIGHT?
HE'S NOT A HORSE, HE'S A GIRAFFE!
HE'S THE BIGGEST RUMINANT ON THE PLANET AND HE EATS 75 POUNDS OF FOLIAGE A DAY!
AND MAYBE--
WE ALREADY HAVE A CAT, MELODY, WE CAN'T HAVE A TIGER.
LOOK AT THE SIZE OF HIS TOE BEANS!
JUST WATCH OUT FOR DOGS.
JOSIE?
OH, MY GOD-- ALAN! I'M SO SORRY!
DON'T WORRY ABOUT IT.
YOU GOT A LITTLE CARRIED AWAY THERE, BUT IT'S NOT YOUR FAULT.

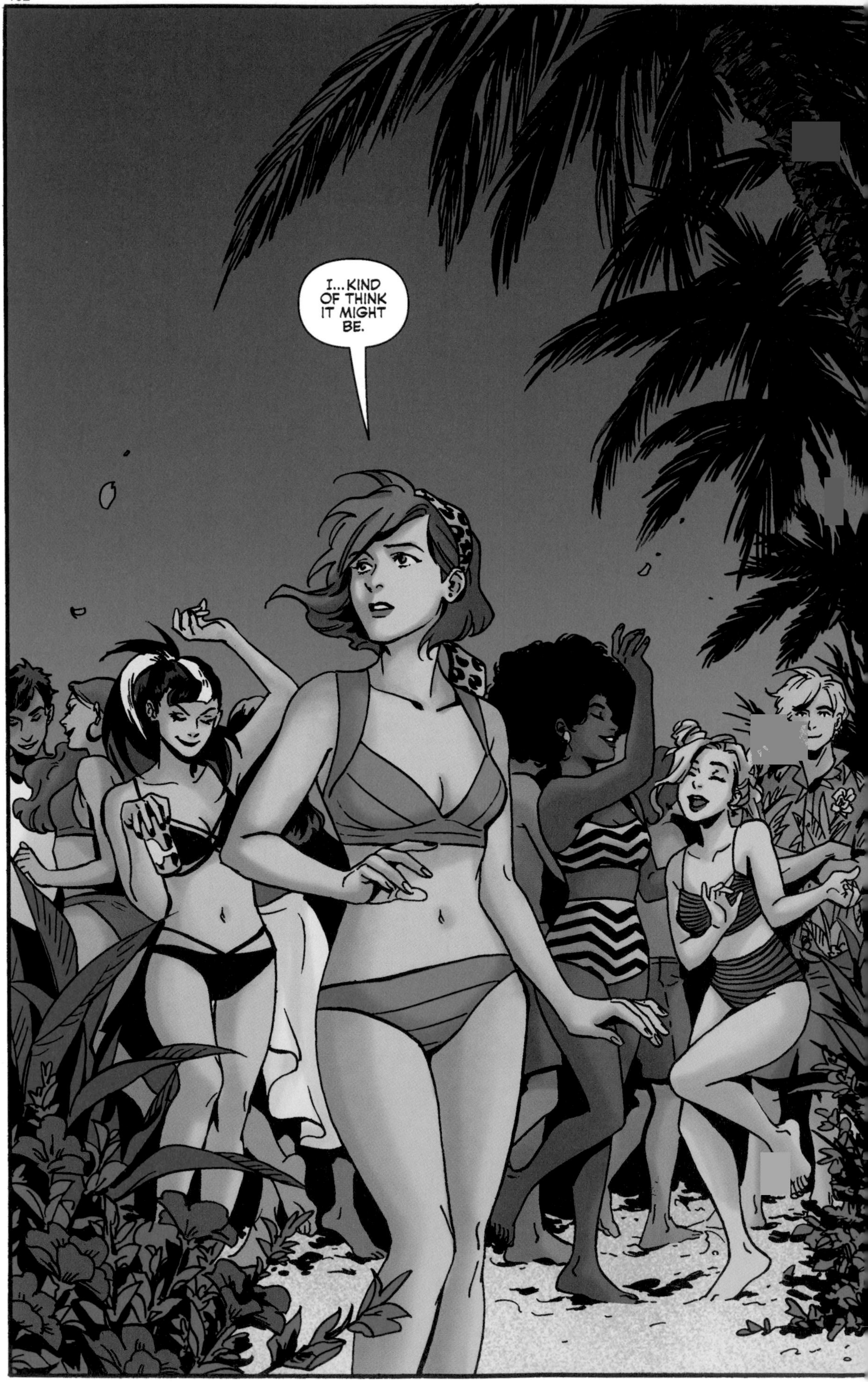
I...KIND OF THINK IT MIGHT BE.

PREVIOUSLY IN THE TOWN OF RIVERDALE...

Reggie Mantle has good looks, a great personality, a sharp wit, an amazing sense of humor and the best friend anyone could ask for in his Dachshund, Vader.

But there's one thing that Reggie doesn't have—and her name is Midge Klump. Unfortunately, Midge is already taken by the big, burly Moose Mason. Reggie's willing to do anything he can to spend some time with Midge, but Moose has other plans for Reggie.

Moose actually wants... to be *Reggie's friend*?

STORY BY
TOM DeFALCO

ART BY
SANDY JARRELL

COLORING BY
KELLY FITZPATRICK

LETTERING BY
JACK MORELLI

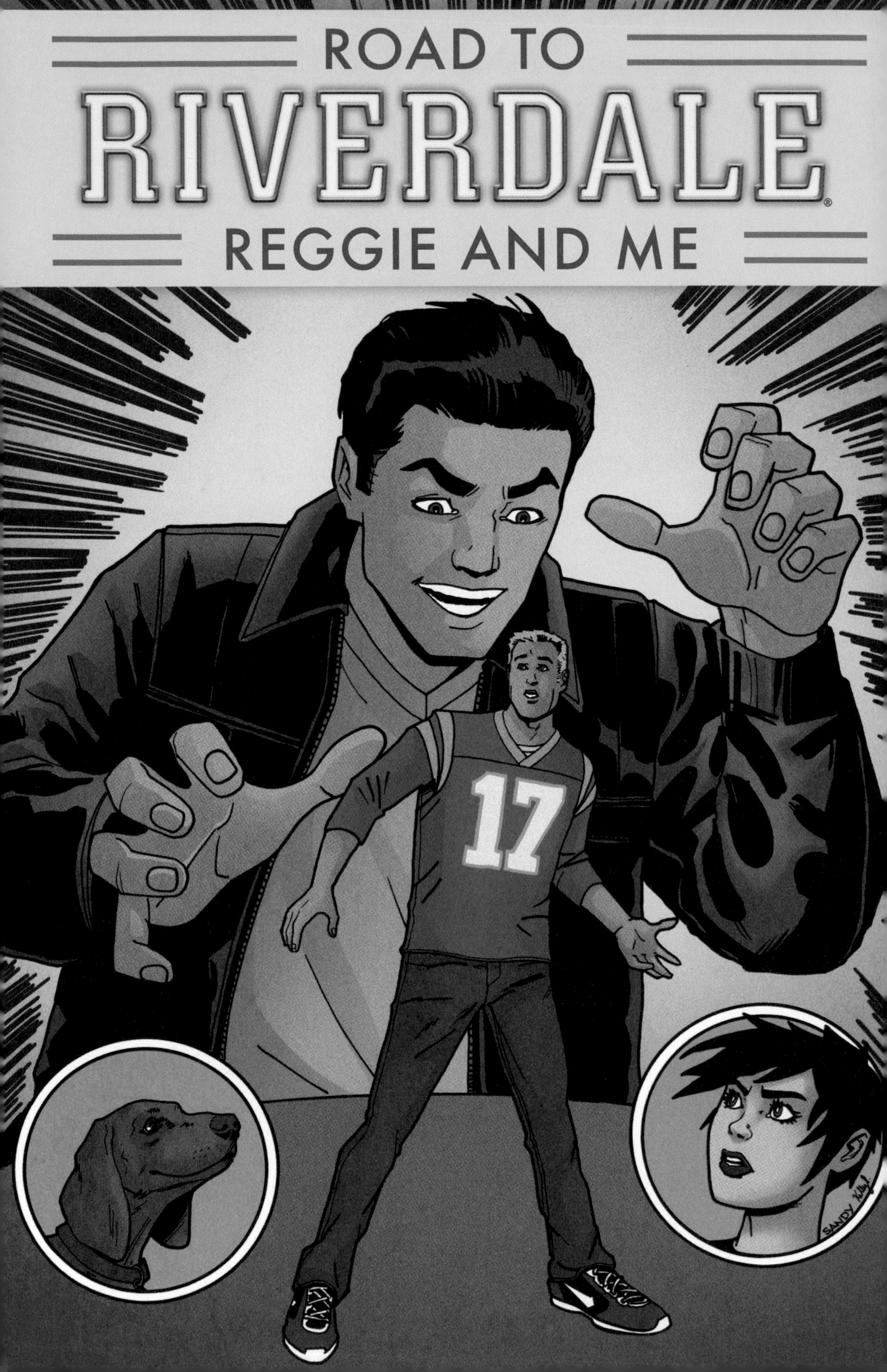
ROAD TO
RIVERDALE®
REGGIE AND ME
17

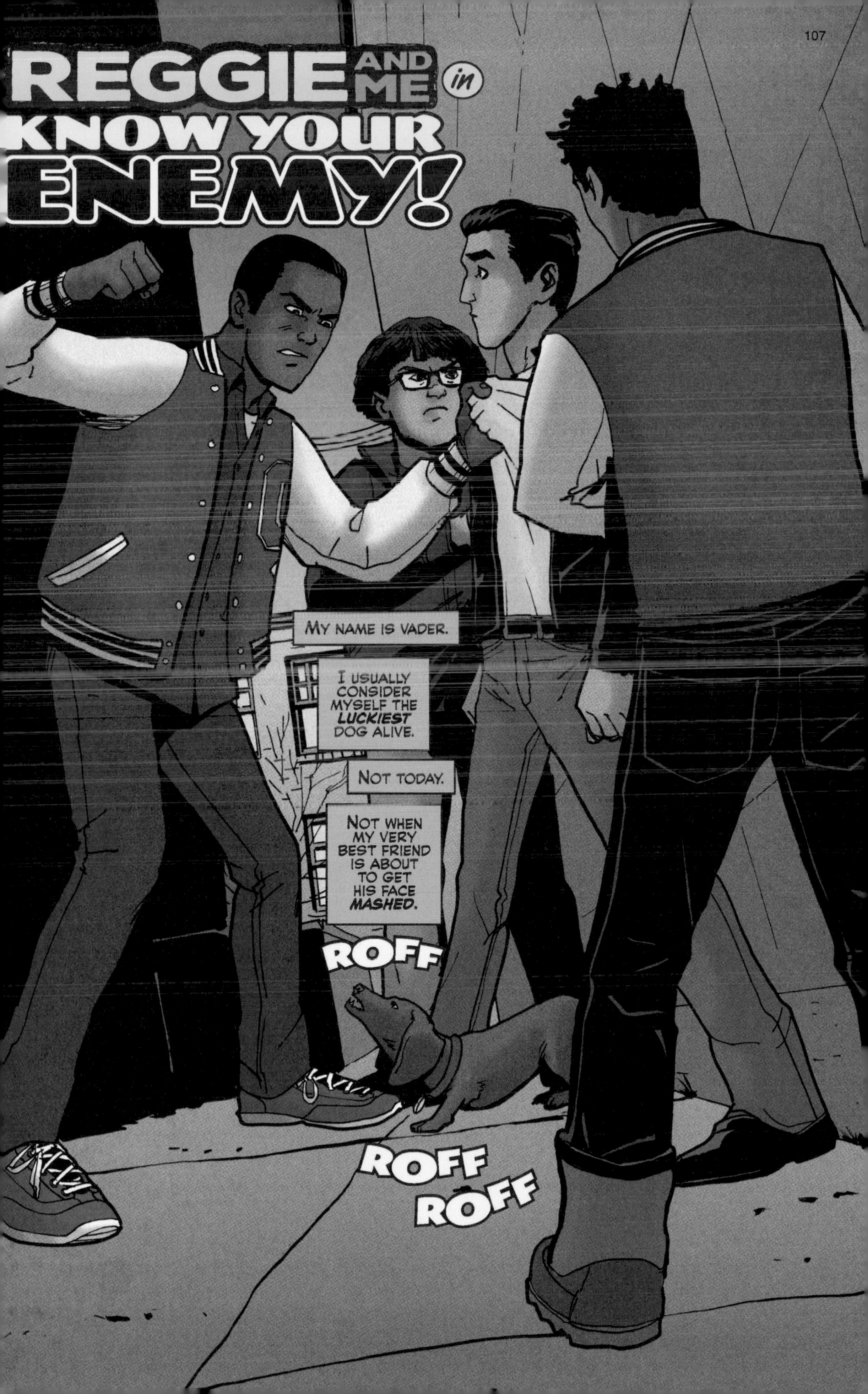
REGGIE AND ME in
KNOW YOUR ENEMY!
MY NAME IS VADER.
I USUALLY CONSIDER MYSELF THE LUCKIEST DOG ALIVE.
NOT TODAY.
NOT WHEN MY VERY BEST FRIEND IS ABOUT TO GET HIS FACE MASHED.
ROFF
ROFF
ROFF

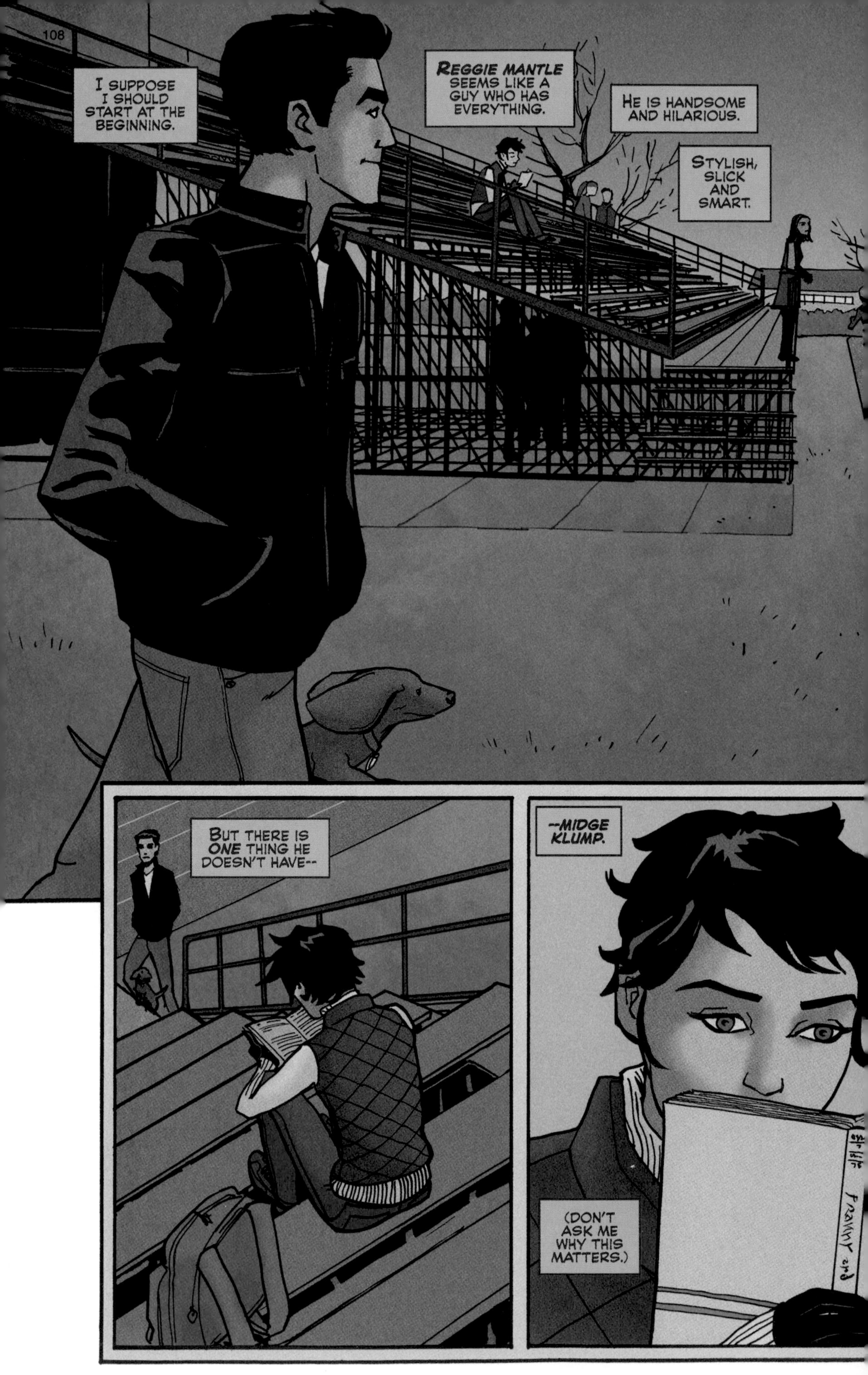
I SUPPOSE I SHOULD START AT THE BEGINNING.
REGGIE MANTLE SEEMS LIKE A GUY WHO HAS EVERYTHING.
HE IS HANDSOME AND HILARIOUS.
STYLISH, SLICK AND SMART.
BUT THERE IS *ONE* THING HE DOESN'T HAVE--
--*MIDGE KLUMP.*
(DON'T ASK ME WHY THIS MATTERS.)

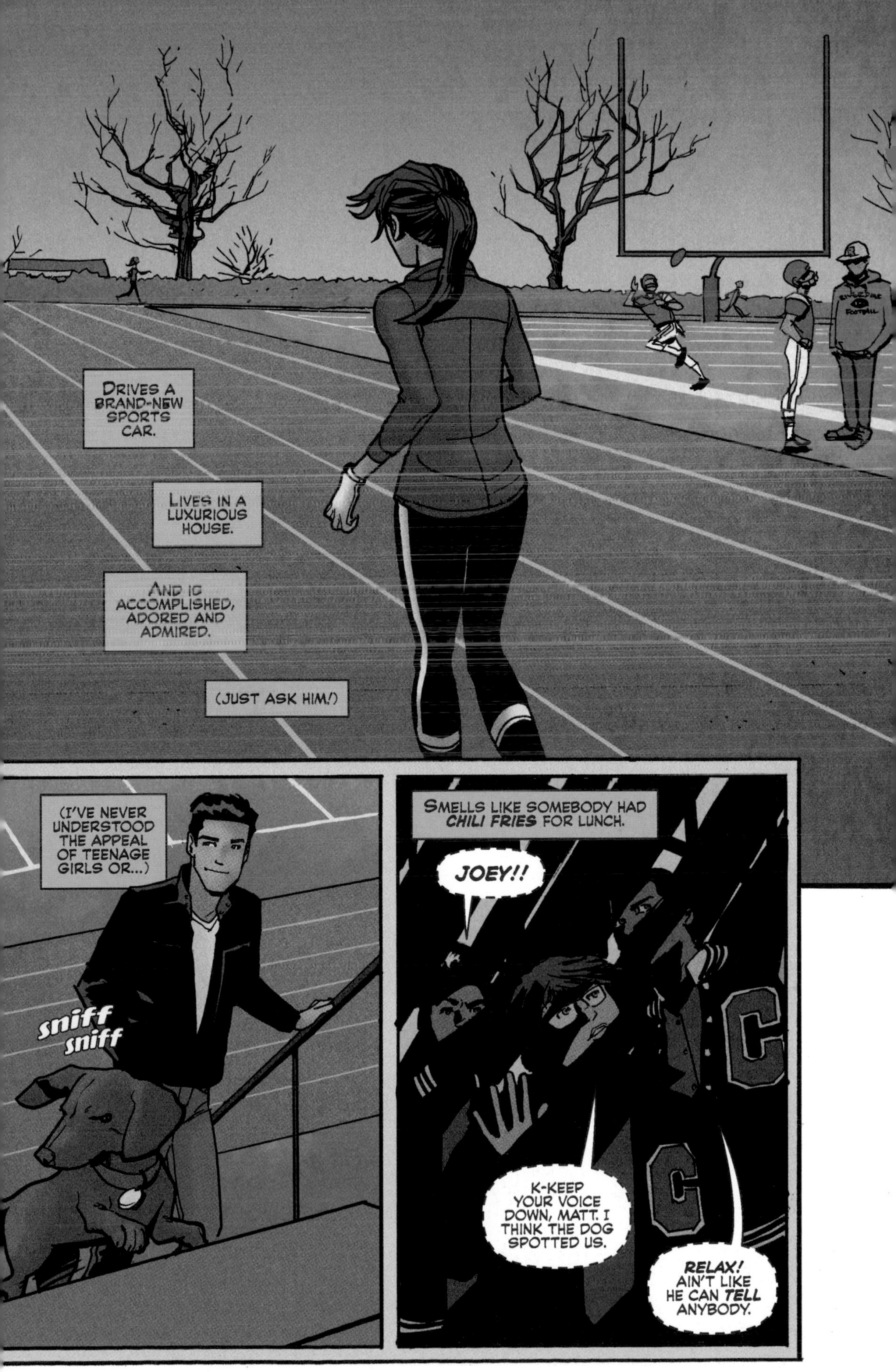
DRIVES A BRAND-NEW SPORTS CAR.
LIVES IN A LUXURIOUS HOUSE.
AND IS ACCOMPLISHED, ADORED AND ADMIRED.
(JUST ASK HIM!)
(I'VE NEVER UNDERSTOOD THE APPEAL OF TEENAGE GIRLS OR...)
sniff sniff
SMELLS LIKE SOMEBODY HAD CHILI FRIES FOR LUNCH.
JOEY!!
K-KEEP YOUR VOICE DOWN, MATT. I THINK THE DOG SPOTTED US.
RELAX! AIN'T LIKE HE CAN TELL ANYBODY.

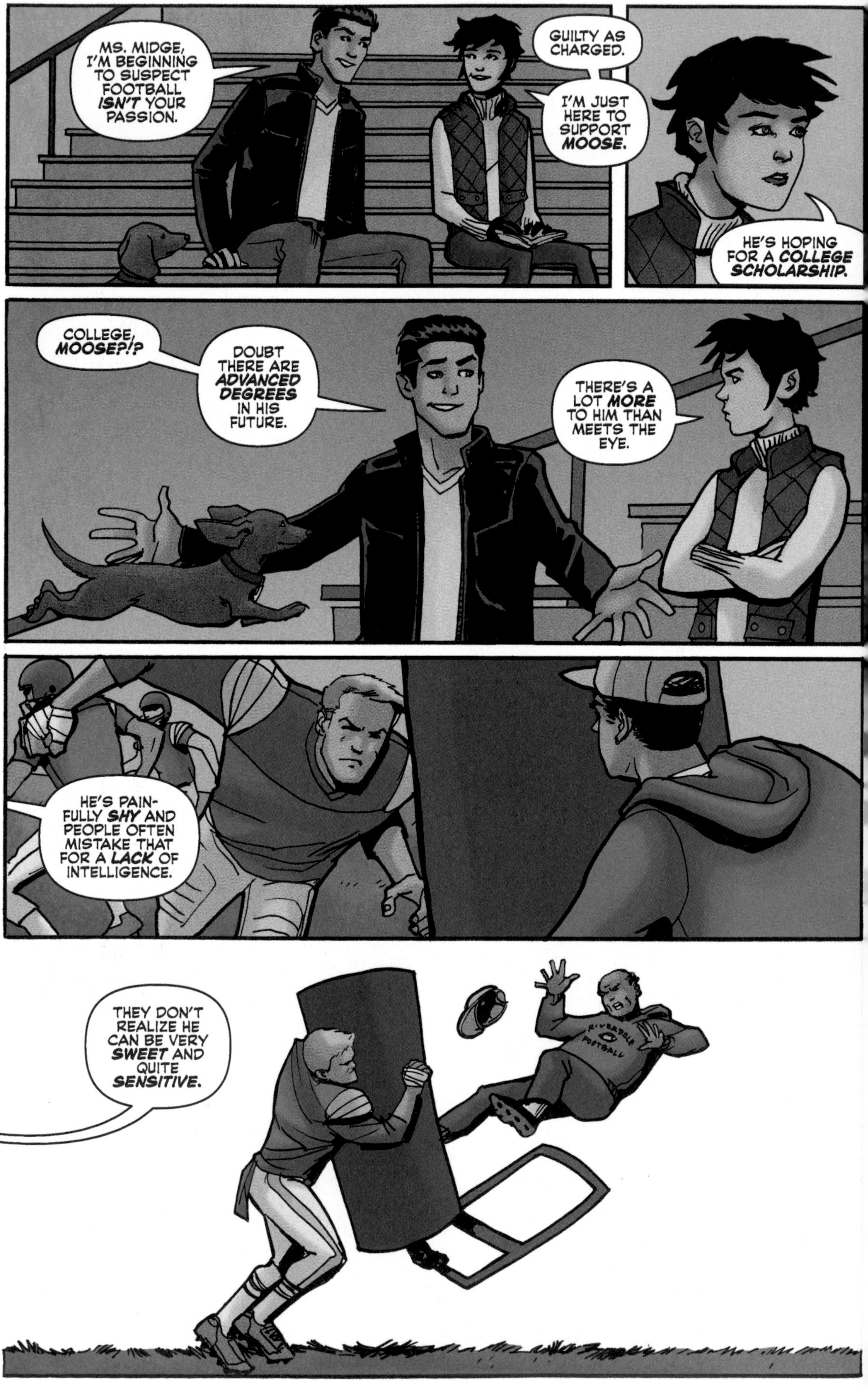
MS. MIDGE, I'M BEGINNING TO SUSPECT FOOTBALL ISN'T YOUR PASSION.
GUILTY AS CHARGED.
I'M JUST HERE TO SUPPORT MOOSE.
HE'S HOPING FOR A COLLEGE SCHOLARSHIP.
COLLEGE, MOOSE?!?
DOUBT THERE ARE ADVANCED DEGREES IN HIS FUTURE.
THERE'S A LOT MORE TO HIM THAN MEETS THE EYE.
HE'S PAIN-FULLY SHY AND PEOPLE OFTEN MISTAKE THAT FOR A LACK OF INTELLIGENCE.
THEY DON'T REALIZE HE CAN BE VERY SWEET AND QUITE SENSITIVE.
RIVERDALE FOOTBALL

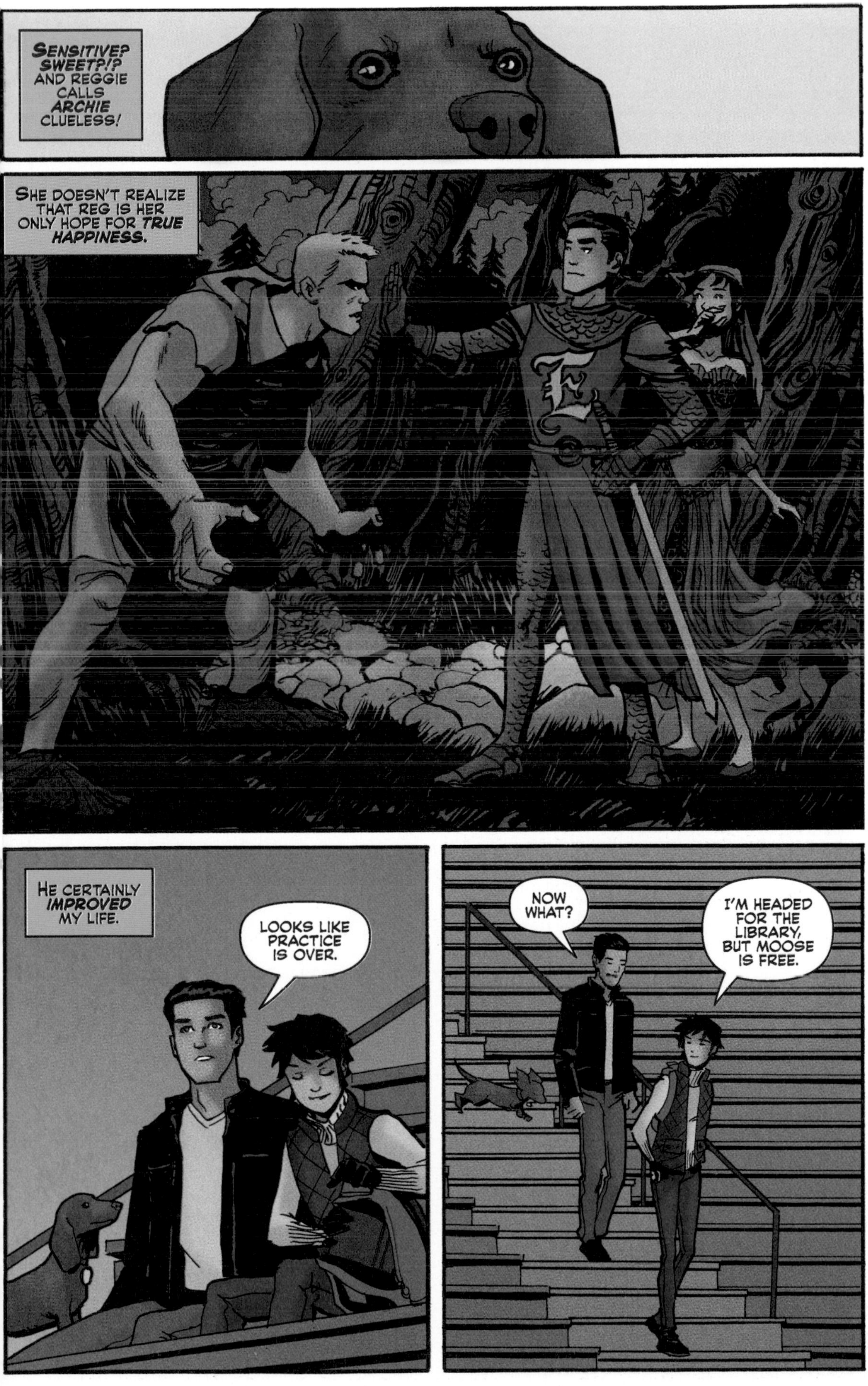
SENSITIVE? SWEET?!? AND REGGIE CALLS ARCHIE CLUELESS!
SHE DOESN'T REALIZE THAT REG IS HER ONLY HOPE FOR TRUE HAPPINESS.
HE CERTAINLY IMPROVED MY LIFE.
LOOKS LIKE PRACTICE IS OVER.
NOW WHAT?
I'M HEADED FOR THE LIBRARY, BUT MOOSE IS FREE.

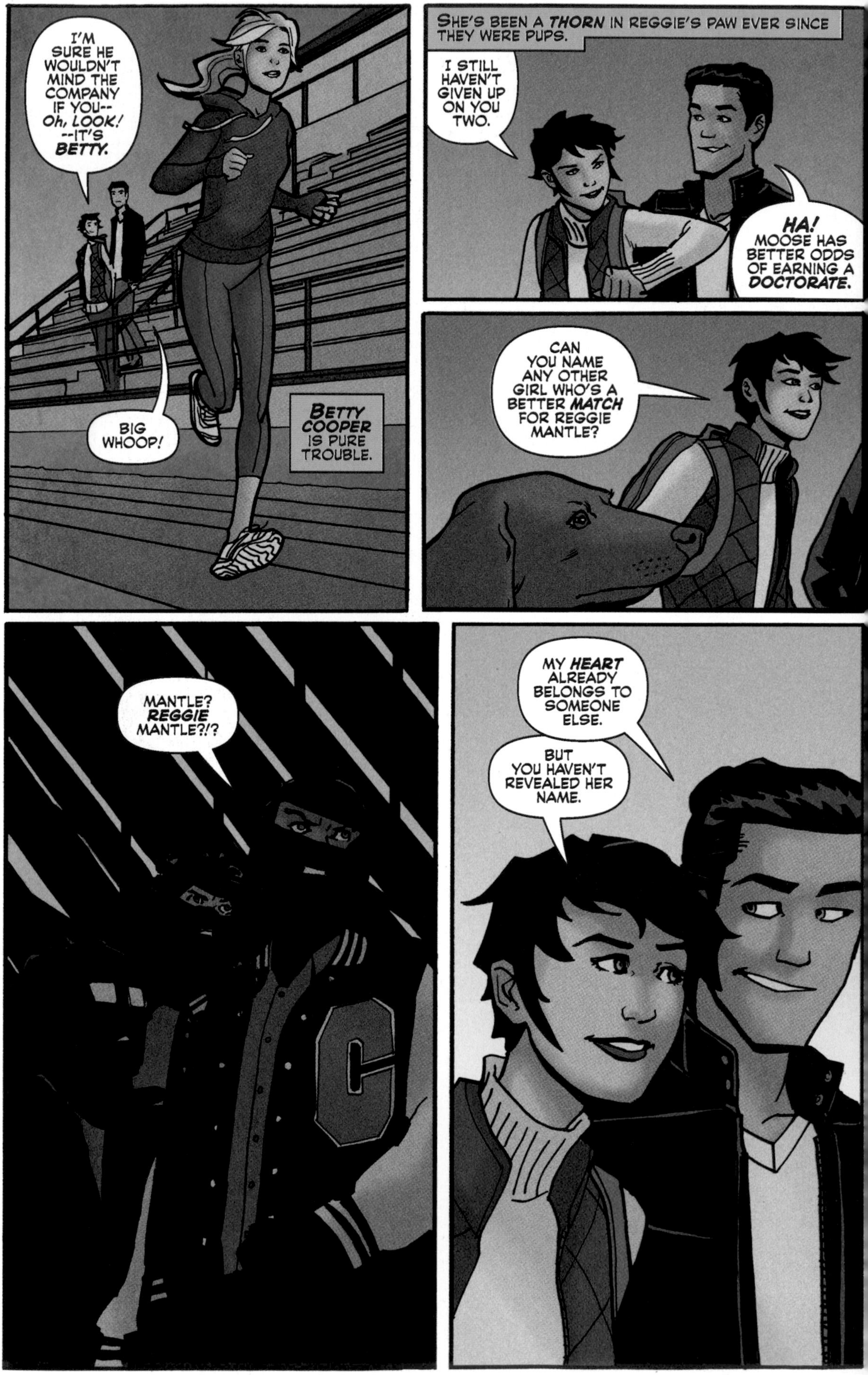
I'M SURE HE WOULDN'T MIND THE COMPANY IF YOU-- Oh, LOOK! --IT'S BETTY.
BIG WHOOP!
BETTY COOPER IS PURE TROUBLE.
SHE'S BEEN A THORN IN REGGIE'S PAW EVER SINCE THEY WERE PUPS.
I STILL HAVEN'T GIVEN UP ON YOU TWO.
HA! MOOSE HAS BETTER ODDS OF EARNING A DOCTORATE.
CAN YOU NAME ANY OTHER GIRL WHO'S A BETTER MATCH FOR REGGIE MANTLE?
MANTLE? REGGIE MANTLE?!?
MY HEART ALREADY BELONGS TO SOMEONE ELSE.
BUT YOU HAVEN'T REVEALED HER NAME.

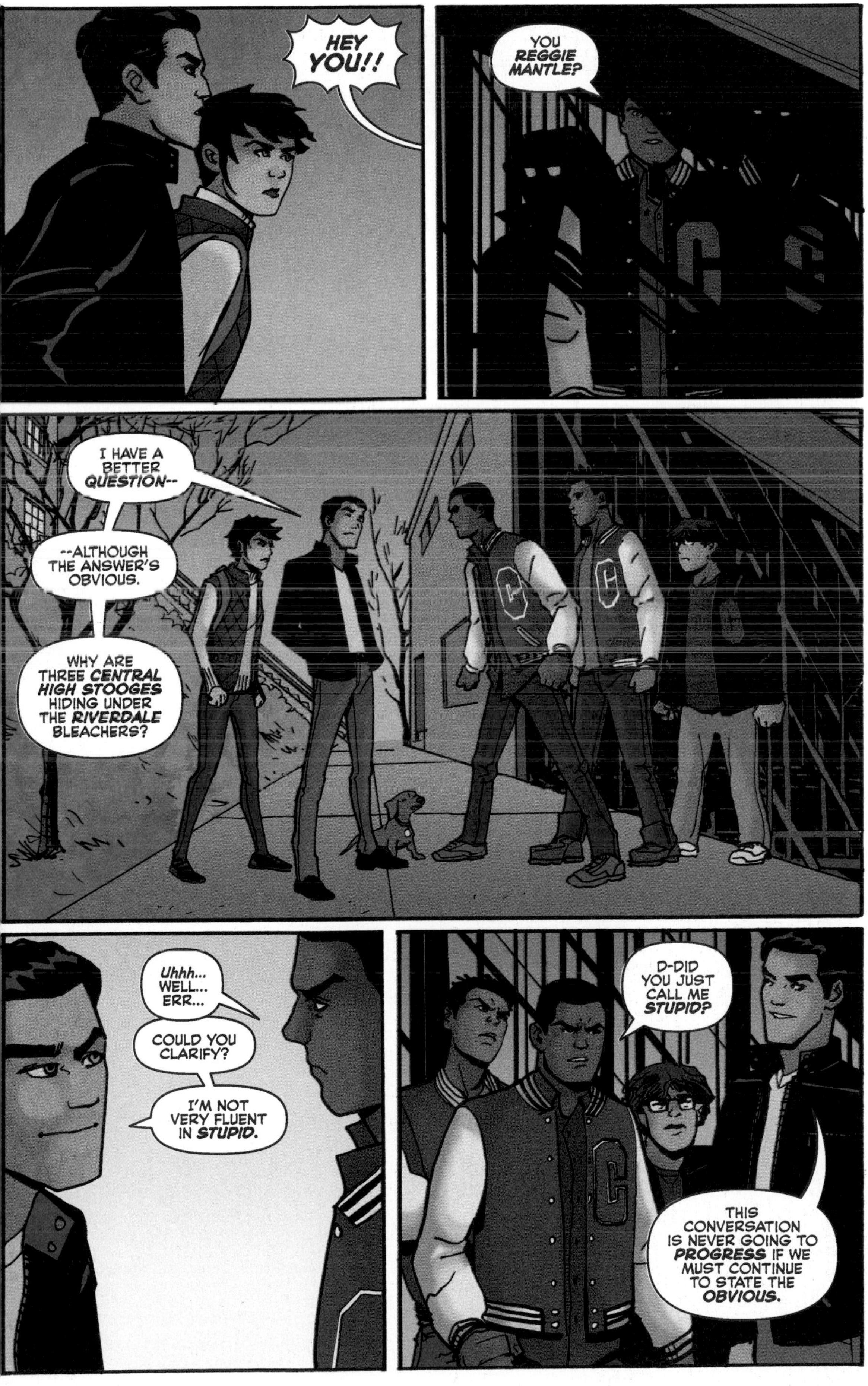
HEY YOU!!
YOU REGGIE MANTLE?
I HAVE A BETTER QUESTION--
--ALTHOUGH THE ANSWER'S OBVIOUS.
WHY ARE THREE CENTRAL HIGH STOOGES HIDING UNDER THE RIVERDALE BLEACHERS?
Uhhh... WELL... ERR...
COULD YOU CLARIFY?
I'M NOT VERY FLUENT IN STUPID.
D-DID YOU JUST CALL ME STUPID?
THIS CONVERSATION IS NEVER GOING TO PROGRESS IF WE MUST CONTINUE TO STATE THE OBVIOUS.

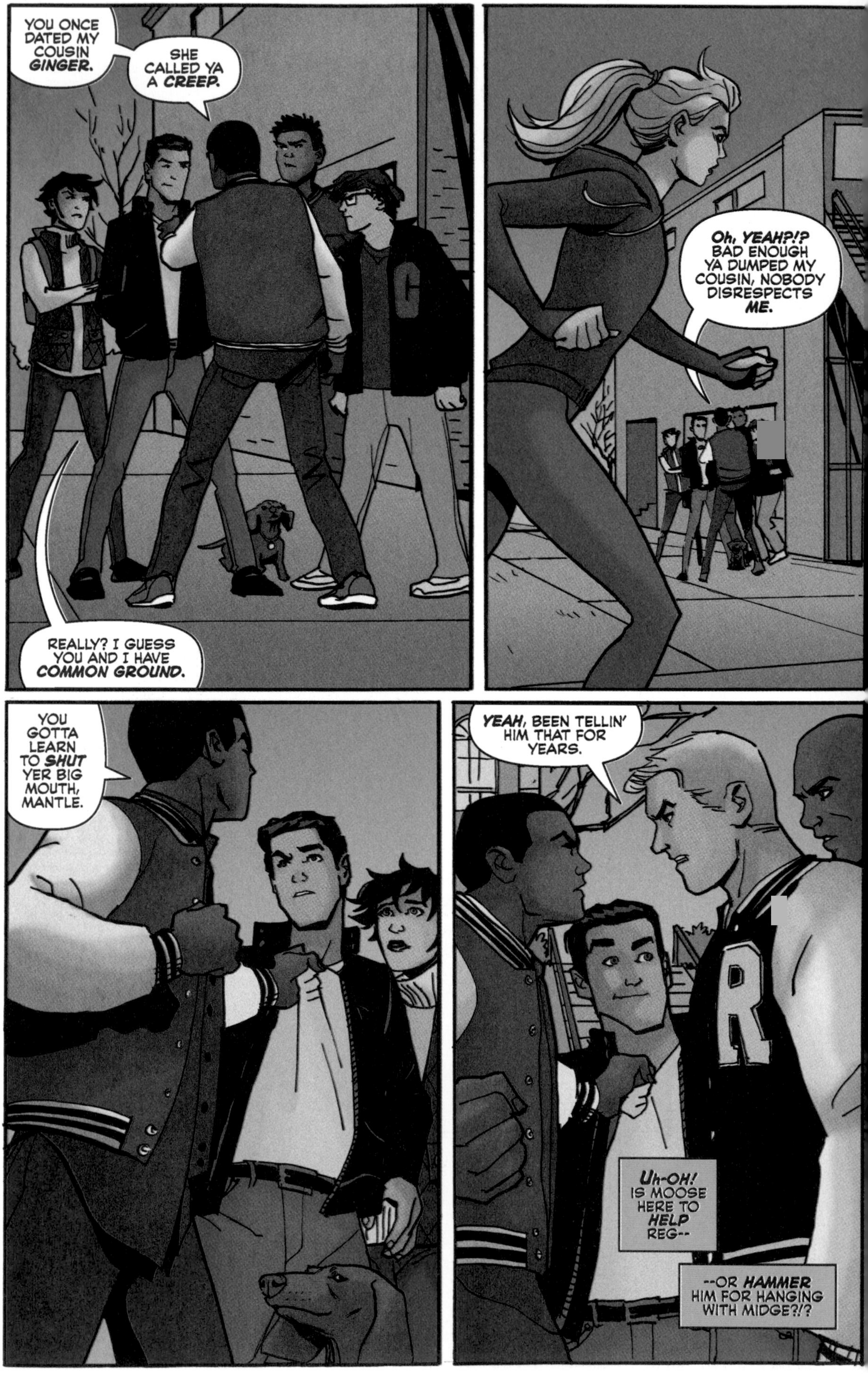
YOU ONCE DATED MY COUSIN GINGER.
SHE CALLED YA A CREEP.
REALLY? I GUESS YOU AND I HAVE COMMON GROUND.
Oh, YEAH?!? BAD ENOUGH YA DUMPED MY COUSIN, NOBODY DISRESPECTS ME.
YOU GOTTA LEARN TO SHUT YER BIG MOUTH, MANTLE.
YEAH, BEEN TELLIN' HIM THAT FOR YEARS.
Uh-OH! IS MOOSE HERE TO HELP REG--
--OR HAMMER HIM FOR HANGING WITH MIDGE?!?

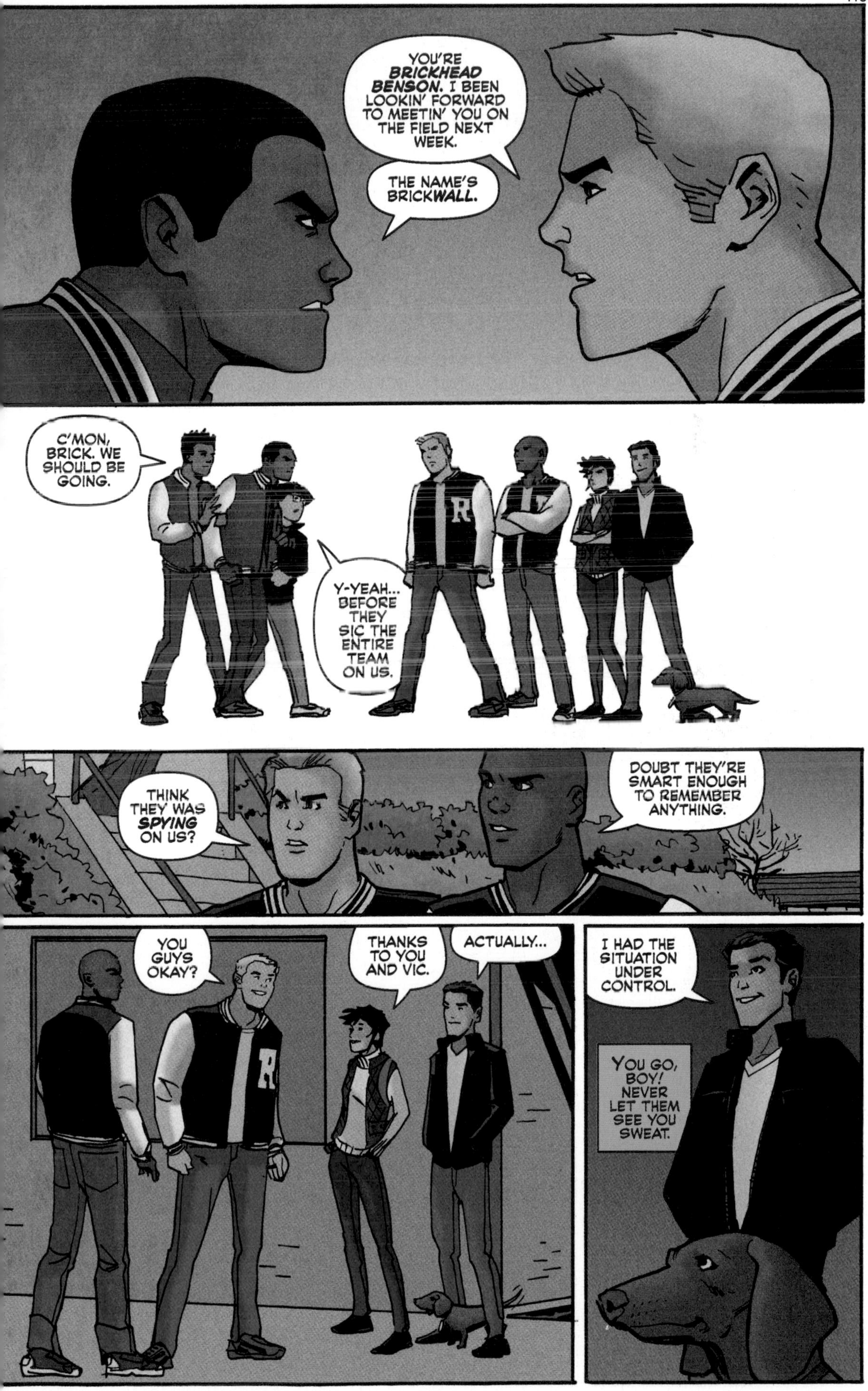
YOU'RE BRICKHEAD BENSON. I BEEN LOOKIN' FORWARD TO MEETIN' YOU ON THE FIELD NEXT WEEK.
THE NAME'S BRICKWALL.
C'MON, BRICK. WE SHOULD BE GOING.
Y-YEAH... BEFORE THEY SIC THE ENTIRE TEAM ON US.
THINK THEY WAS SPYING ON US?
DOUBT THEY'RE SMART ENOUGH TO REMEMBER ANYTHING.
YOU GUYS OKAY?
THANKS TO YOU AND VIC.
ACTUALLY...
I HAD THE SITUATION UNDER CONTROL.
YOU GO, BOY! NEVER LET THEM SEE YOU SWEAT.

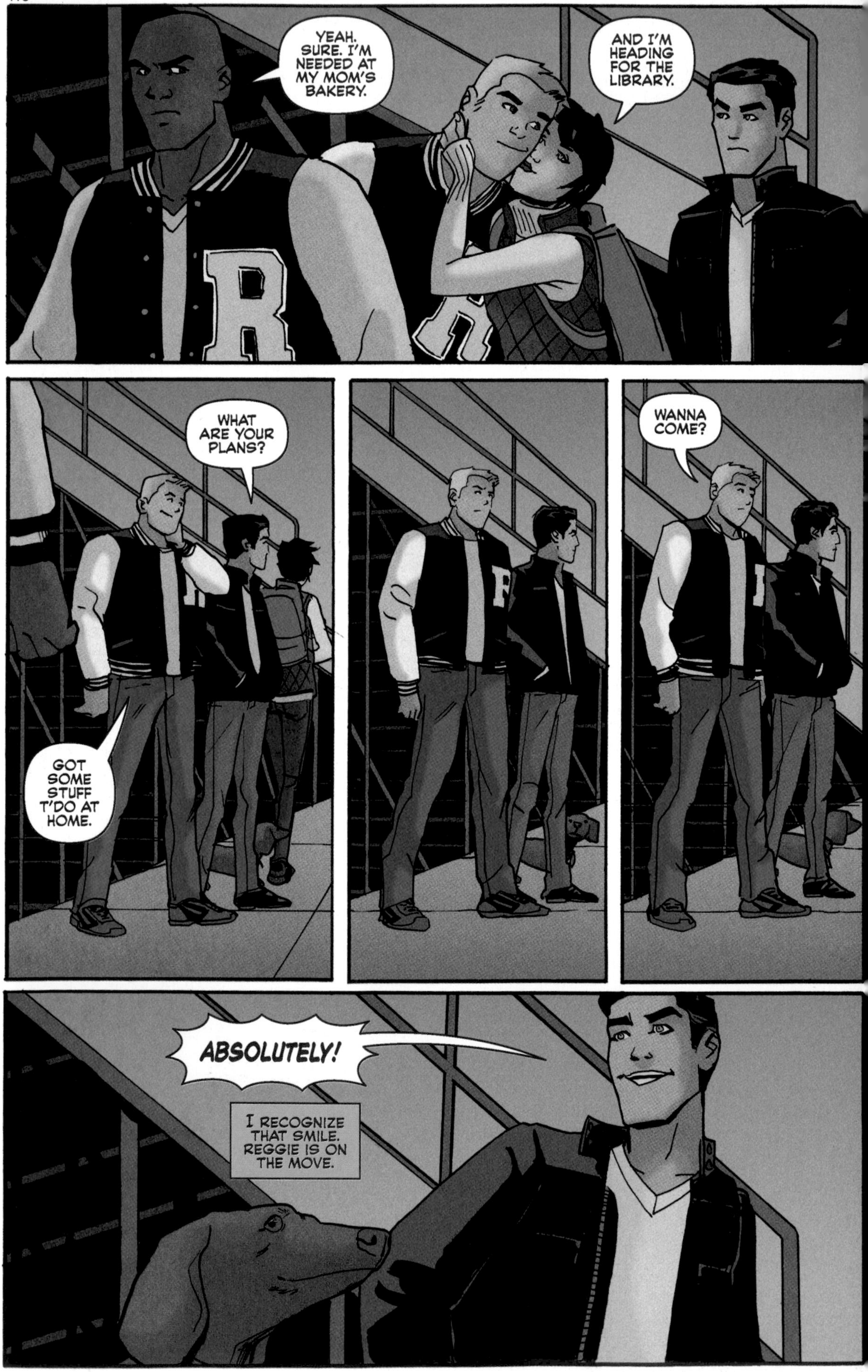
YEAH. SURE. I'M NEEDED AT MY MOM'S BAKERY.
AND I'M HEADING FOR THE LIBRARY.
WHAT ARE YOUR PLANS?
GOT SOME STUFF T'DO AT HOME.
WANNA COME?
ABSOLUTELY!
I RECOGNIZE THAT SMILE. REGGIE IS ON THE MOVE.

YOU WERE PRETTY CONFIDENT AGAINST THEM CENTRAL GUYS. BEEN IN A LOT OF FIGHTS?

NOT AS MANY AS YOU.

BUT ≷SIGH≶ THERE ARE BALLS TO CATCH AND STICKS TO FETCH.

ME?!? NOBODY EVER FIGHTS WITH ME.

THEY JUST RUN AWAY!

SPEAKING OF RUNNING AWAY, I WISH ANDREWS WOULD TAKE THE HINT.

YOU DON'T LIKE ARCHIE?

I ALWAYS THOUGHT HE WAS A GOOD GUY.

HA! BENEATH HIS CAREFULLY CONSTRUCTED FACADE, LIES A CRAFTY, CONNIVING, MANIPULATIVE SNAKE--

--WHO CAN'T BE TRUSTED WITH ANY-ONE'S GIRLFRIEND.

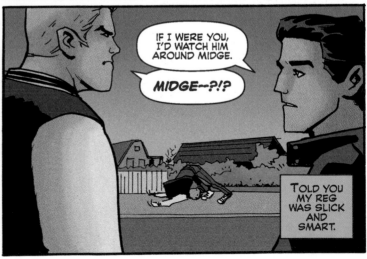

IF I WERE YOU, I'D WATCH HIM AROUND MIDGE.

MIDGE--?!?

TOLD YOU MY REG WAS SLICK AND SMART.

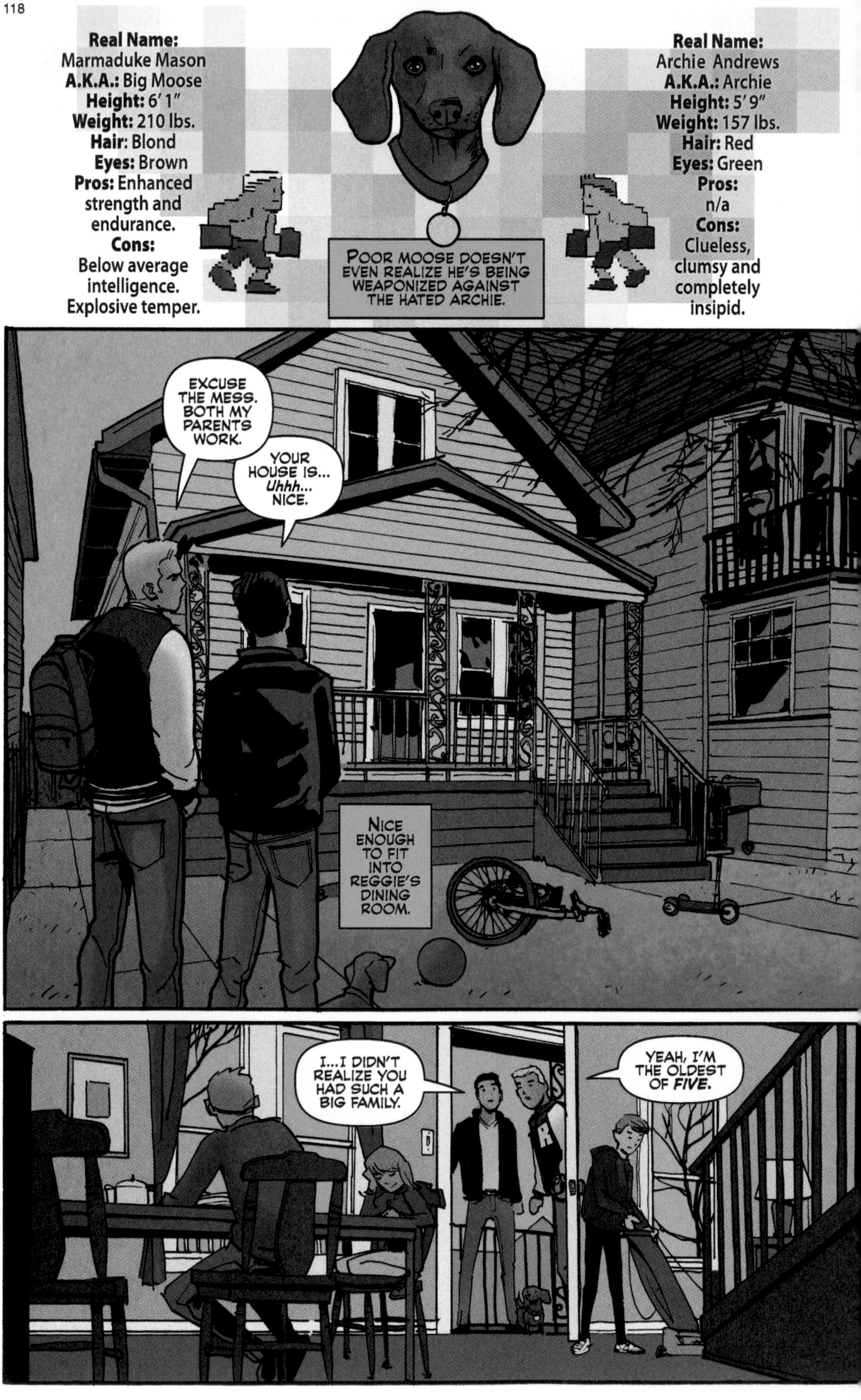
Real Name:
Marmaduke Mason
A.K.A.: Big Moose
Height: 6′ 1″
Weight: 210 lbs.
Hair: Blond
Eyes: Brown
Pros: Enhanced strength and endurance.
Cons:
Below average intelligence.
Explosive temper.
POOR MOOSE DOESN'T EVEN REALIZE HE'S BEING WEAPONIZED AGAINST THE HATED ARCHIE.
Real Name:
Archie Andrews
A.K.A.: Archie
Height: 5′ 9″
Weight: 157 lbs.
Hair: Red
Eyes: Green
Pros:
n/a
Cons:
Clueless, clumsy and completely insipid.
EXCUSE THE MESS. BOTH MY PARENTS WORK.
YOUR HOUSE IS... *Uhhh*... NICE.
NICE ENOUGH TO FIT INTO REGGIE'S DINING ROOM.
I...I DIDN'T REALIZE YOU HAD SUCH A BIG FAMILY.
YEAH, I'M THE OLDEST OF *FIVE*.

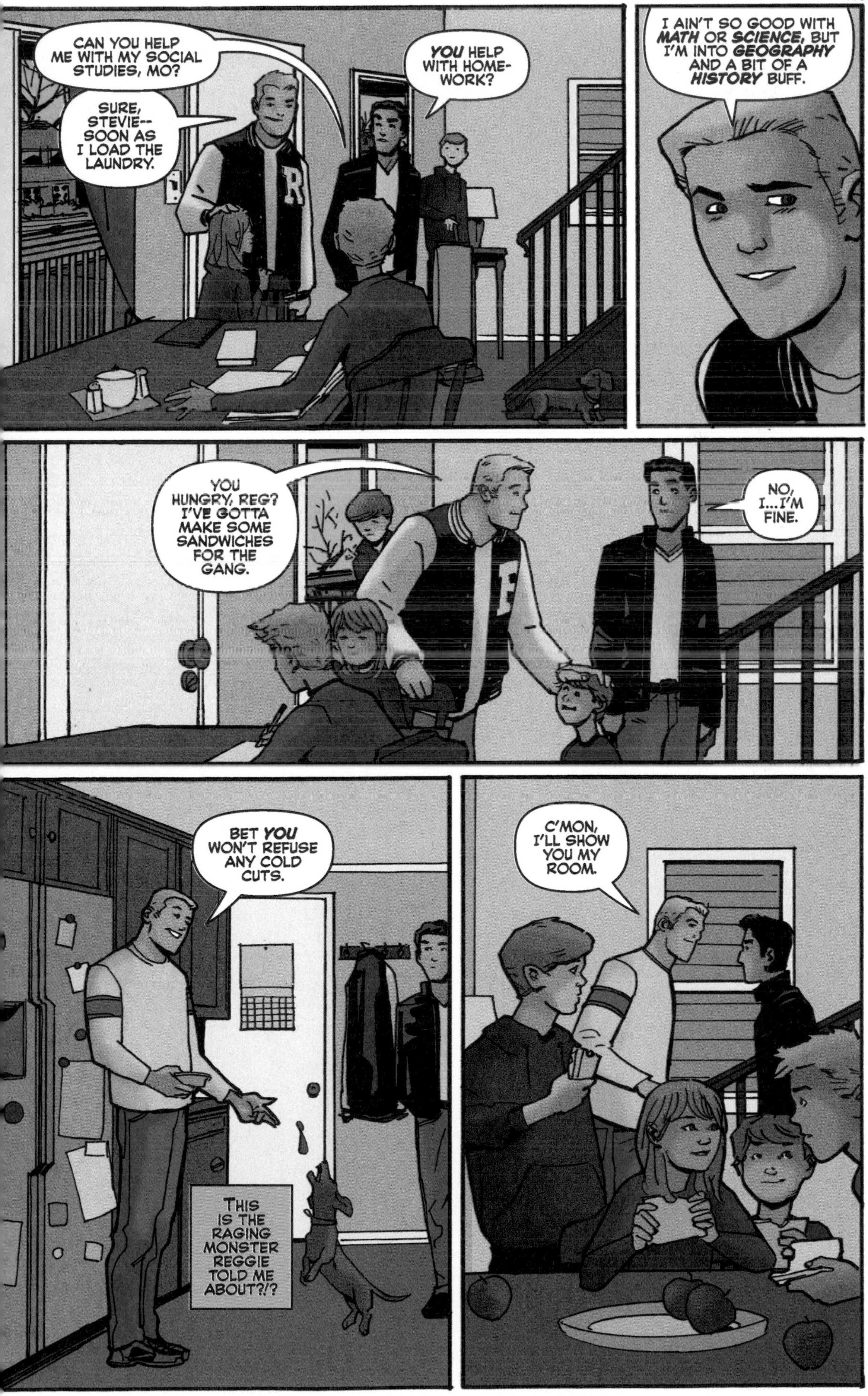
CAN YOU HELP ME WITH MY SOCIAL STUDIES, MO?
SURE, STEVIE-- SOON AS I LOAD THE LAUNDRY.
YOU HELP WITH HOME-WORK?
I AIN'T SO GOOD WITH MATH OR SCIENCE, BUT I'M INTO GEOGRAPHY AND A BIT OF A HISTORY BUFF.
YOU HUNGRY, REG? I'VE GOTTA MAKE SOME SANDWICHES FOR THE GANG.
NO, I...I'M FINE.
BET YOU WON'T REFUSE ANY COLD CUTS.
THIS IS THE RAGING MONSTER REGGIE TOLD ME ABOUT?!?
C'MON, I'LL SHOW YOU MY ROOM.

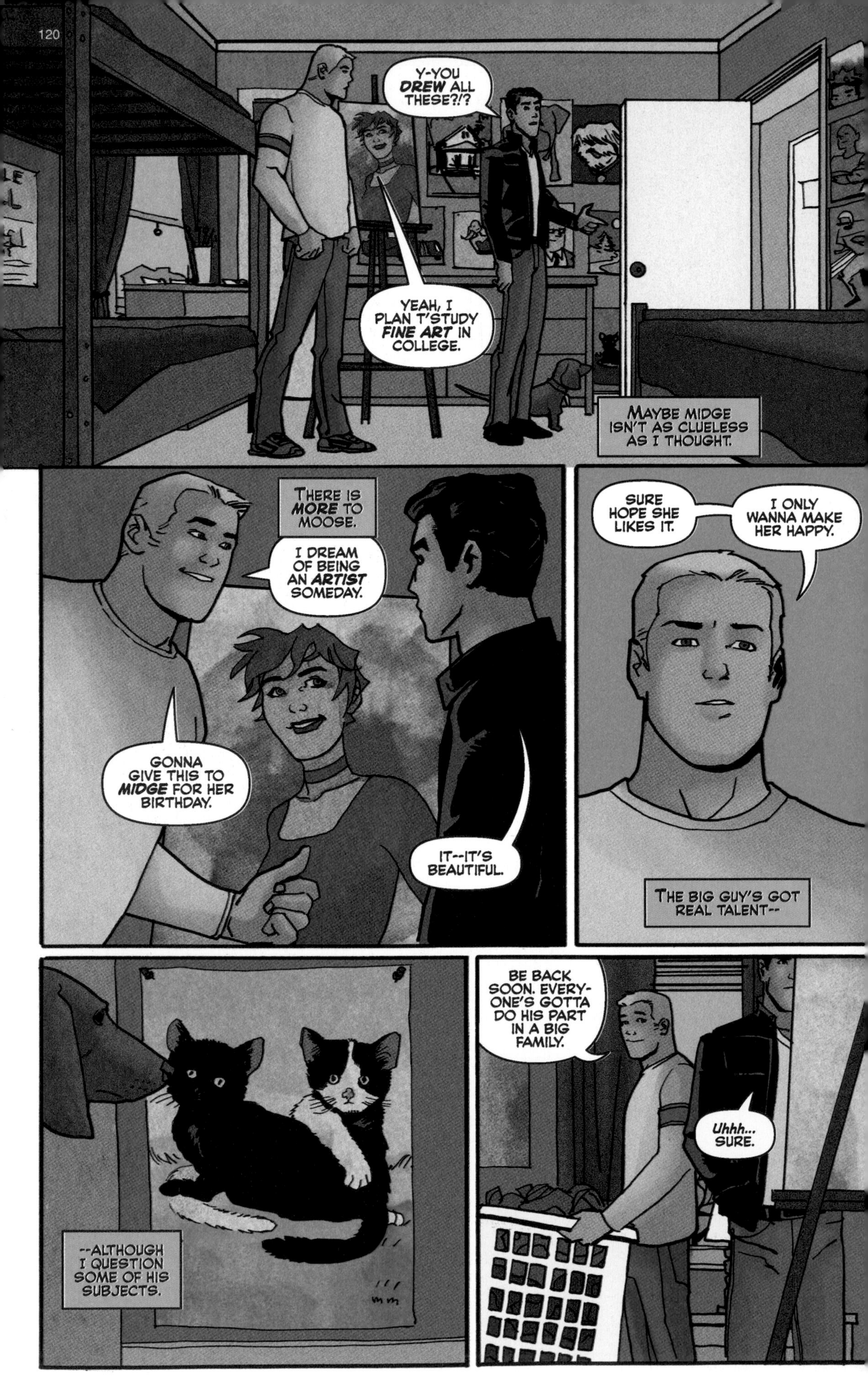
Y-YOU *DREW* ALL THESE?!?
YEAH, I PLAN T'STUDY *FINE ART* IN COLLEGE.
MAYBE MIDGE ISN'T AS CLUELESS AS I THOUGHT.
THERE IS *MORE* TO MOOSE.
I DREAM OF BEING AN *ARTIST* SOMEDAY.
GONNA GIVE THIS TO *MIDGE* FOR HER BIRTHDAY.
IT--IT'S BEAUTIFUL.
SURE HOPE SHE LIKES IT.
I ONLY WANNA MAKE HER HAPPY.
THE BIG GUY'S GOT REAL TALENT--
--ALTHOUGH I QUESTION SOME OF HIS SUBJECTS.
BE BACK SOON. EVERY-ONE'S GOTTA DO HIS PART IN A BIG FAMILY.
Uhhh... SURE.

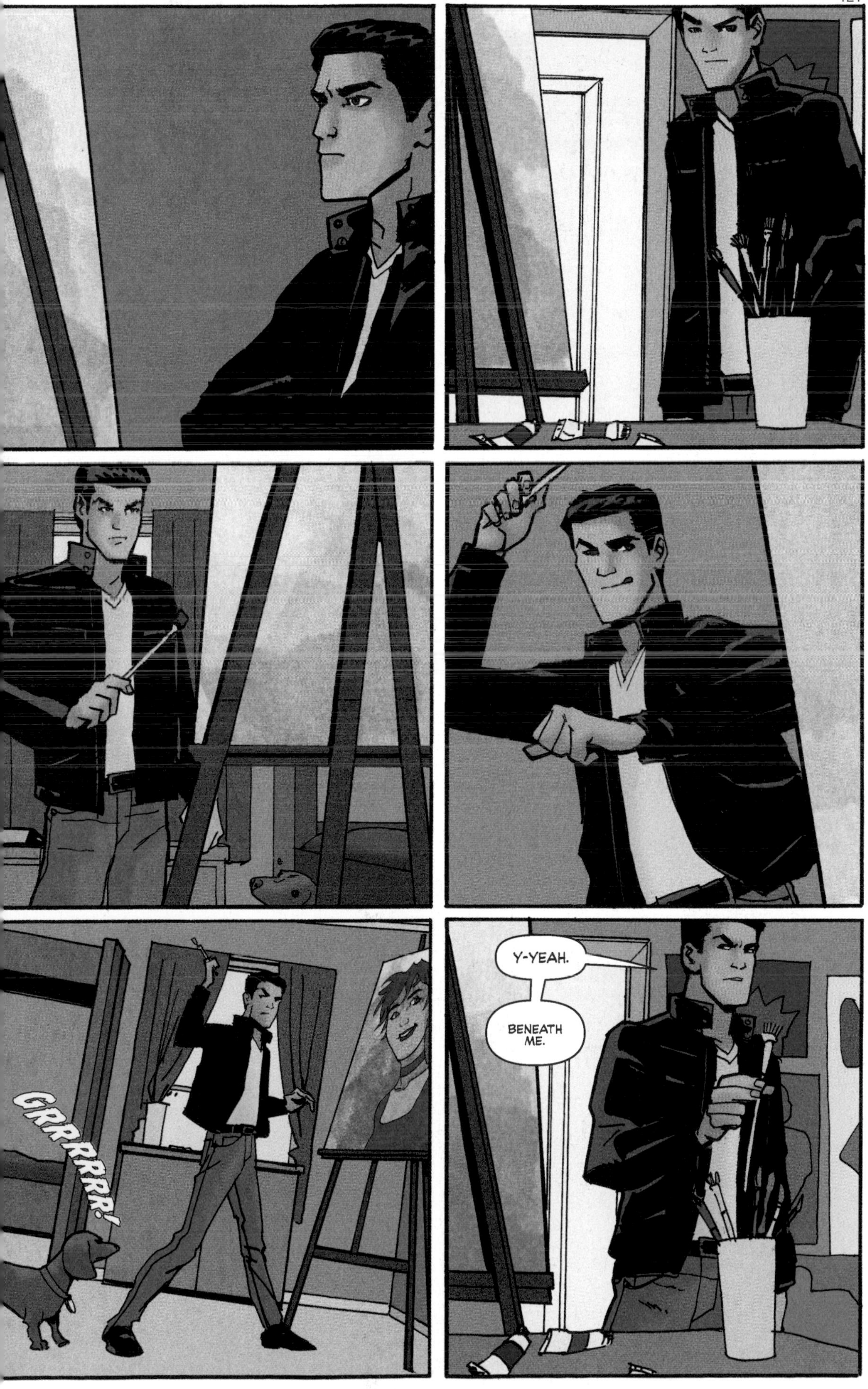
GRRRRRR!
Y-YEAH.
BENEATH ME.

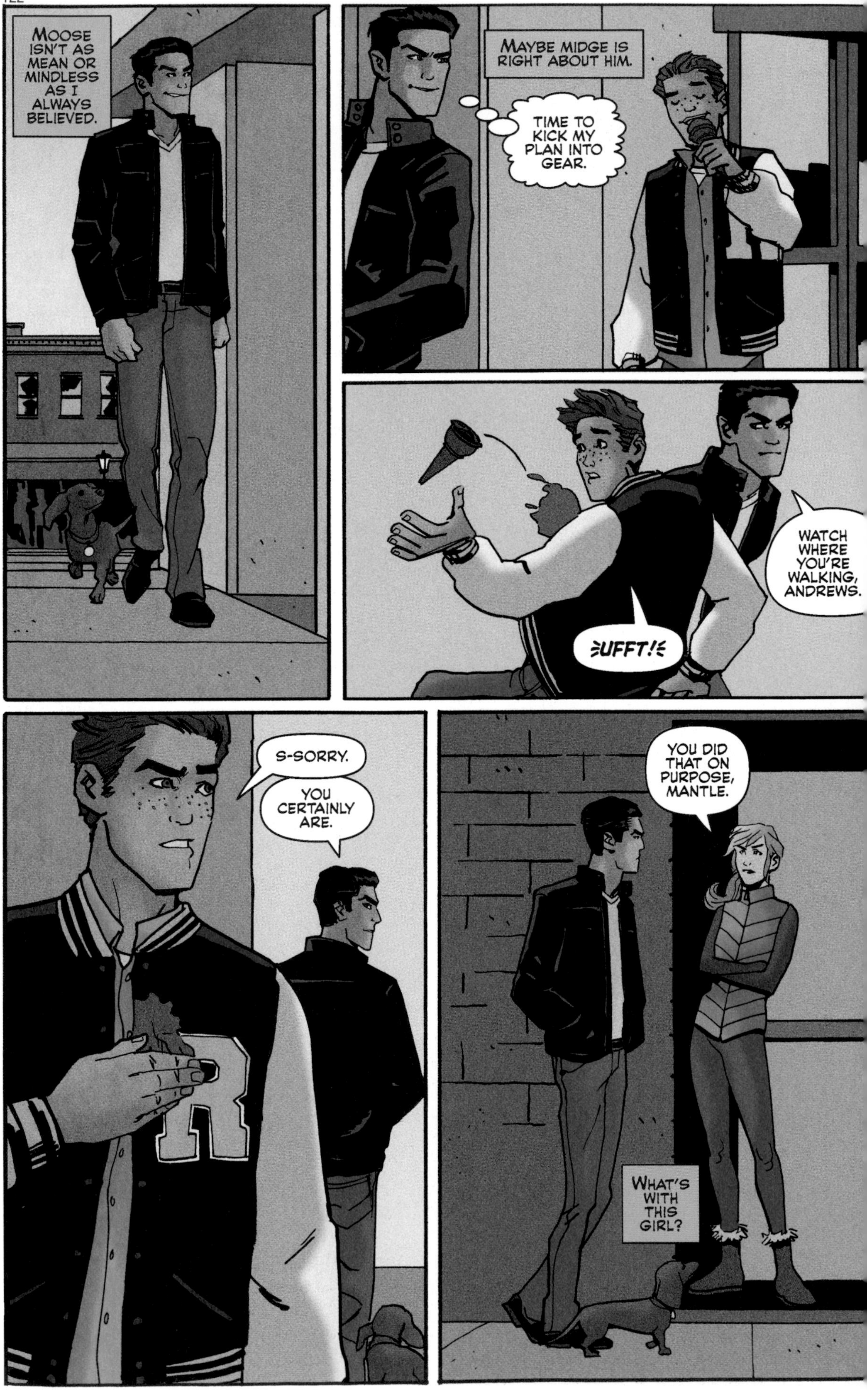
MOOSE ISN'T AS MEAN OR MINDLESS AS I ALWAYS BELIEVED.
MAYBE MIDGE IS RIGHT ABOUT HIM.
TIME TO KICK MY PLAN INTO GEAR.
WATCH WHERE YOU'RE WALKING, ANDREWS.
UFFT!
S-SORRY.
YOU CERTAINLY ARE.
YOU DID THAT ON PURPOSE, MANTLE.
WHAT'S WITH THIS GIRL?

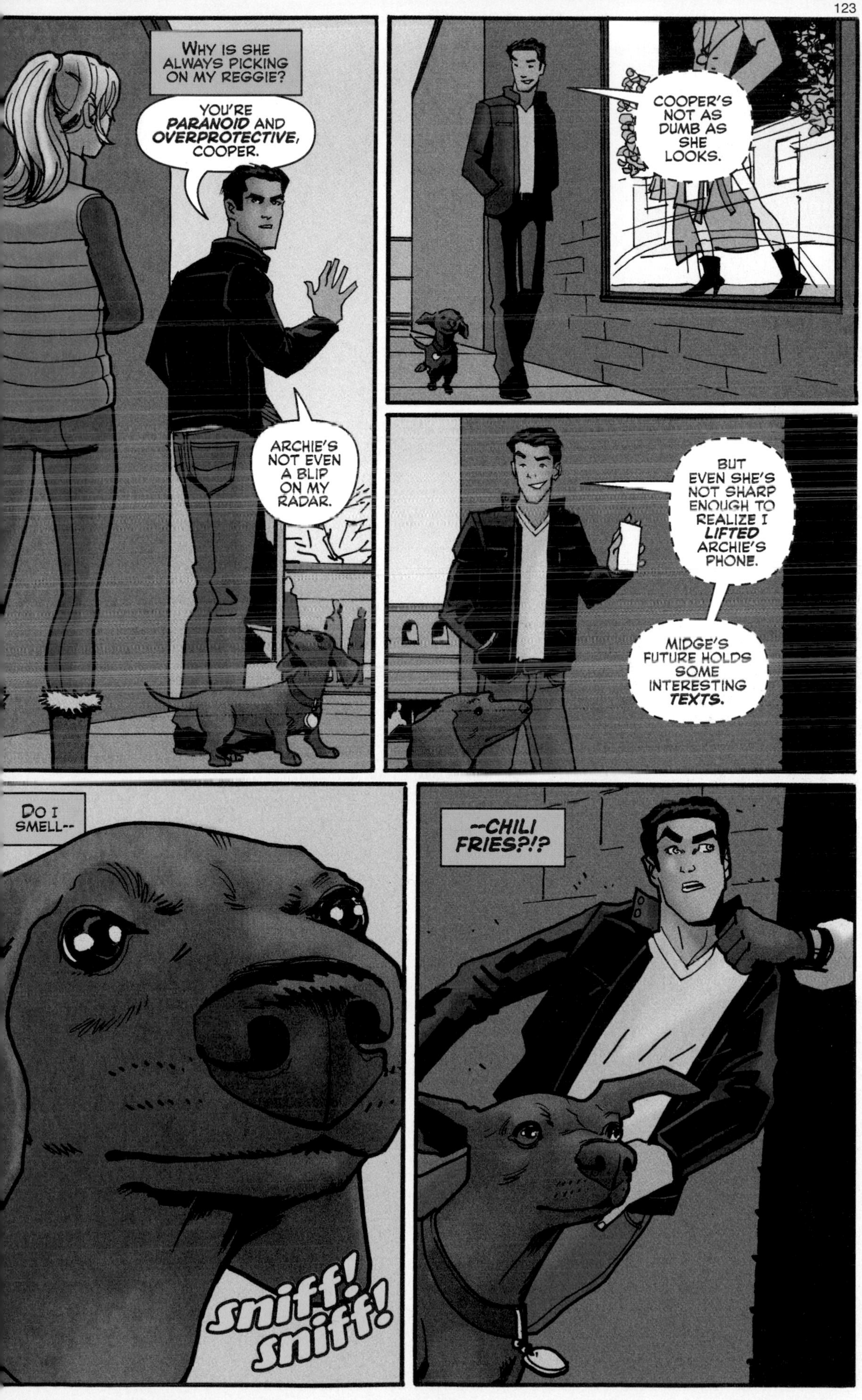
WHY IS SHE ALWAYS PICKING ON MY REGGIE?
YOU'RE PARANOID AND OVERPROTECTIVE, COOPER.
ARCHIE'S NOT EVEN A BLIP ON MY RADAR.
COOPER'S NOT AS DUMB AS SHE LOOKS.
BUT EVEN SHE'S NOT SHARP ENOUGH TO REALIZE I LIFTED ARCHIE'S PHONE.
MIDGE'S FUTURE HOLDS SOME INTERESTING TEXTS.
DO I SMELL--
sniff! sniff!
--CHILI FRIES?!?

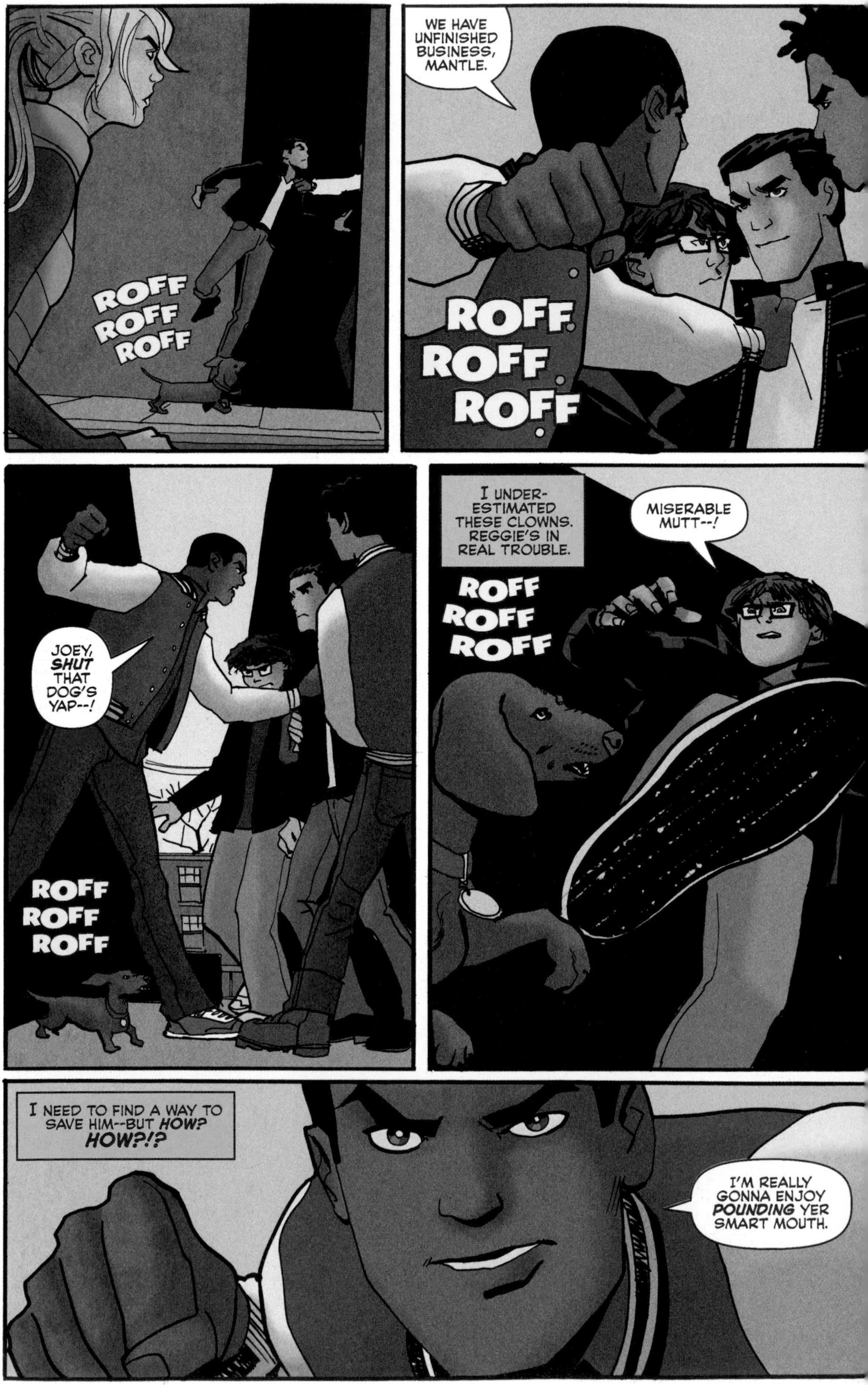
ROFF
ROFF
ROFF
WE HAVE UNFINISHED BUSINESS, MANTLE.
ROFF
ROFF
ROFF
JOEY, **SHUT** THAT DOG'S YAP--!
ROFF
ROFF
ROFF
I UNDER-ESTIMATED THESE CLOWNS. REGGIE'S IN REAL TROUBLE.
MISERABLE MUTT--!
ROFF
ROFF
ROFF
I NEED TO FIND A WAY TO SAVE HIM--BUT ***HOW? HOW?!?***
I'M REALLY GONNA ENJOY ***POUNDING*** YER SMART MOUTH.

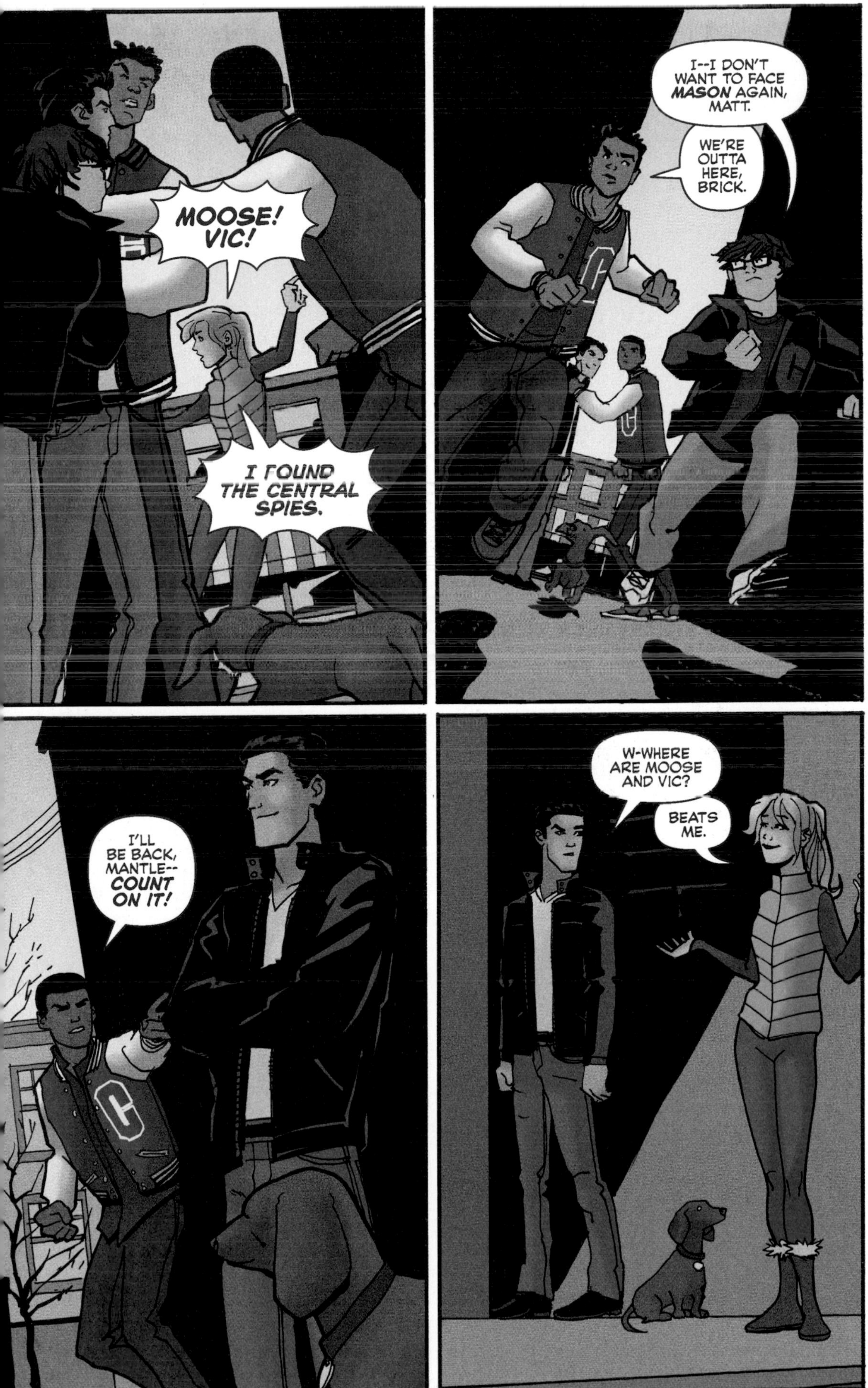
MOOSE! VIC!
I FOUND THE CENTRAL SPIES.
I--I DON'T WANT TO FACE MASON AGAIN, MATT.
WE'RE OUTTA HERE, BRICK.
I'LL BE BACK, MANTLE-- COUNT ON IT!
W-WHERE ARE MOOSE AND VIC?
BEATS ME.

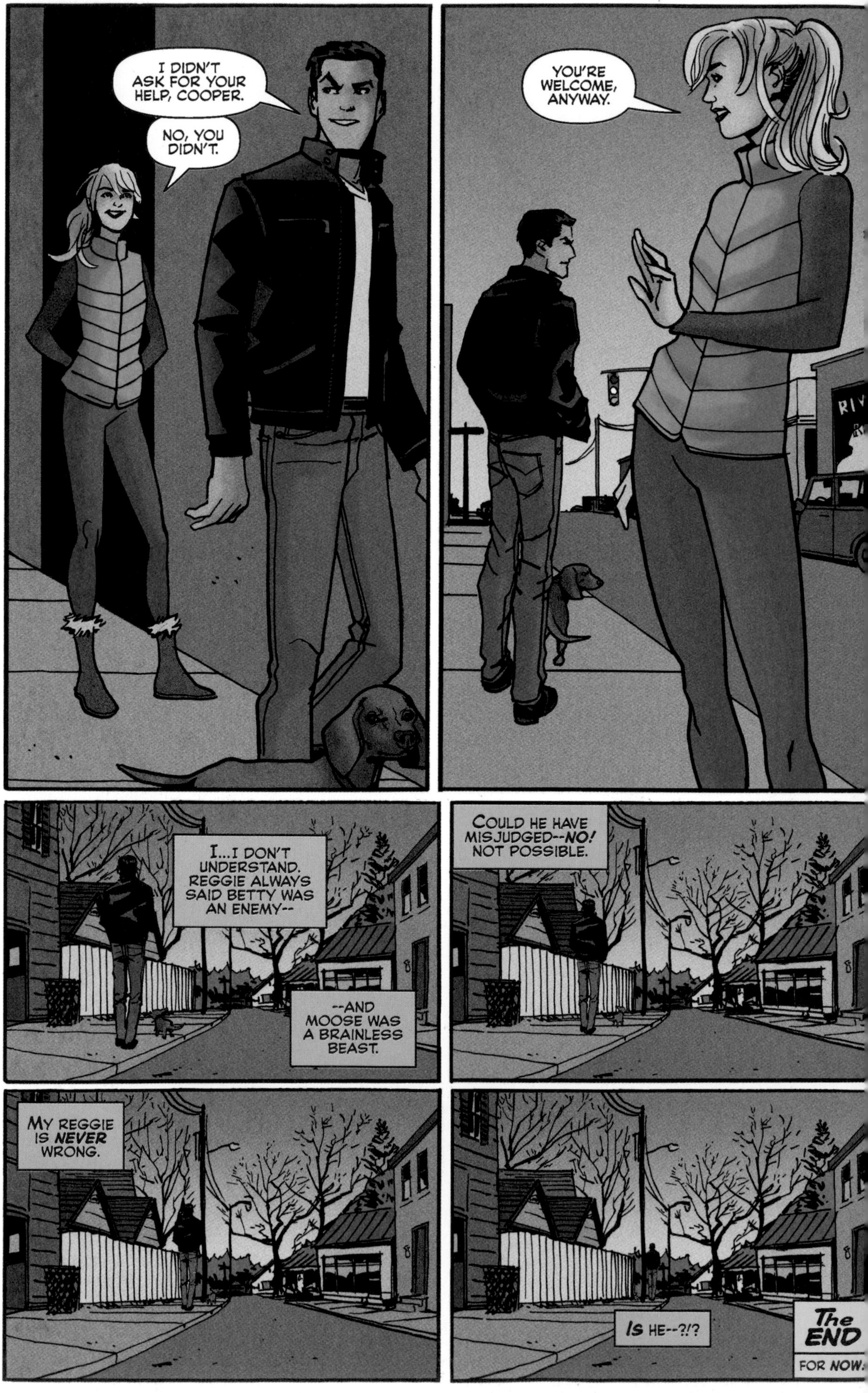
I DIDN'T ASK FOR YOUR HELP, COOPER.
NO, YOU DIDN'T.
YOU'RE WELCOME, ANYWAY.
I...I DON'T UNDERSTAND. REGGIE ALWAYS SAID BETTY WAS AN ENEMY--
--AND MOOSE WAS A BRAINLESS BEAST.
COULD HE HAVE MISJUDGED--NO! NOT POSSIBLE.
MY REGGIE IS NEVER WRONG.
IS HE--?!?
The END
FOR NOW.

ROAD TO RIVERDALE® SPECIAL FEATURES

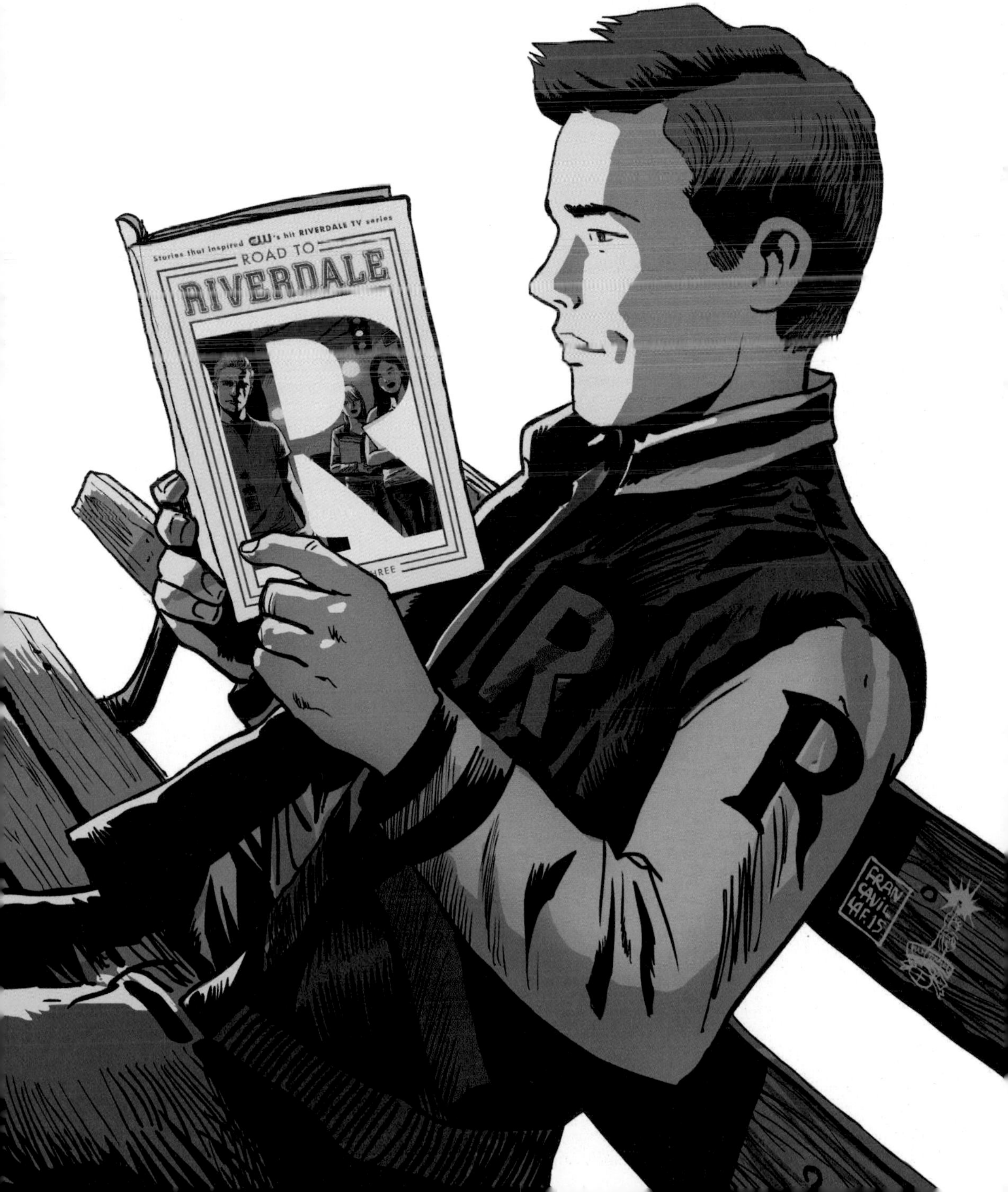
Stories that inspired CW's hit RIVERDALE TV series
ROAD TO
RIVERDALE

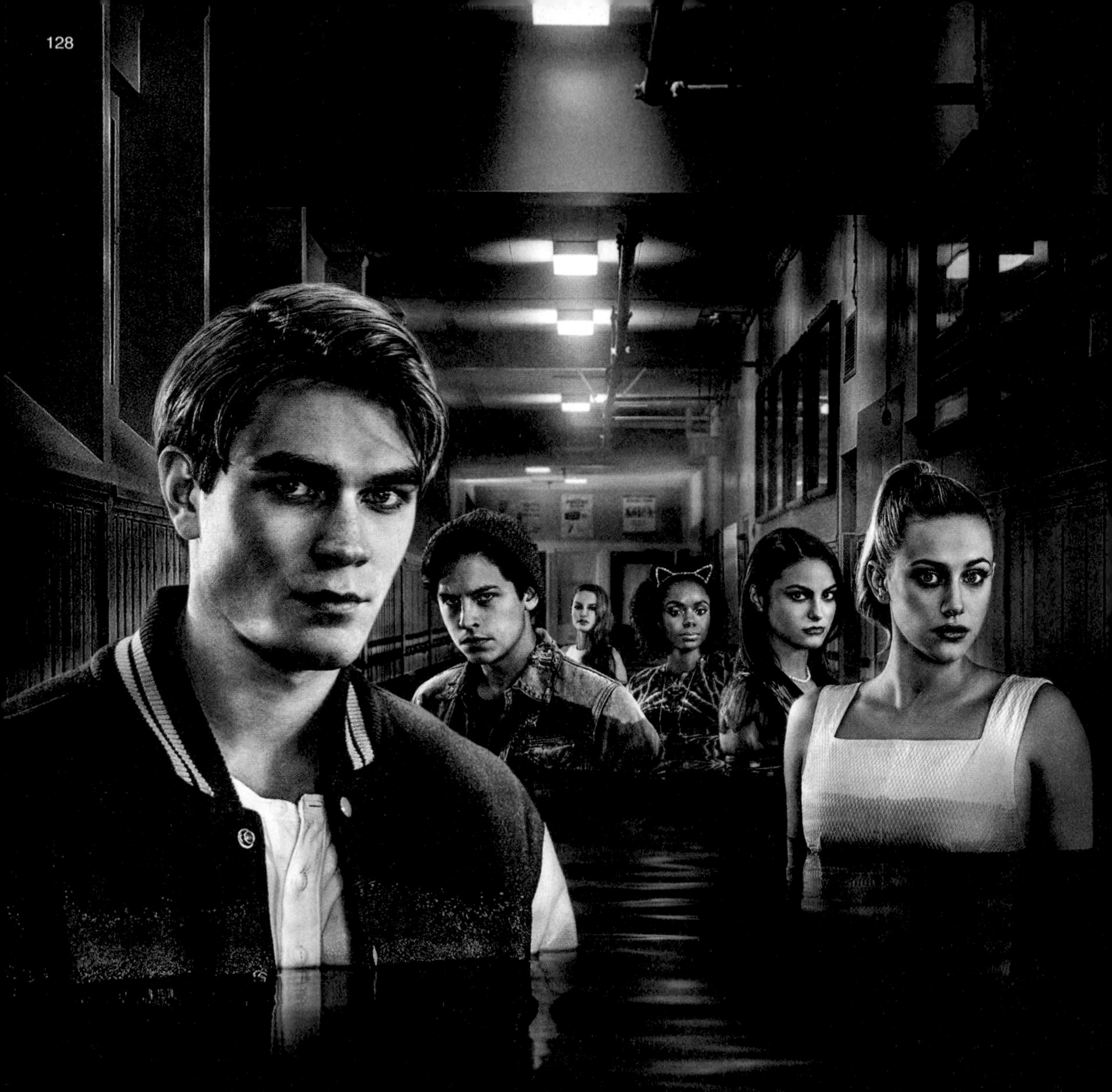

RIVERDALE

Welcome to this special look at The CW's **RIVERDALE**. If you haven't already been following the drama and suspense of the TV series, here's an inside peek at how the show has taken the beloved Archie characters and brought them to new life on the small screen.

Follow @ArchieComics on Twitter for even more Riverdale updates, including live tweets during each episode!

All photos courtesy The CW/Warner Bros.

Meet Me At Pop's!

Our special tour starts at, where else, **Pop's Chock'lit Shoppe**! Pop's is a long-time staple in the Archie Universe, the meeting place for everyone who passes through the town of Riverdale.

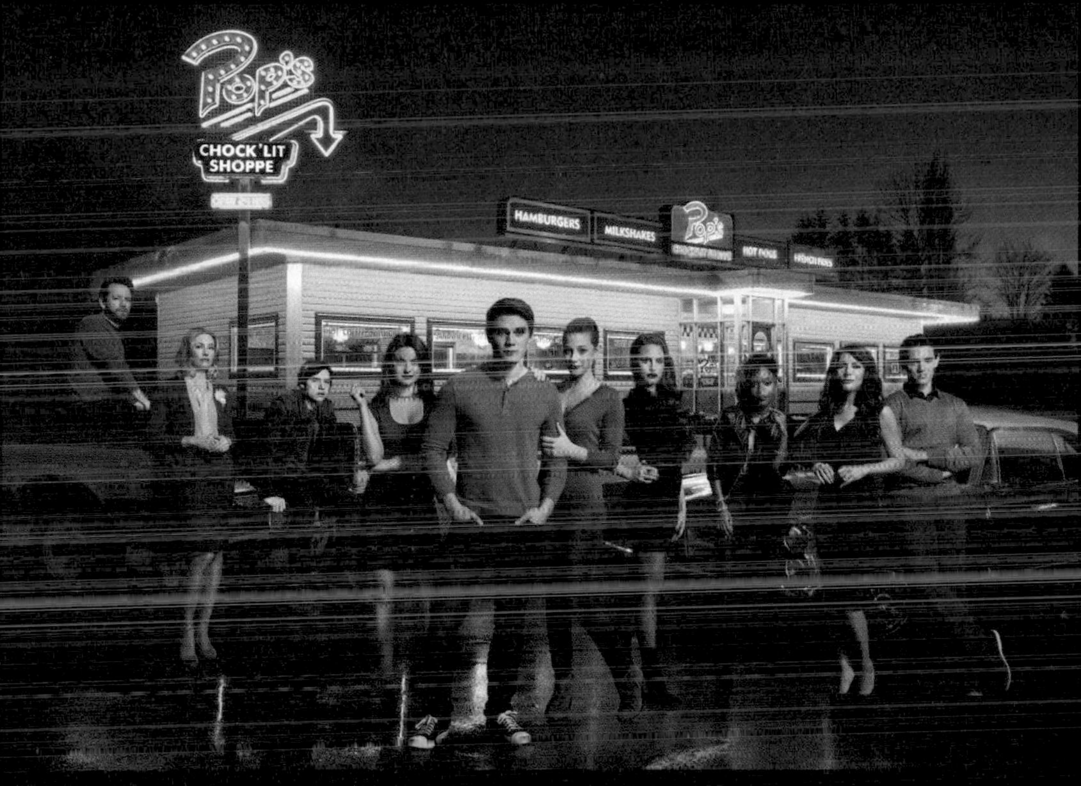
Pop's
CHOCK'LIT SHOPPE
HAMBURGERS
MILKSHAKES
Pop's

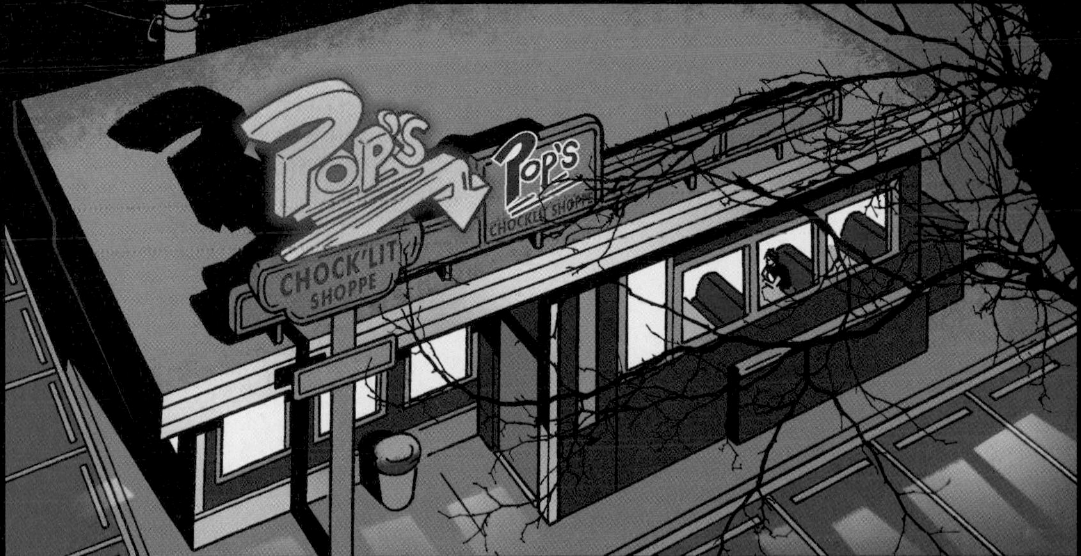
Pop's
CHOCK'LIT SHOPPE
Pop's

The Gang's All Here!

Archie (**KJ Apa**), **Josie** (**Ashleigh Murray**), **Veronica** (**Camila Mendes**), **Betty** (**Lili Reinhart**) and **Jughead** (**Cole Sprouse**) may have some updated looks, but they translate from comic pages to screen and vice-versa perfectly!

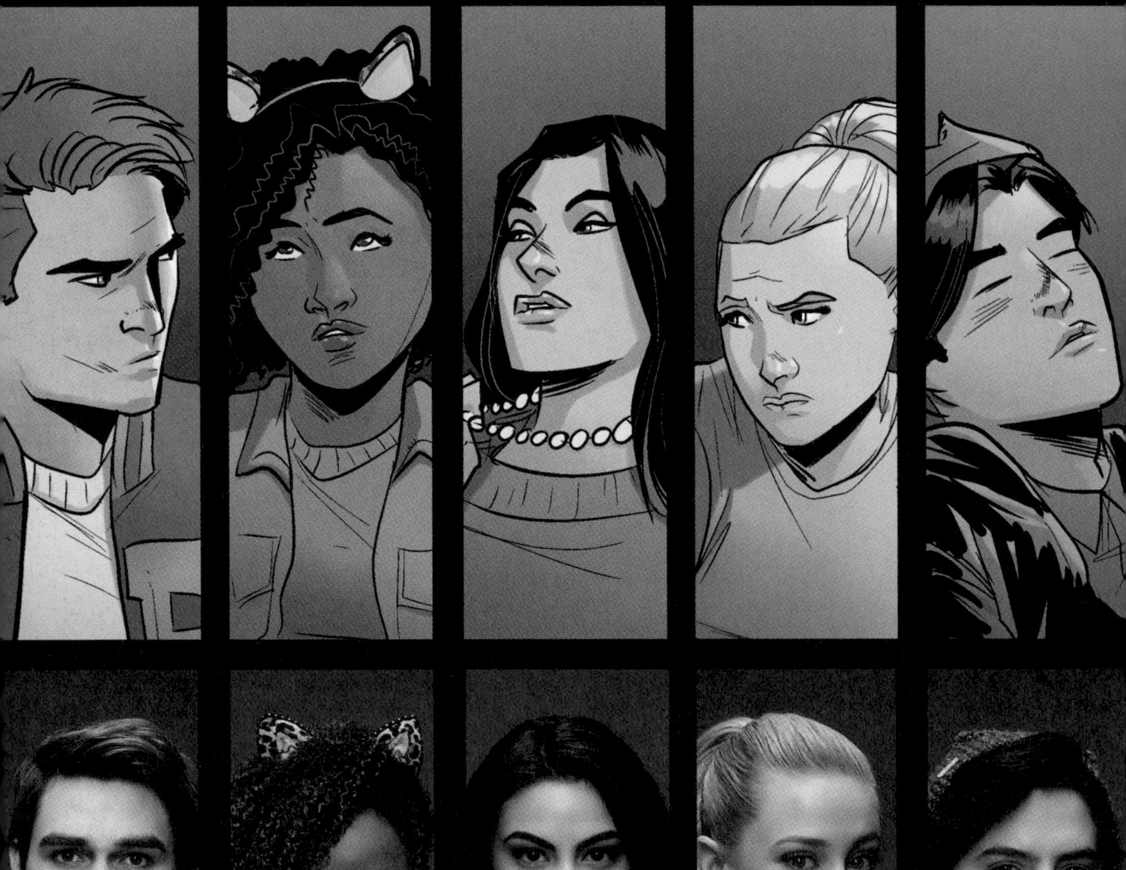

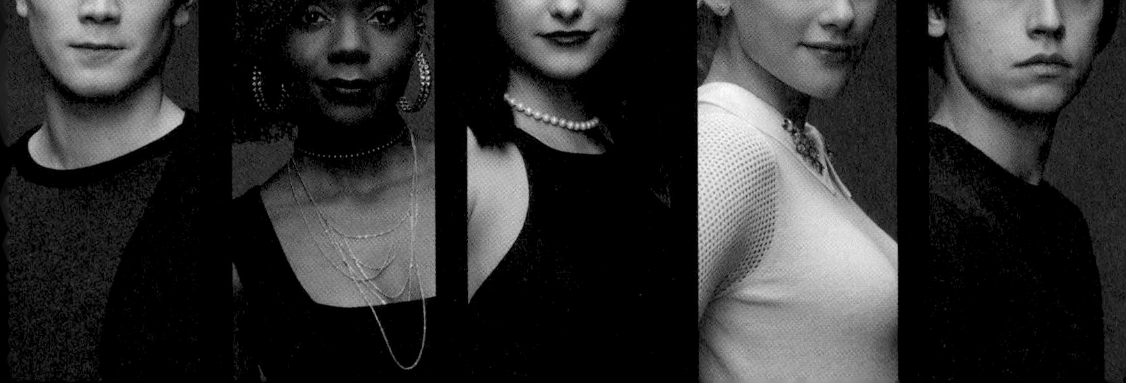

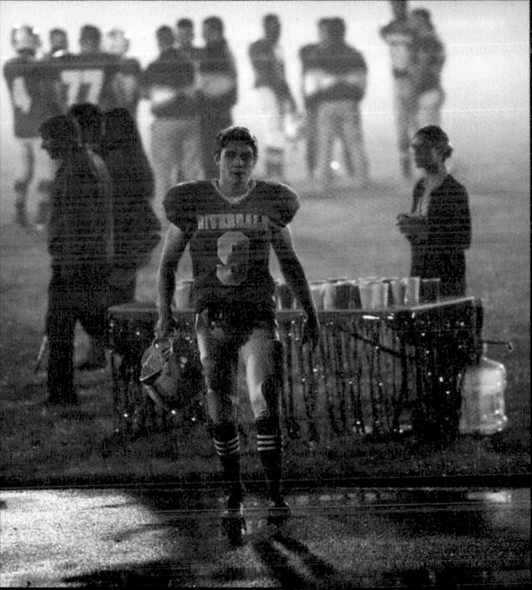

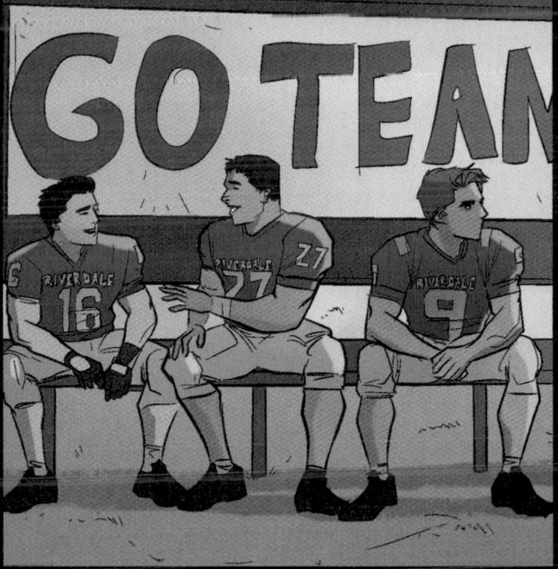
GO TEAM

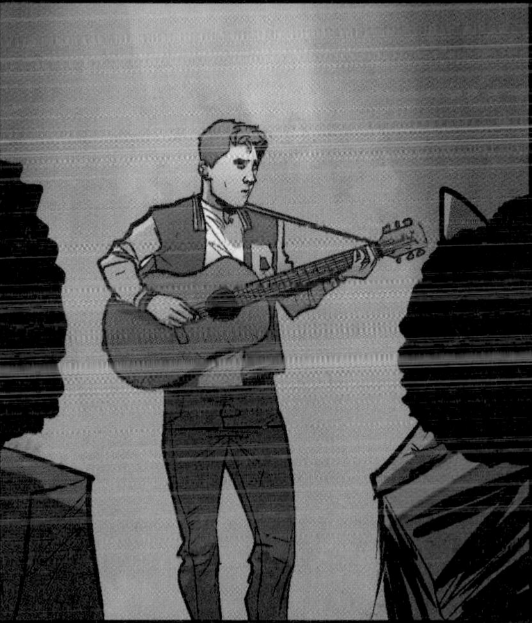

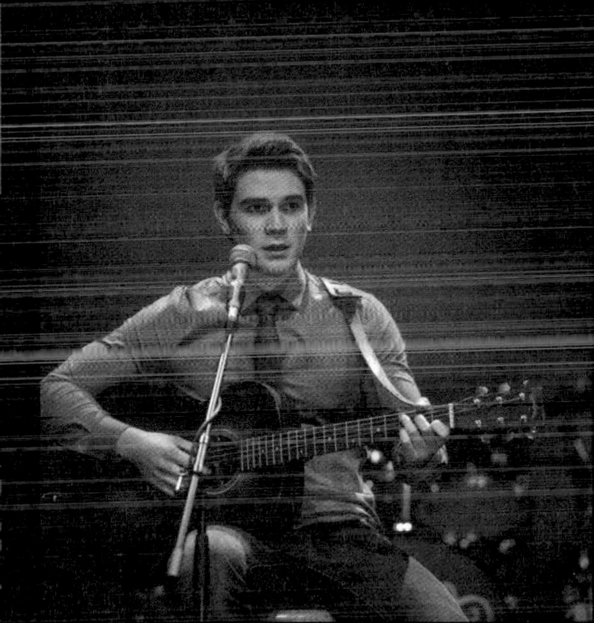

Torn Between Two Worlds

Archie's a new recruit on the football team, and he's quickly becoming a star player. However, his true passion is writing and playing music, and he'll take every opportunity he can get to showcase his talent in front of others.

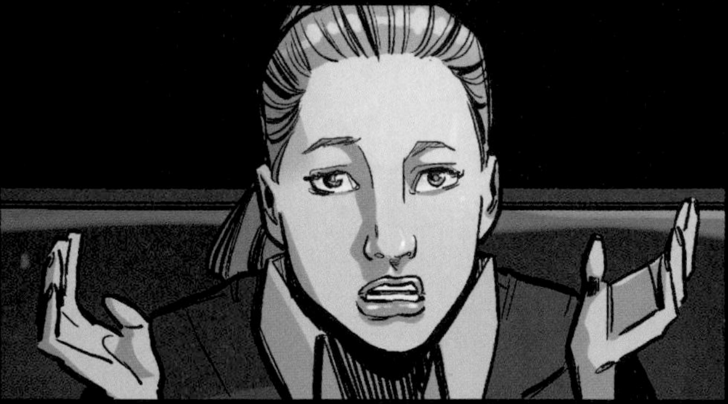

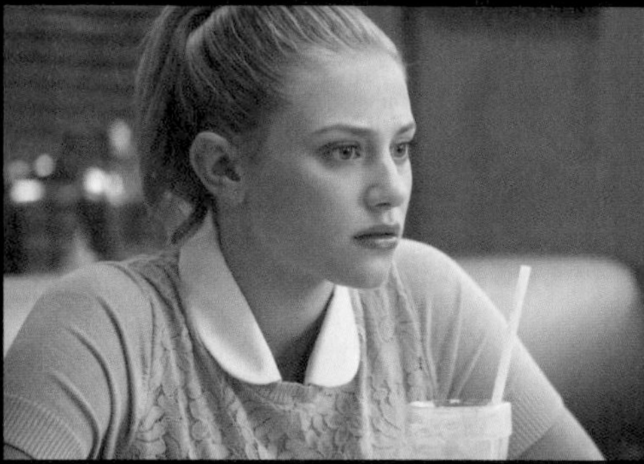

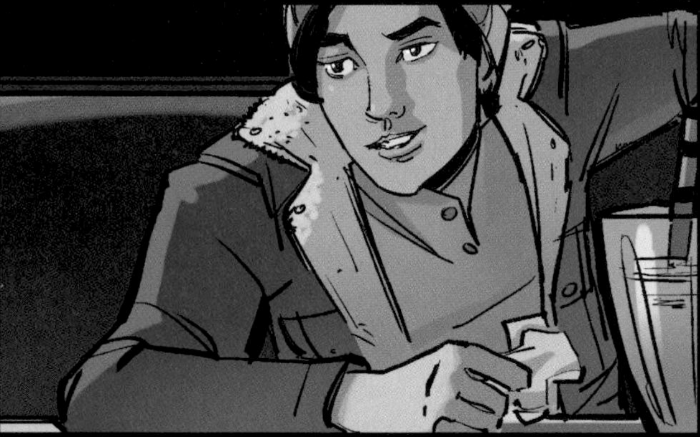

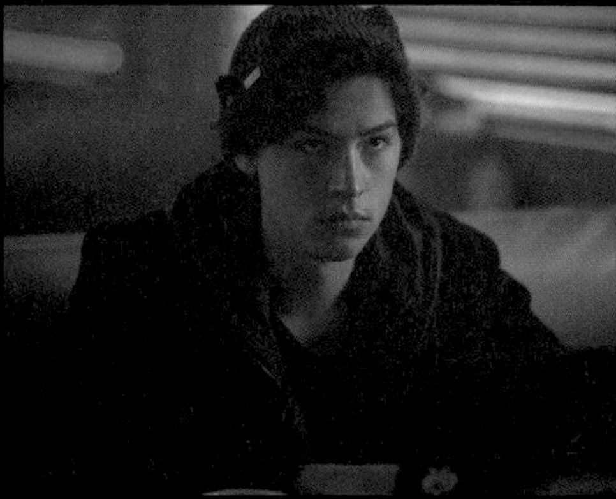

Meet #Bughead!

Betty and **Jughead** have formed a special bond over the course of the show, whether it be discussing life over milkshakes at Pop's or doing detective work to bring **Jason Blossom**'s murderer to justice.

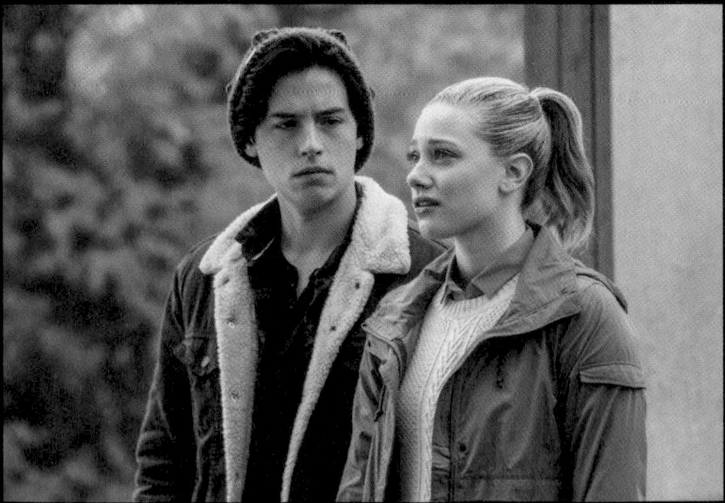

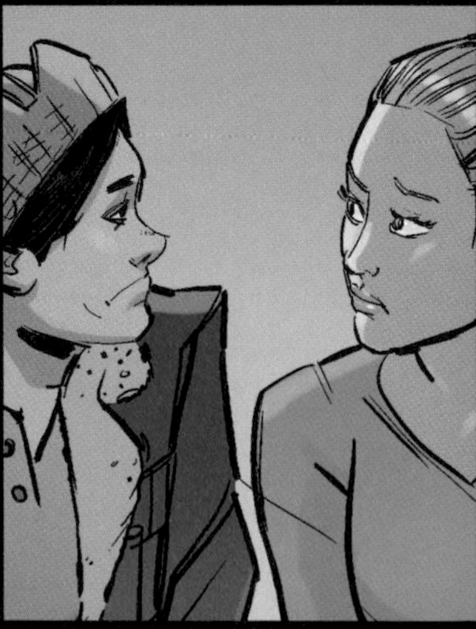

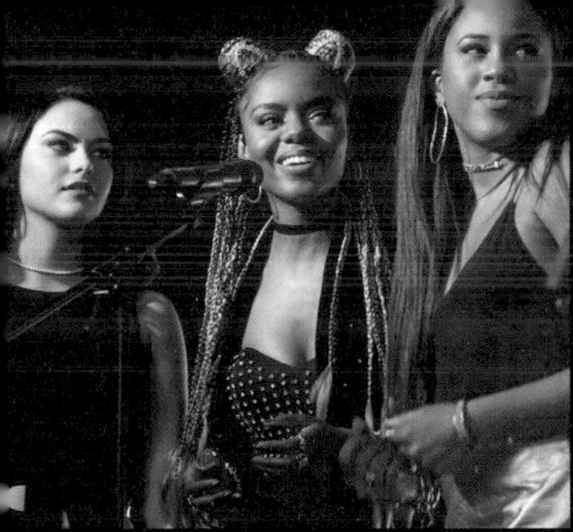

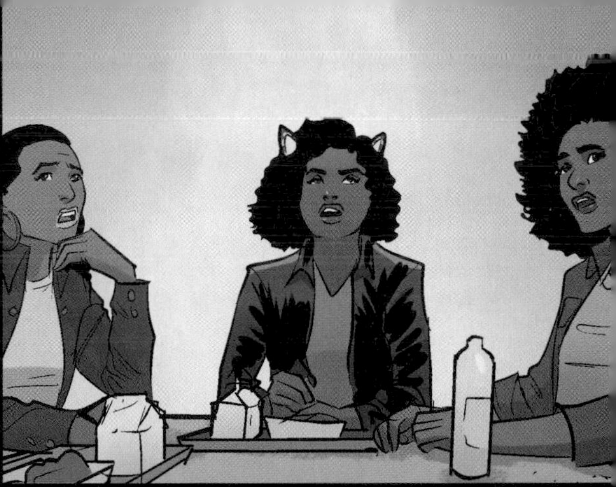

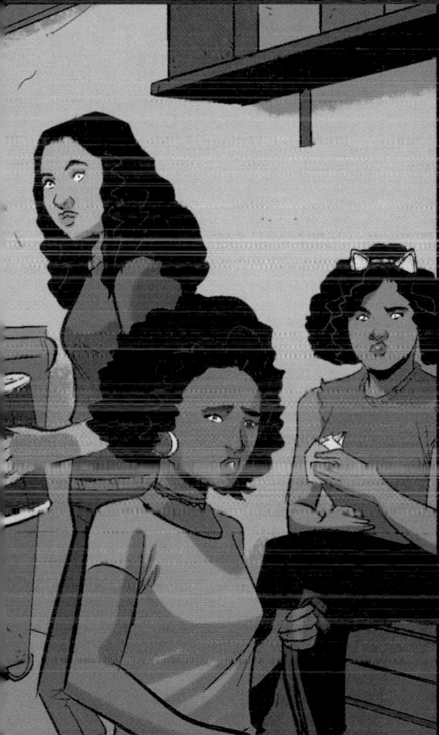

What's New, Pussycats?

Josie, **Valerie (Hayley Law)** and **Melody (Asha Bromfield)** welcome a new member: **Veronica Lodge**! The 'cats are fierce, fun and talented so adding Veronica Lodge to that mix is a recipe for success!

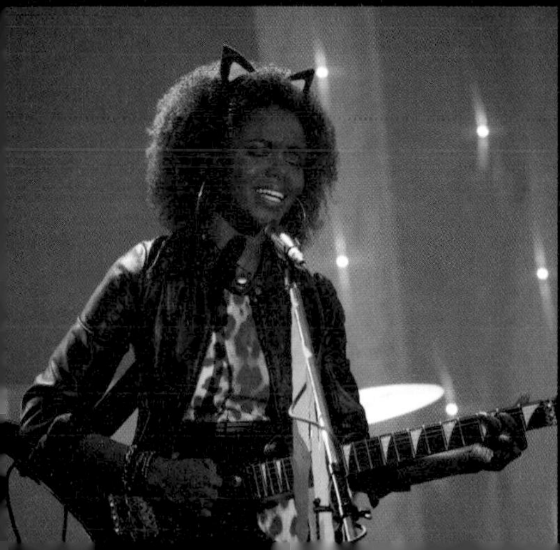

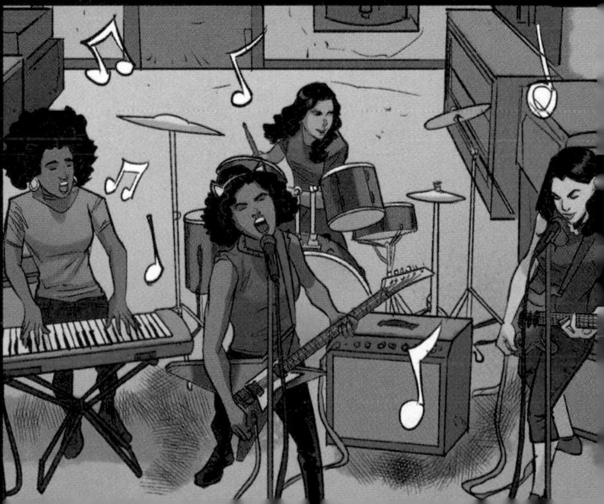

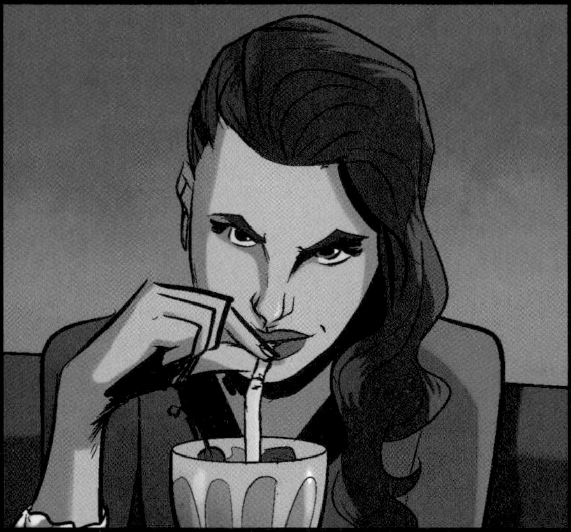

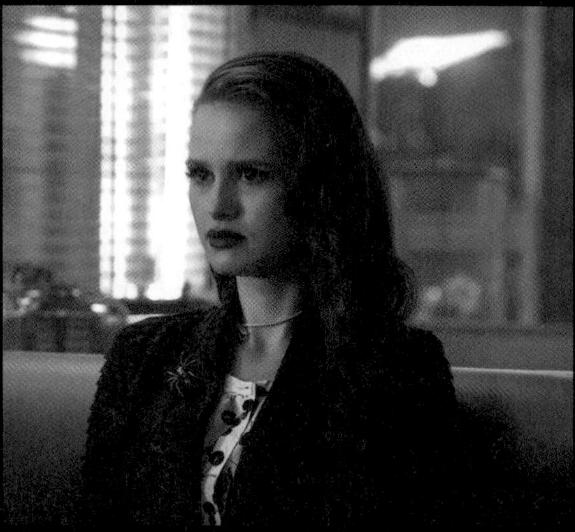

The Vermilion Vixen!

Cheryl (Madelaine Petsch) is just as witty, devious and charming on *Riverdale* as she is in the comics. While she can come off as harsh, she too is struggling under the pressure of upholding the Blossom family name while mourning the loss of her brother, Jason.

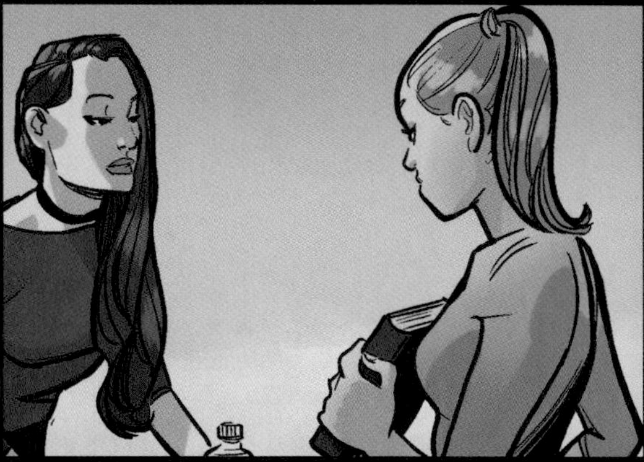

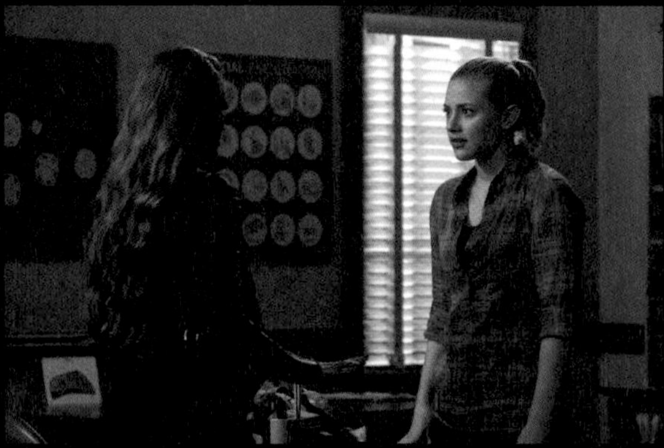

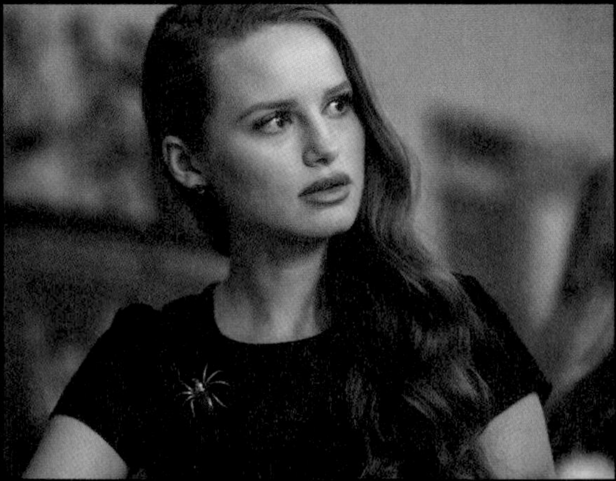

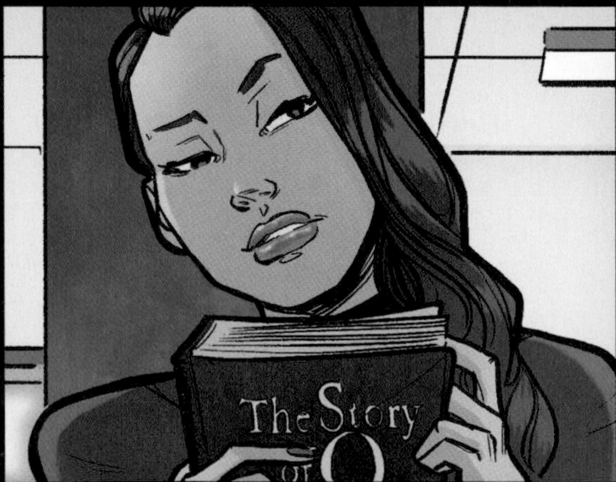
The Story

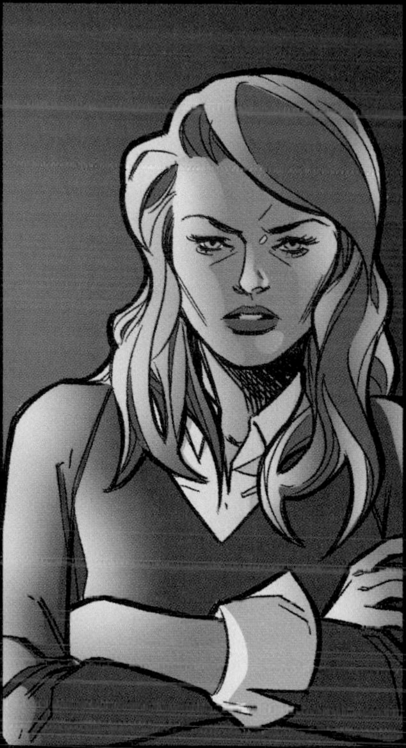

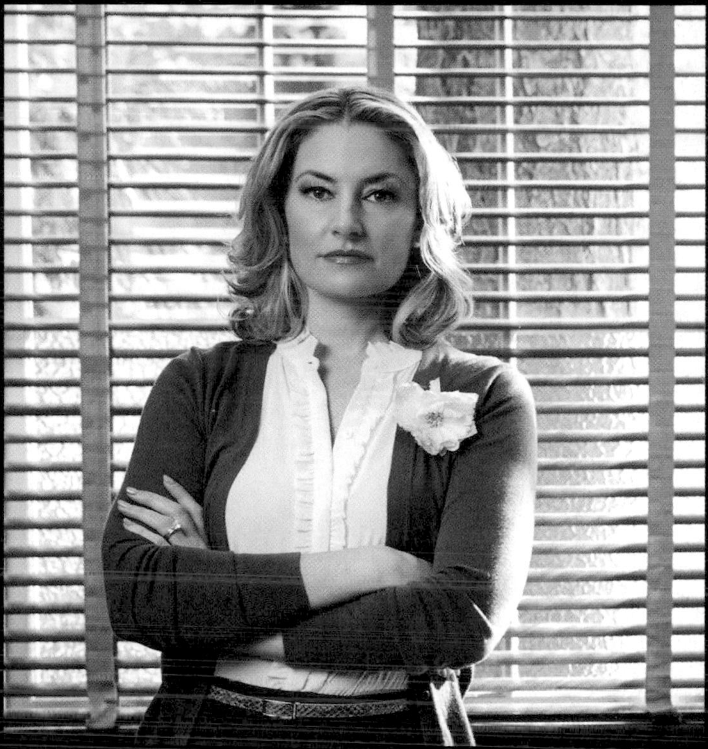

Mother Knows Best

Alice Cooper, played by **Mädchen Amick**, loves her daughters **Betty** and **Polly**, though her parenting is strict. **Hermione Lodge**, played by **Marisol Nichols**, had to leave her debutante NYC lifestyle behind her and settle with her daughter **Veronica** in **Riverdale**, after the arrest of her husband, **Hiram**.

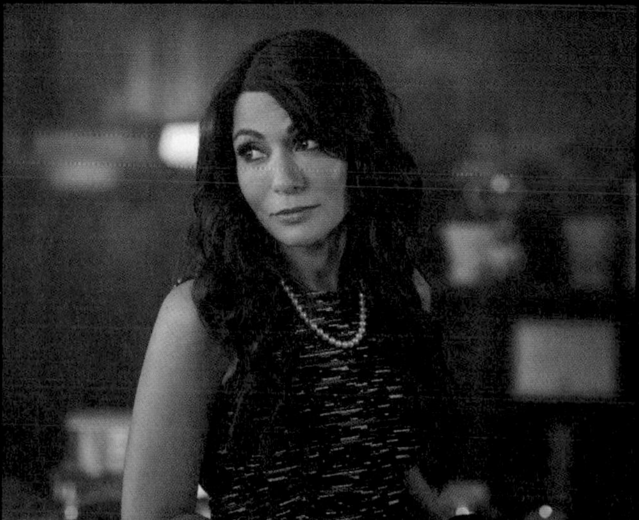

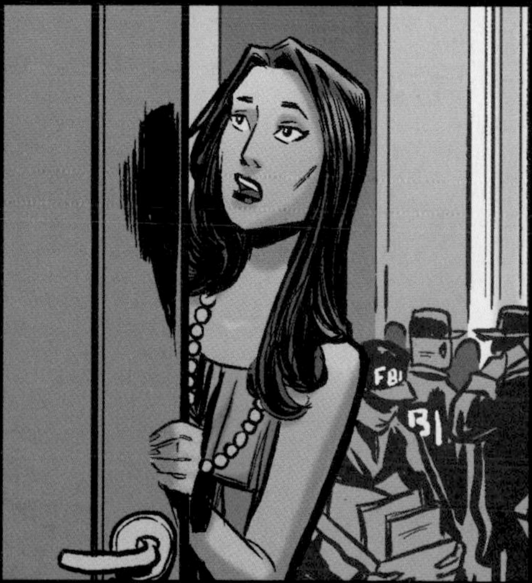
FBI
FBI

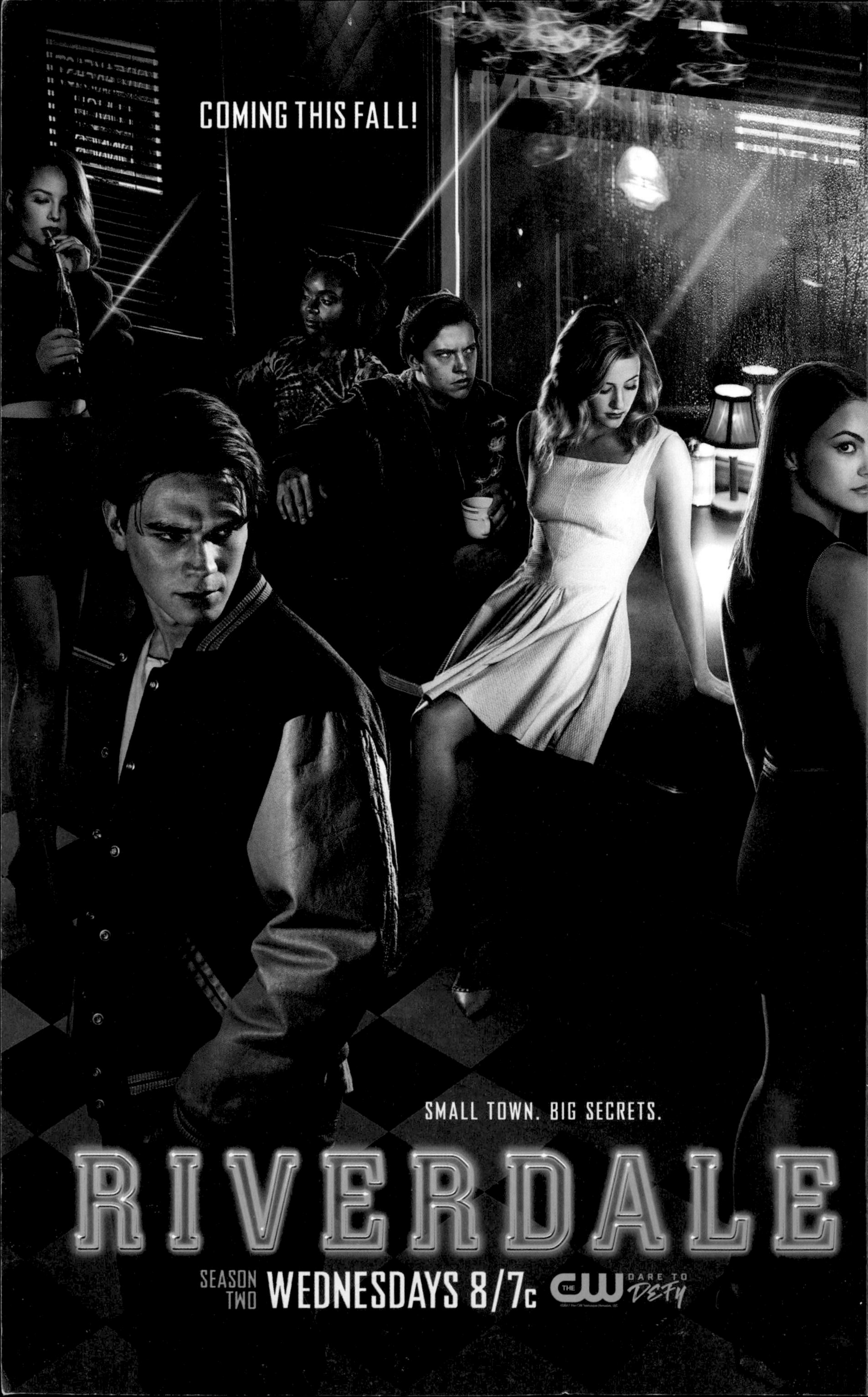
COMING THIS FALL!
SMALL TOWN. BIG SECRETS.
RIVERDALE
SEASON TWO WEDNESDAYS 8/7c
THE CW
DARE TO DEFY